LEGENDS *of the* CAPILANO

FIRST VOICES, FIRST TEXTS

SERIES EDITOR: WARREN CARIOU

First Voices, First Texts aims to reconnect contemporary readers with some of the most important Aboriginal literature of the past, much of which has been unavailable for decades. This series reveals the richness of these works by providing newly re-edited texts that are presented with particular sensitivity toward Indigenous ethics, traditions, and contemporary realities. The editors strive to indigenize the editing process by involving communities, by respecting traditional protocols, and by providing critical introductions that give readers new insights into the cultural contexts of these unjustly neglected classics.

1. *Devil in Deerskins: My Life with Grey Owl* by Anahareo
2. *Indians Don't Cry / Gaawiin Mawisiiwag Anishinaabeg* by George Kenny
3. *Life Among the Qallunaat* by Mini Aodla Freeman
4. *From the Tundra to the Trenches* by Eddy Weetaltuk
5. *Honouring the Strength of Indian Women: Plays, Stories, Poetry* by Vera Manuel
6. *Legends of the Capilano* by E. Pauline Johnson with Chief Joe Capilano and Mary Agnes Capilano

LEGENDS *of the* CAPILANO

E. Pauline Johnson (Tekahionwake)
with Chief Joe Capilano (Sahp-luk)
and Mary Agnes Capilano (Lixwelut)
Edited by Alix Shield

Legends of the Capilano

27 26 25 24 23 1 2 3 4 5

University of Manitoba Press
Winnipeg, Manitoba, Canada
Treaty 1 Territory
uofmpress.ca

Cataloguing data available from Library and Archives Canada
First Voices, First Texts, ISSN 2291-9627 ; 6
ISBN 978-1-77284-017-9 (PAPER)
ISBN 978-1-77284-019-3 (PDF)
ISBN 978-1-77284-018-6 (EPUB)
ISBN 978-1-77284-020-9 (BOUND)

Cover images: Mary Capilano, 1938, UBC Library Rare Books and Special Collections, BC1849/175a; and The Lions, Capilano Creek in foreground, c. 1900, City of Vancouver Archives, CVA 13-2.
Cover design: Mike Carroll
Interior design: Jess Koroscil

The University of Manitoba Press acknowledges the financial support for its publication program provided by the Government of Canada through the Canada Book Fund, the Canada Council for the Arts, the Manitoba Department of Sport, Culture, and Heritage, the Manitoba Arts Council, and the Manitoba Book Publishing Tax Credit.

Funded by the Government of Canada | Canada

CONTENTS

List of Figures
vii

Foreword
xi

Author's Foreword to the 1911 Edition
xiii

Introduction
1

The Two Sisters
77

The Siwash Rock
82

The Recluse
87

The Lost Salmon Run
95

The Deep Waters
101

The Sea-Serpent
107

The Lost Island
113

Point Grey
117

The Tulameen Trail
121

The Grey Archway
127

Deadman's Island
134

A Squamish Legend of Napoleon
140

The Lure in Stanley Park
146

Deer Lake
151

A Royal Mohawk Chief
156

The Legend of the Two Sisters
163

The Legend of the Squamish Twins
169

The Legend of the Seven Swans
176

The Legend of Lillooet Falls
184

The Legend of the Ice Babies
190

Interview with Rick Monture
197

Interview with Rudy Reimer
206

Glossary
215

Acknowledgements
217

Notes
219

Selected Bibliography
236

LIST OF FIGURES

Figure 1: "Sko-Mish-Oath: The Territory of the Squamish Indian Peoples; Indian Villages and Landmarks; Burrard Inlet and Howe Sound Before the Whitemans Came," 1937. Major James Skitt Matthews, aided by August Jack Haatsalano [Khahtsahlano]. City of Vancouver Archives, AM54-S13-: MAP 351b. / x

Figure 2: Agnes (Agi) Mathias Paul at the Kia'palano exhibit (Capilano Suspension Bridge, North Vancouver, BC). October 2018. Photo by A. Shield. / xiii

Figure 3: Portrait of E. Pauline Johnson, n.d. Vancouver Public Library, Special Collections Historical Photographs, Accession no. 9430. / 7

Figure 4: Chief Joe Capilano, 1908. Photographed by George G. Nye. MONOVA Archives of North Vancouver, Inventory no. 2849. / 11

Figures 5 and *6:* British news coverage from Chief Joe Capilano's 1906 trip to visit King Edward VII. Left: *Over-Seas Magazine* (with names wrongly attributed below cover image), 1 September 1906. E. Pauline Johnson fonds, The William Ready Division of Archives and Research Collections, McMaster University Library, Box 4, file 30. Right: *The Graphic*, 18 August 1906. MONOVA Archives of North Vancouver, Inventory no. 1906-5. / 12

Figure 7: "Indians—Capilano genealogy," n.d. Compiled by Major James Skitt Matthews. City of Vancouver Archives, Major Matthews collection, Ref. AM54-S23-1. / 13

Figure 8: "Mrs. Mary 'Lay-hu-lette' Capilano," 31 May 1939. City of Vancouver Archives, Major Matthews collection, Ref. AM54-S4-: Port P430. / 17

Figure 9: "Map of Stanley Park, Vancouver, B.C.," 1911. City of Vancouver Archives, Ref. AM1594-: MAP 368b. / 22

Figure 10: Images of Cedar basket woven by Mary Capilano. Property of the Mathias family. Images by A. Shield, 2018. / 31

Figure 11: Order slip that was returned by mail to Johnson at the Bute Street Hospital, requesting one autographed copy of *Legends* for the price of $2.00. E. Pauline Johnson Fonds, The William Ready Division of Archives and Research Collections, McMaster University Library, Box 1, File 41. / 40

Figure 12: Excerpt of a letter from Evelyn H.C. Johnson to Mr. James Goulet, July 1, 1913. E. Pauline Johnson fonds, The William Ready Division of Archives and Research Collections, McMaster University Library, Box 11. / 41

Figure 13: Legends of Vancouver, First edition, privately printed (1911). Image courtesy of SFU Special Collections and Rare Books, PR 9220 O35 L4 1911b. / 45

Figure 14: Legends of Vancouver, Thomson Stationery Illustrated edition (1912). Image courtesy of SFU Special Collections and Rare Books, PR 9220 O35 L4 1912d. / 47

Figure 15: Line drawing signed by O.B.A in Johnson's "The Grey Archway." Image courtesy of SFU Special Collections and Rare Books, PR 9220 O35 L4 1911a [miscatalogued; published in 1912]. / 48

Figure 16: Advertisement for *Legends of Vancouver* published in the *BC Federationist* newspaper, 12 December 1913, 4. / 48

Figures 17 and *18: Legends of Vancouver,* Saturday Sunset Presses edition (1913) and *Legends of Capilano* Geo. S. Forsyth subedition (1913). Images courtesy of SFU Special Collections and Rare Books, PR 9220 O35 L4 1913l & PR 9220 O35 L4 1913h. / 51

Figure 19: Legends of Vancouver, McClelland and Stewart 1926 edition. Image courtesy of SFU Special Collections and Rare Books, PR 9220 O35 L4 1926. / 52

Figure 20: Legends of Vancouver, McClelland and Stewart 1961 edition. Image courtesy of SFU Special Collections and Rare Books, PR 9220 O35 L4 1961. / 53

Figure 21: Legends of Vancouver, Quarry Press edition (1991). Image courtesy of SFU Special Collections and Rare Books, PR 9220 O35 L4 1991. / 55

Figure 22: Legends of Vancouver, Douglas and McIntyre edition (1997). Image courtesy of SFU Special Collections and Rare Books, PR 9220 O35 L4 1997. / 60

Figure 23: Legends of Vancouver, Midtown Press edition (2013). Image by A. Shield, scanned from personal collection. / 61

Figure 24: "Canoeing on Clayquot Sound" by Edward S. Curtis (c. 1910). Library of Congress, LOT 12328-B. / 63

Figure 25: Presses de Bras-d'Apic *Légendes de Vancouver* French edition (2012). Image by A. Shield, scanned from personal collection. / 64

Figure 26: The Legend of the Salt-Chuck Oluk (c. 1920). Image courtesy of SFU Special Collections and Rare Books, PR 9220 O35 L3 1902. / 69

Figure 1: "Sko-Mish-Oath: The Territory of the Squamish Indian Peoples; Indian Villages and Landmarks; Burrard Inlet and Howe Sound Before the Whitemans Came," 1937. Major James Skitt Matthews, aided by August Jack Haatsalano [Khahtsahlano]. City of Vancouver Archives, AM54-S13-: MAP 351b.

FOREWORD

The Mathias family are the great-grandchildren of Mary Agnes Capilano and Chief Joe Capilano. We are a large family of eleven girls and five boys. During our childhood, we were told the stories of our family heritage. Our grandparents, Chief Mathias Joe and Ellen Joe taught us the traditional songs and dances, and we performed for many events up until the death of Chief Mathias Joe in 1969.

After the passing of our mother in 1972, the family was broken up and placed in residential schools. The family eventually came back together, each of us in our own time. Our older brother, Chief Joe Mathias, started the annual Christmas gatherings, which still continue today. Many years later, with the encouragement of our elder sister Agnes Paul, we also began practising the old songs and dances again, this time passing on the knowledge to the younger generations.

During our performances at "The Drum Is Calling" festival in 2017, we came to know Alix Shield, who was working on a new edition of the old stories that were in the book *Legends of Vancouver* by E. Pauline Johnson. We were thrilled to meet Alix and to share the stories that we had all heard as children growing up.

During visits to the Mathias family, Alix was told the stories, and shown photos and artifacts from our family. Many of these were lent to Alix to use in the writing of this book. Our family had heard of *Legends of Vancouver,* and many of the stories featured in the book had been passed down in the family for generations in the traditional oral manner.

We are very excited to be a part of this new edition and to have our stories included here. With many thanks and good thoughts for the opportunity.

—The Mathias Family, July 2018

AUTHOR'S FOREWORD TO THE 1911 EDITION

THESE legends (with two or three exceptions) were told to me personally by my honoured friend, the late Chief Joe Capilano, of Vancouver, whom I had the privilege of first meeting in London in 1906, when he visited England and was received at Buckingham Palace by their Majesties King Edward VII and Queen Alexandra.

To the fact that I was able to greet Chief Capilano in the Chinook tongue, while we were both many thousands of miles from home, I owe the friendship and the confidence which he so freely gave me when I came to reside on the Pacific Coast. These legends he told me from time to time, just as the mood possessed him, and he frequently remarked that they had never been revealed to any other English-speaking person save myself.

—E. Pauline Johnson (Tekahionwake)

Figure 2: Agnes (Agi) Mathias Paul standing between portraits of Mary Capilano and Chief Mathias Joe (son of Mary Capilano and Chief Joe Capilano) at the Kia'palano exhibit (Capilano Suspension Bridge, North Vancouver, 2018).

INTRODUCTION

"These Legends Were Told to Me": The Disappearing Legacy of Chief Joe Capilano (Sahp-luk) and Mary Capilano (Lixwelut) in E. Pauline Johnson's *Legends of Vancouver* (1911)

ALIX SHIELD

"How did he get there? It's written in the books that they don't know. They have no knowledge. Nobody even came and talked to anybody, from what I understand from my Dad. And what had happened is that Sahp-luk walked all over B.C. and collected whatever he could from people, because he was going to go over and talk to the King about land claims in the province of British Columbia. That's why he went there [London, England] in 1906, to talk about land claims. He talked to King Edward VII, *who also died in 1910—they both died that year. But he got there because he went to all the people in B.C. and got pennies, dimes, and nickels, and they got him there and back."*

—Agi Mathias Paul, great-granddaughter of Chief Joe and Mary Capilano, daughter of William Joseph Mathias Capilano Joe (son of Mathias Capilano Joe), November 2017

Though Mohawk[1] poet, performer, and writer Emily Pauline Johnson first met Chief Joe Capilano in London in 1906, it wasn't until Johnson's retirement and relocation to Vancouver in 1909 that their collaborative relationship would begin. It was during this time, and in a mixture of English and Chinook (a hybridized trade language used on the west coast of British Columbia), that Joe and Mary Capilano shared their traditional Sḵwx̱wú7mesh stories with Johnson, which she later penned from memory for publication and as a form of cultural safekeeping. Different versions of the stories appeared in periodicals such as *The Boys' World* and *The Mother's Magazine* (1909–1911), as well as the weekend edition of the Vancouver newspaper *The Daily Province* (1910–1911). When Johnson became ill with inoperable breast cancer in 1909, a selection of these stories was gathered from *The Daily Province* by a group who called themselves "the Pauline Johnson Trust," and the book *Legends of Vancouver* was published in 1911—with all proceeds going towards Johnson's medical bills. Though Johnson would die from breast cancer within two years of the book's publication, *Legends* has remained in print ever since; it has been reissued (including unique editions, subeditions, and additional impressions of existing editions by different publishers) approximately thirty times over the last century.

But despite the longevity of *Legends* within the Canadian publishing industry, my research into its publishing history revealed how the authorial contributions of Joe and Mary Capilano have been gradually dismissed from the book entirely. For instance, in over 100 years of publication, neither Joe or Mary Capilano has been acknowledged alongside Johnson on the cover as co-authors; and only in the most recent edition of *Legends* (2013) did biographical information appear for Chief Capilano. Furthermore, despite Mary Capilano's recurring role as narrator in Johnson's stories, very little is known of her life and accomplishments (or the stories she narrated beyond those chosen for *Legends*). On a research trip in 2017 to McMaster University's Special Collections, I found a letter written by Johnson's sister, Evelyn, in which she explicitly states, "The name 'Legends of Vancouver' was given the book by the Trustees of the Fund in the hope that it would prove a better seller. My sister was greatly disappointed as she had called it 'Legends of the Capilano'—the tribe of Indians on the Coast."

In determining that Johnson's wishes for a different title had been documented, and that due to various factors (including the author's declining health and limited involvement in the book's publication) these wishes were not observed, I decided to undertake the project of republishing this book as Johnson had intended.

As an English/Scottish-descended Canadian-born settler scholar working in the field of Indigenous literature, my position in relation to the work of this new edition is one that has required a necessary "unsettling" and "unlearning" of colonial approaches to scholarship, research, and knowing. Though I was raised on the ancestral and unceded territories of the xʷməθkʷəy̓əm (Musqueam), Sḵwx̱wú7mesh Úxwumixw (Squamish), and Səl̓ílwətaʔ/Selilwitulh (Tsleil-Waututh) Nations in Vancouver, where many of the legends in this volume take place, I found myself having to unlearn my relationship to these lands in order to make space for a different perspective—and for stories about the land that I did not know. It was during my master's program at Dalhousie University, in a course on Indigenous literatures, that I first read Johnson's *Legends of Vancouver*. Being on the other end of the country and reading stories of familiar places and landmarks felt like some small reminder of home; but I was also surprised by these stories, because despite recognizing in them places like Stanley Park and Siwash Rock that I knew from my childhood, the stories shared a perspective that I hadn't yet heard; voices I hadn't taken the time to listen to before. When I returned to BC to begin my PhD at Simon Fraser University (SFU), my research focused on *Legends of Vancouver* and looked more broadly at the Canadian publishing industry and its historical marginalization of Indigenous women's writing and literary agency. I looked for ways that my research could contribute meaningfully in response to the TRC's Calls to Action, and to what Métis author Maria Campbell refers to as *kwaskastahsowin* or conciliation ("putting things to right"[2]) within the context of Canada's publishing industry. However, in doing this work as a settler and cultural outsider,

I must also acknowledge the inherent limitations of my own understanding; I am always learning and am grateful to those who have helped teach me along the way.

In this new Introduction, I provide biographical information for Johnson and, for the first time, for the Capilanos; I also draw on archival research to outline the publication history of *Legends of Vancouver*, with a particular focus on the "disappearing" legacies of Chief Joe Capilano and Mary Capilano—how their lives and stories were excluded from the various editions of *Legends* published throughout the past 100 years. As this updated edition seeks to reconnect the *Legends of Vancouver* stories to the Sḵwx̱wú7mesh and Six Nations communities, I consulted two widely respected Indigenous scholars, Rick Monture (Mohawk) and Rudy Reimer (Sḵwx̱wú7mesh), whose own work demonstrates ongoing collaborations with their home Nations; I draw on insights from interviews conducted with Monture and Reimer (separately) throughout this introduction.[3] Other community voices in this edition include those of descendants of Chief Joe and Mary Capilano, the Mathias family, who collaborated on this work with me and to whom I dedicate this updated edition.

E. Pauline Johnson (Tekahionwake)

Emily Pauline Johnson (Tekahionwake) was born 10 March 1861 on Six Nations of the Grand River territory (near Brantford, Ontario). Her father, Mohawk Chief George Henry Martin Johnson (Onwanonsyshon), built the impressive family home known as "Chiefswood" for his English bride, Emily Susanna Howells (a relative of American writer William Dean Howells). The house boasted a unique dual-entrance design, with one door facing the road and the other facing the Grand River—for access by canoe.

As the youngest of four children, Johnson enjoyed a middle-class upbringing and was educated mostly from home; she attended the reserve school for two years and then Brantford Collegiate Institute from the ages of fourteen to sixteen. In 1877, Johnson returned to the family home and spent her time reading, writing, visiting with friends, and canoeing on the Grand River. When her father died in 1884, the family could no longer afford to live at Chiefswood and relocated to a smaller home in Brantford. Johnson, now twenty-three years old and unmarried, began publishing her poetry in periodicals including *Gems of Poetry* (New York) and *The Week* (Toronto). By 1886 her literary reputation was growing, and she began signing her work with both her English name and adopted Mohawk name, Tekahionwake—a name that belonged first to her great-grandfather, Jacob Johnson. She began using this name shortly after the death of her grandfather, John Smoke Johnson, in 1886, and began signing all her poems "E. Pauline Johnson" and "Tekahionwake."[4] Of her use of both names, scholars Veronica Strong-Boag and Carole Gerson suggest that Tekahionwake was "adopted largely to enhance Johnson's professional status," as in her personal life she was known as "Pauline" to her friends and "Paul" to her siblings.[5]

In 1892, Johnson's newspaper article, "A Strong Race Opinion: On the Indian Girl in Modern Fiction," made a critical interjection into the field of Canadian literature, demanding more realistic literary representations of Indigenous women. Though largely ignored at the time,[6] Johnson identified key issues relating to race, gender, and colonialism (including the lack of cultural specificity and awareness of distinct Indigenous nations) that would continue impacting Indigenous women writers into the twentieth century and beyond. That same year, Johnson delivered a captivating recitation of the politically charged poem, "A Cry from an Indian Wife," to a crowd of Toronto's literary select. This began her career as a performer for the next seventeen years, when she toured throughout Canada, the United States, and England. Often, Johnson would appear onstage wearing a "Native" buckskin dress for the first half of the program

and then change into a Victorian evening gown for the second half, thereby encapsulating the performative "dual" identity of poet E. Pauline Johnson, Tekahionwake.

As an Indigenous woman writing at the turn of the nineteenth century and in the wake of the 1876 Indian Act, Johnson stood at a particular intersection of race, gender, and colonialism—an historical moment evidenced by the notable absence of Indigenous or female voices in the literary canon. As such, even Johnson's writing was not immune to the twentieth-century colonial movement of "salvage ethnography," an anthropological trend that positioned Indigenous culture as something dying that needed to be saved.[7] In fact, while Johnson used her unique position as both author and Indigenous proto-feminist to rewrite the "Indian" heroine, her stories have nonetheless attracted criticism for the stereotypes of Indigenous women—through overly romanticized language and references to a melancholic past—that she so vehemently rejected. Forced to find the balance between the competing roles of Indigenous advocate and struggling freelance writer, the superficial tensions often palpable in her writing speak to the difficulty of this position. For instance, Johnson's early stories for *Boy's World* prompted editor Elizabeth Ansley to seek more: "The Indian stories and legends that you have sent us for the *Boys' World* have all been extremely interesting, and it has occurred to us that you might have something equally pleasing suitable for *The Mother's Magazine*."[8] In reality, such editorial demands meant that Johnson often needed to rework existing material based on the publisher's readership. Furthermore, as Monture notes, it's important to acknowledge that Johnson wasn't raised traditionally at Six Nations; he argues, she "had an imperfect understanding of our culture and ceremony . . .

Figure 3: Portrait of E. Pauline Johnson, n.d. Vancouver Public Library, Special Collections Historical Photographs, Accession no. 9430.

and wasn't that interested in understanding or portraying traditional culture accurately."[9] This non-traditional upbringing, paired with Johnson's career involving constant nationwide and international travelling and touring, meant that she had limited opportunities to connect with her home community—particularly as she moved further west to Winnipeg and, ultimately, Vancouver. In 1895, Johnson published her first book of poetry, titled *The White Wampum*, which met with great success. Johnson moved to Winnipeg after the death of her mother (1898) and was briefly engaged to Charles Robert Lumley Drayton that same year. Her second poetry collection, *Canadian Born*, was published in 1903. *The White Wampum* clearly pays tribute to Johnson's Mohawk ancestry, placing her adopted name Tekahionwake as the only text on the book's cover and featuring some of Johnson's most iconic Indigenous-centred poems (including "Ojistoh" and "The Cattle Thief").[10] On the other hand, *Canadian Born* opens with a poem proclaiming Johnson's nationalistic pride in a country ruled "beneath the British flag"—an approach that decidedly ignores the sovereignty of the Kanien'kehá:ka (Mohawk) people.

After retiring from the stage in 1909 due to declining health, Johnson moved to Vancouver, BC, where she reconnected with Sḵwx̱wú7mesh Chief Joe Capilano (Sahp-luk) and wrote the stories that would be gathered together for *Legends of Vancouver*. A collection of her poetry, titled *Flint and Feather* (Toronto: Musson), was published in 1912, also to raise money for her medical bills. Both collections remain in print today.

Johnson eventually succumbed to cancer and passed away on 7 March 1913. The City of Vancouver held a funeral several days later, with the grand procession taking place between the Bute Street hospital and Christ Church Cathedral: "Throughout the city, public offices were closed and flags flew at half-mast. This was the largest funeral the young city had ever seen."[11] Johnson's ashes were interred near Ferguson Point in Stanley Park, within view of her beloved Siwash Rock. A memorial service was also held at the Mohawk

Church on the Six Nations Reserve. There were two prose collections published following her death: *The Moccasin Maker* (Toronto: Briggs), which includes many stories from *The Mother's Magazine*, and *The Shagganappi* (Toronto: Briggs), a collection of stories from *The Boys' World* periodical. In 1922 the Women's Canadian Club raised a monument at her gravesite in Stanley Park.[12]

Chief Joe Capilano (Sahp-luk)

Chief Joe Capilano (Sahp-luk),[13] known also as Sahp-luk Joe, was born around 1854 at Yekw'ts (near Squamish, BC).[14] His father, Letekwamcheten, was also from Yekw'ts.[15] After becoming orphaned at a young age, Joe began working for the government in Fort Langley—this helped to develop his skills as an English-speaker and gain confidence in his abilities as a public orator.

Sahp-luk Joe married Mary Agnes (Lixwelut) on 21 May 1872, likely at a Roman Catholic church in New Westminster;[16] he was baptized as a Catholic on their wedding day.[17] Joe and Mary then moved to the Catholic reserve known as Eslhá7an (or Mission Indian Reserve No. 1[18]) in North Vancouver to start a family. When Chief Lahwa (of the Sḵwx̱wú7mesh Nation) died in 1895, Joe was selected as the next Chief because of Mary—as the grand-niece of "Old" Chief Ki-ap-a-la-no, she was the nearest blood relative to the former hereditary chief. Beyond these blood ties, however, Sḵwx̱wú7mesh Elder Louis Miranda believes that Catholic missionary Bishop Paul Durieu may have influenced the decision to choose Joe as chief. As a devout Catholic and respected orator, Sahp-luk Joe was considered the most acceptable leader by the church—and the best chance the missionaries had of converting the nearby Capilano Reserve to Catholicism.[19] Chief Joe Capilano and Mary Agnes later relocated from Mission to Homulchesun (Capilano Creek) Reserve. Joe Capilano began working as a longshoreman in Moodyville (close to the Second Narrows Bridge

in North Vancouver) and eventually became a foreman. As Vancouver author James Morton writes, Joe Capilano "was first known to the white settlers around Burrard Inlet as Hyas [or Hi-Ash] Joe meaning big, strong, powerful, and later as Capilano Joe, to distinguish him from all the other Joes up and down the inlet."[20]

In 1906, Chief Capilano, along with Chief Charlie Silpaymilt (Cowichan) and Chief Basil Bonaparte (Kamloops), travelled to London, England, to protest to King Edward VII about seasonal restrictions being enforced over Indigenous land and fishing rights. According to Chief Simon Baker, elected chief of the Sḵwx̱wú7mesh Nation (1942–2001)[21] and grandson of Joe Capilano, Joe was lent the name "Capilano" prior to this trip, so that he might meet the King bearing a respected Coast Salish name.[22] The three Chiefs plus their interpreter, Simon Pierre (of the Keatzie Reserve, Port Hammond), left Vancouver for England on 3 July 1906; there was a great gathering to send off the delegation at the Canadian Pacific Railway (CPR) station. They took the train to Ottawa, visiting Parliament Hill and obtaining a letter of introduction to Canada's High Commissioner in London, Lord Strathcona.[23] During their trip abroad, the *Vancouver Daily Province* published an excerpt of one of Chief Capilano's London speeches, addressing concerns relating to seasonal hunting and fishing: "In the past few years, white men have so increased that they are like a storm of locusts, leaving the earth bare where they pass by. They have extinguished the buffalo, and moose is each year getting less and less. The caribou is doomed and our rivers no longer give forth that abundance of fish that was the heritage of our forefathers. The close season should be made more restrictive for the whites and more open for us. With them it is a recreation; with us it is our living."[24] In

---

Figure 4: Chief Joe Capilano, 1908. MONOVA Archives of North Vancouver, Inventory no. 2849.

Over-Seas

Facts and Opinions from Greater Britain.

THE GRAPHIC

Figures 5 and *6:* British news coverage from Chief Joe Capilano's 1906 trip to visit King Edward VII. Left: *Over-Seas Magazine* (with names wrongly attributed below cover image), 1 September 1906. E. Pauline Johnson fonds, The William Ready Division of Archives and Research Collections, McMaster University, Box 4 file 30. Right: *The Graphic*, 18 August 1906. MONOVA Archives of North Vancouver, Inventory no. 1906-5.

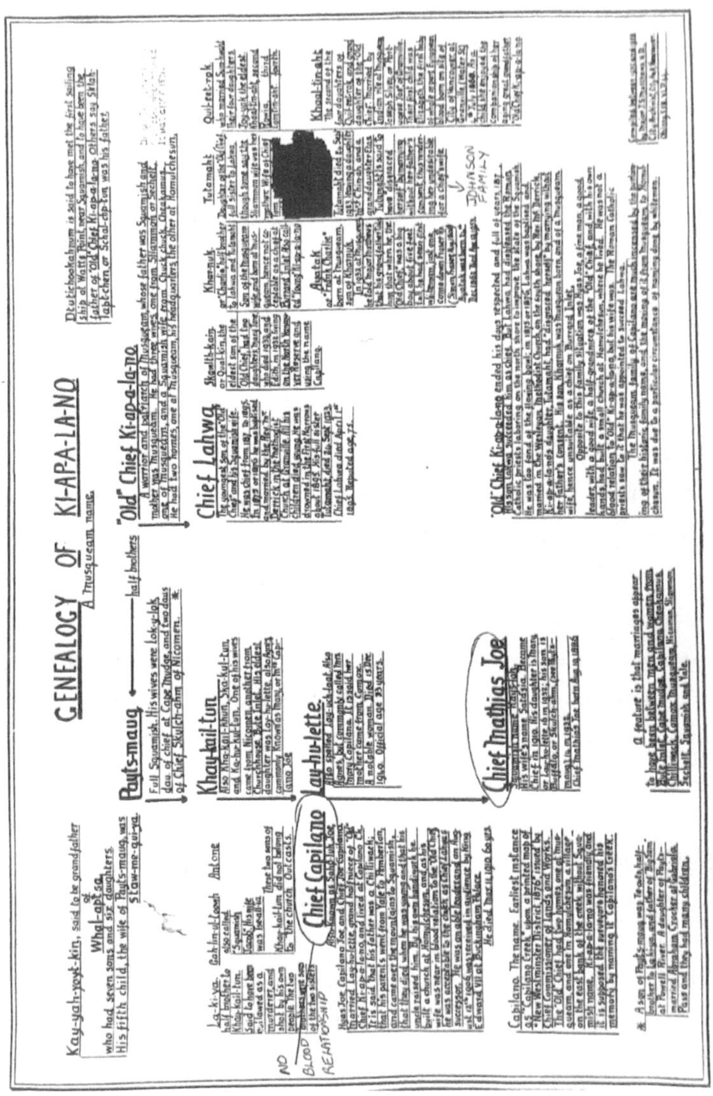

Figure 7: "Genealogy of Ki-ap-a-la-no: A Musqueam Name" n.d. Compiled by Major James Skitt Matthews. City of Vancouver Archives, Major Matthews collection, "Indians—Capilano genealogy" file, Ref. AM54-S23-1.

London, Chief Capilano was introduced to E. Pauline Johnson for the first time. Johnson had been asked by Sir Arthur Pearson, friend of Lord Strathcona, to interview the delegation, and while she did not speak any of the West Coast dialects, she was able to greet them using the Chinook greeting, "Klahowya Tillicum" ("How do you do, friend?").[25] The Chiefs returned to Vancouver with vague promises and hopes that King Edward VII would take their concerns to heart.

Back in Vancouver, Joe Capilano had garnered the reputation of "agitator"[26] as he continued lobbying local politicians for the return to year-round traditional hunting rights. In June 1908, Capilano travelled to Ottawa to see Governor-General Earl Grey and voice these concerns; he instead had an audience with Prime Minister Sir Wilfrid Laurier but met with little success.[27] Not content to stop fighting for their traditional rights, Joe Capilano travelled to different local Indigenous communities, spreading the news of his trip to London and the meeting with the King.[28] Upon his return, Chief Capilano began speaking out against the Catholic Church, arguing that their lack of support for his trip to London had rendered them an unwelcome presence on the reserve.[29] During the next two years, Joe and Mary Capilano, along with their young children, reunited with Johnson and shared with her their stories of the Sḵwx̱wú7mesh Úxwumixw (Squamish peoples).

In March of 1910, Chief Joe Capilano died from tuberculosis. His funeral was held at the Catholic Church at Mission Reserve, and people from all over British Columbia attended. Johnson was said to have "laid upon his coffin her bunch of lilies 'as a token of Peace and Power from the Mohawks.'"[30] Joe Capilano was succeeded as Chief by his son, Mathias Joe.

Mary Capilano (Lixwelut)

"For one must voice his thoughts delicately if one hopes to extract a tradition from my good old ancient Klootchman."

—"The Legend of the Ice Babies," November 1911

"My Grandfather's mother, Mary Agnes Capilano, did a lot for the people that live on our land... Great-grandma worked hard—every day she would go on her canoe with all the seafood. She brought to the Hotel Vancouver fresh seafood. And also she made cedar baskets, and other things she made and sold them in downtown Vancouver, then came back in her canoe. I think about how strong she was."

—Katherine (Katie) Phyllis Mathias Joe August, December 2017

Mary Agnes Capilano (Lixwelut, also spelled Lay-hu-lette[31] or Lay-Kho-Lote,[32] meaning "the beginning of the world") was born around 1840. She was the granddaughter of Paytsamauq, who was half-brother of Old Chief Ki-ap-a-la-no—the same Chief that welcomed Captain Vancouver into Burrard Inlet in 1792.[33] Though some descendants understand that Mary Capilano was born at Potlatch Creek in Howe Sound, off the eastern coast of Vancouver Island,[34] it is also known in the Sḵwx̱wú7mesh community that she came from X̱wáýx̱way (Lumberman's Arch) in what is now known as Stanley Park. Mary Capilano was the first-born daughter of a marriage that united two previously warring First Nations, the Yaculta (now known as the Kwakwaka'wakw) and the Sḵwx̱wú7mesh. For this, she became known by many as "The Princess of Peace." According to members of the Sḵwx̱wú7mesh Nation, Mary Capilano moved at one time to Potlatch Creek, where she built a longhouse and fought to protect the traditional ceremonies against colonial anti-Potlatch legislation.[35]

Mary Capilano's first husband, Charley Tihomak, came from the Catholic Mission Reserve in New Westminster; they were married on 10 May 1866.[36] After his death from smallpox, Mary met her second husband, Sahp-luk Joe. After they married in 1872,[37] the Capilanos relocated first to Mission Reserve No. 1, and then near the Capilano River to Homulchesun (now known as Xwmelch'sten) or Capilano Indian Reserve No. 5. Although the Catholic Church wanted to build a church on Capilano land, Mary Capilano said no; instead, a church was built nearby at the Mission Reserve No. 1 (also on Sḵwx̱wú7mesh territory).[38] Together, the Capilanos had three surviving children—Mathias Joe, Emma, and Susan—and raised four of their grandsons, Simon, Dan, William, and Joe Baker.[39]

Mary Capilano could speak many languages, including Sḵwx̱wú7mesh, hən̓q̓əmin̓əm̓ (Musqueam), Tsilhqot'in (Chilcotin), St'at'imcets (Lillooet), Chinook, and some English.[40] Those who knew her often described her as good-natured and clever. Noel Robinson, a Vancouver journalist and acquaintance of Mary's, said, "She has the keenest sense of humor and is often very witty, and I am convinced that, as a small child she must have been what we call precocious."[41] She was known widely for her talents as a basket weaver (see Figure 10), and was often seen paddling her dugout canoe, even in her older years when her legs were "not quite skookum,"[42] to cross the First Narrows between the Capilano Reserve and downtown Vancouver to sell her wares—a round-trip journey of about six kilometres. As Mary Capilano's great-granddaughter, Agi Mathias Paul, explains: "Sahp-luk lived the traditional way; Mary Agnes knew the city."[43] She made a living by selling her basketry and mats, along with fresh clams and berries, to residents of the West End and guests at the Hotel Vancouver. According to her grandson, Chief

---

Figure 8: "Mrs. Mary 'Lay-hu-lette' Capilano," 31 May 1939. City of Vancouver Archives, Major Matthews collection, Ref. AM54-S4-: Port P430.

Simon Baker, Mary Capilano "used to keep busy going there about three times a week, even if she got only five cents a pound."[44] Mary Capilano was also known to enjoy smoking tobacco from a pipe—or "tobac," as she called it.[45]

After the death of her second husband in 1910, Mary Capilano held two memorial Potlatches in his honour—one shortly afterwards, and another about fifteen years later. Vancouver columnist Mamie Moloney wrote about her Potlatch in the *Vancouver Sun*: "A chieftainess in her own right, Mary gave one of the last of the famous potlatches before they were outlawed by the white man. With the proceeds from her clam beds, her orchard and her berry-picking, she saved money to buy hundreds of blankets which she gave away, with all the cash she possessed, to her potlatch guests."[46]

As the Mathias family remembers, Mary Capilano was well known throughout BC, and many First Nations from up and down the coast would come to her for advice. For example, when traders from the Hudson's Bay Company would travel around the coast to buy or trade (often blankets) for carvings or hides, people would ask her if these traders were trustworthy. The family remembers stories of runners coming down from northern First Nations communities, like Gitxsan, Wet'suwet'en, and Nisga'a, to learn what money was along with negotiation tactics, since Mary herself spoke English and had first-hand experience from years of selling her own goods.

Mary Capilano was also an activist for Indigenous rights, standing as witness during the City of Vancouver and Government of Canada's 1923 dispossession cases against the families of Brockton Point, Stanley Park. The "Dispossession Cases" were launched by the City of Vancouver and the Canadian Government in April 1923, against eight families in an effort to dispossess those residing at Whoi Whoi, Kanaka Ranch and Brockton Point of their land and dwellings. These legal cases followed the 1886 petition to the government by Vancouver's city council to turn all of the Coal Harbour peninsula into a public park.[47] Of the four court cases, commonly referred to in newspapers as the "Stanley Park Squatters," Mary Capilano testified as a defence witness for sisters Agnes Cummings and Margaret West as they attempted to prove, through succession, their "squatter's rights" to the land in Stanley Park; their mother was First Nations from Bella Coola, and their father was a white settler.[48] As Jean Barman notes, these cases relied on the concept of "adverse possession," i.e. "whereby occupation that went unchallenged for a specified period of time overrode legal ownership."[49] Mary Capilano spoke to the court in Sḵwx̱wú7mesh (translated in court to English by her son Chief Mathias Joe), testifying that she remembered previous residents of the Cummings' house from her childhood: "She knows Dr. Johnson. She says she never visit him, but she sees the old Dr. Johnson when she used to dig clams near to the beach there."[50]

In October 1940, Mary Capilano had a near-death experience that likely led to her passing several weeks later. After visiting her husband's mausoleum at the Capilano cemetery, she got lost on her return home, and decided to wade across the Capilano River at dusk. She ended up in shoulder-deep water and spent most of the night resting alongside the river, too exhausted to continue home. When she eventually made it home, it was nearly sunrise. Mary Capilano spent the next two days in bed, semi-conscious, before she was able to resume her normal activities. This incident was reported in the *Province* on 29 October 1940, in an article titled "Matriarch of Capilano Escapes Torrent." Mary Capilano never fully recovered from her injuries and died on 15 December 1940, when she was approximately 100 years old.[51] Her family laid her to rest next to her late husband, Chief Joe Capilano.

From London (1906) to Vancouver (1909)

When Johnson was first introduced to Chief Capilano in London, England, speaking the little Chinook that she knew at the time, she provided a small sense of home to the Sḵwx̱wú7mesh leader.[52] It is unlikely, however, that following her introduction to Chief Capilano, Johnson had any sense of the complex backstory behind the mighty Capilano name. Known prior to his London trip as Hyas Joe or Sahp-luk Joe, he had embarked on a massive fundraising effort in order to make the trek to visit the King—collecting whatever he could, "pennies, dimes, and nickels" from anyone in BC that was willing to support their cause.[53] Though Sahp-luk Joe had already been an elected chief for the Capilano Reserve since 1895, the community decided that it was not quite proper to visit the King of England without a respected name to accompany him. Chief Simon Baker explains that prior to Joe's trip to England, "the BC Indian leaders got together on the Cambie Street grounds where the old bus depot used to be. He was officially given that Capilano name and a blanket was put on him in a ceremony."[54] According to Sḵwx̱wú7mesh Elder Louis Miranda (1892–1990), a distinguished Sḵwx̱wú7mesh community member and language revitalist, the name was given to Chief Sahp-luk Joe to borrow but was kept even after his return to Vancouver:

> So when Chief Sahp-luk—they were calling him Chief Joe at that time, so Kiapalano from Musqueam said, "I don't think it's right for you to go down there as 'Chief Joe.' Take an Indian name with you. The man who really was the Chief of that reserve—My father," he says. "And I got that name, Kiapalano. I'll loan you this name, with the understanding that you'll use it over there, but when you come back, you'll return that name to me. Because it's my name," he says. "I'm the direct descendant." So Chief Joe

> got the name Kiapalano when he went over, and when he came back, he never returned it.[55]

In this sense, Chief Joe was never really a "Kiapalano" or Capilano—not like his wife, Mary Agnes, who was a descendant of the Old Chief through her father's side.[56] As elected chief of the Capilano Reserve, Joe kept the Capilano name after his visit with the King and later passed it to his son, Mathias Joe. As Chief Simon Baker explains, "There was a lot of controversy over the Capilano name, so he didn't use it except once in a while when he was referred to as Chief Mathias Joe Capilano. Some of the descendants of the four Capilano brothers are to this day wanting to reclaim the Capilano name. So, it seemed better not to use the name any more for the descendants of Hi-Ash Joe, Chief Joe Capilano."[57] After Chief Mathias Joe used the Capilano name, only Mathias and Joe, not Capilano, have been passed through the family line.

After a brief visit for a month in 1908—when Joe Capilano welcomed her at the Hotel Vancouver—and a final year of touring between 1908 and 1909, Johnson settled in Vancouver permanently. A modest apartment located at 1117 Howe Street became the site for most of her final writing. As to why Johnson chose to retire in Vancouver, literary scholar Martha L. Viehmann suggests:

> She was seeking a place to retire from her stage career but would need to continue to write to support herself. Therefore, Vancouver may have been a more appealing choice than the Six Nations area because of its mild climate and beautiful landscape. In addition, the presence of friends, such as her former partner Walter McRaye,[58] and acquaintances, such as Suápuluck, would have been a draw, and perhaps she foresaw that her friendship with the Squamish chief would provide her with new material,

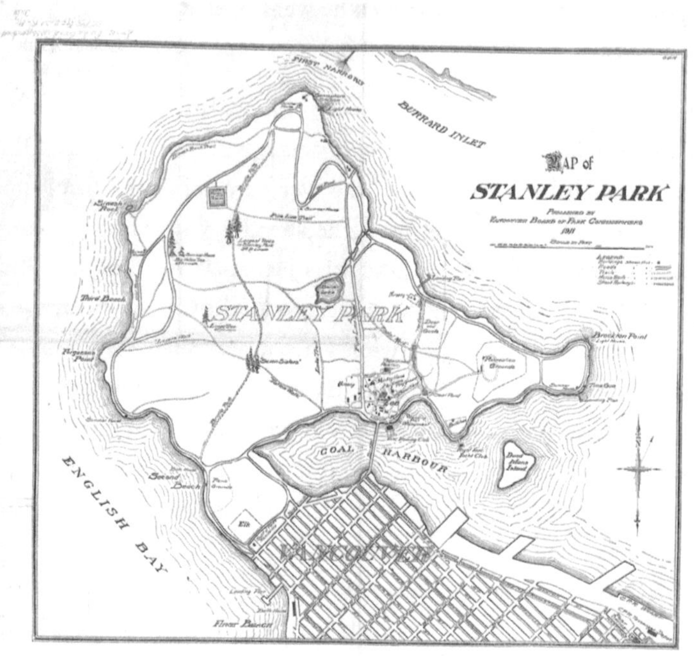

Figure 9: "Map of Stanley Park, Vancouver, B.C.," 1911. City of Vancouver Archives, Ref. AM1594-: MAP 368b.

> and the publishing opportunities in the northwest may have seemed better.[59]

Johnson often spent time with the Capilanos—at her home in Downtown Vancouver, across the Inlet at the Capilano Reserve, or paddling a canoe around Stanley Park. In those days, the only way across the Narrows was by boat; the Harris family, who lived in Stanley Park until 1949, owned several rowboats and often received telephone calls from Johnson asking about hiring a boat to travel to the north shore: "When the famous Indian poetess, Pauline Johnson, wished to visit the Indian reserve at Capilano, she would call Mrs. Harris and ask her to keep a boat close at hand."[60] During those visits, Johnson listened to the stories, spoken in a mixture of Chinook and English, told by her Sḵwx̱wú7mesh friends. Not much is documented about how she recorded the stories being shared with her. However, from what little is known, we can assume that Johnson relied mainly on some combination of memory and literary imagination to produce the stories. In Linda Quirk's extensive descriptive bibliography on *Legends*, she argues that "Johnson took few notes because she did not want to distract the storyteller."[61] In fact, in Charlotte Gray's *Flint & Feather: The Life and Times of E. Pauline Johnson, Tekahionwake* (2002), Gray points to a privately published collection of newspaper columns written by Bertha Jean Thompson Stevinson (a close Vancouver friend of Johnson's) for insight into Johnson's methodology: "If she needed to make a note to assist her memory she went into the kitchen on the pretense of getting a drink of water and there jotted down the note. Never did she do this before her guest."[62] Though the majority of the "legends" are narrated by Chief Joe Capilano, descendants of the Capilanos believe that Mary Capilano was the actual source for the stories of the Coast—that she had learned these stories and then told them to her husband, who then eventually shared them with Johnson, or sometimes directly to Johnson.[63]

"Periodicals First": *The Mother's Magazine* and the *Vancouver Daily Province*[64]

The "legends" were published mainly between 1909 and 1912, with most appearing in the weekend edition of the *Vancouver Daily Province*, and others in the American women's periodical, *The Mother's Magazine* (Elgin, IL). These two publication venues targeted very different readerships; and aside from illustrating Johnson's far-reaching, international literary audience, these distinct venues also underscore her adaptability as a writer to ensure a steady income.[65] *Mother's Magazine* (published by David C. Cook, who also published the *Boys' World* magazine) was a mass-circulation magazine directed at "predominantly white, middle-class" women.[66] For this U.S. periodical, Johnson crafted stories that centred on themes of motherhood and femininity; in fact, when the editor of *Mother's*, Elizabeth Ansley, corresponded with Johnson about writing for their magazine, she suggested that "some humour and bright, happy stories" would be most suitable.[67] Johnson's stories in *Mother's* were often those narrated by Mary Capilano and were written with a more "sentimental" tone than those that appeared in the *Province*.[68]

The "urban" readers of the Vancouver newspaper, on the other hand, expected something a bit more literary and sophisticated;[69] in early twentieth-century Vancouver, this meant catering to a presumed readership of mostly male, non-Indigenous readers. Though Johnson's first "legend" was narrated by Mary Capilano and published in *Mother's* ("The Legend of the Two Sisters"), a slightly different version appeared in the *Province*. After Johnson's initial meeting with Lionel Makovski, then editor of the *Vancouver Daily Province Magazine Section* (the weekend supplement of the *Province* newspaper), he suggested that adjustments to the legends would be necessary: "Mr. Makovski took the manuscript of 'The Two Sisters' under consideration, and in a few days reported to Pauline that he would use the story with a few changes, and asked if she would undertake to provide a series."[70] The most notable of these "changes" involved switching the narrative voice from Mary Capilano's to that of Chief Capilano, trading Mary's voice for something more authoritative—presumably to better appeal to male readers.

Though Johnson had initially "doubted her ability" to convey the Capilanos' stories, Makovski played an instrumental role in convincing Johnson to continue.[71] As Alfred Buckley notes in a 1913 article for the *Vancouver News-Advertiser*, Johnson had a special connection with the Capilanos that Makovski recognized: "Others of us had talked with Chief Joe and found him a benevolent old man, expressing himself in English with difficulty and retiring too suddenly and frequently behind the monosyllable.... Only Pauline Johnson had the sympathetic key to his mind."[72] But Johnson's translations were not received without issue, as J.N.J. Brown, former superintendent of the Sḵwx̱wú7mesh Nation, noted: "Pauline simply did not fully understand the chief's mixture of Chinook and English, which had been thinly stretched to provide words to explain the symbolism and subtle meanings in the legends. The mistakes, he suggested, were in the passage from the teller to the recorder."[73]

Furthermore, the *Province* may have recognized an opportunity to capitalize on the notoriety of Chief Capilano, who was already known to many newspapers in Vancouver and throughout British Columbia. In fact, shortly before the publication of their first "legend," the *Province* published a three-page profile for their weekend magazine dedicated to Chief Capilano, who had recently passed. Until the profile, the *Province* had been hostile towards Indigenous issues.[74] Their unexpected and favourable tribute to Chief Capilano may have come from a position of comfortably looking back on Capilano with "settler nostalgia for an imagined Indianness assumed to be already or almost already extinct."[75] In other words, it may have seemed easier for journalists to celebrate Chief Capilano with exaggerated fondness when viewing him as one of the "last Indians."[76]

We can also look to the short passages that often preceded Johnson's newspaper stories to get a sense of Makovski's editorial motivations, and how *The Province's* readership informed the ways the legends were editorially framed. For example, in the Preface to "The Lure in Stanley Park" (20 August 1910), Makovski emphasizes Johnson's Mohawk heritage and, by extension, her authority on the subject. He writes, "We may remind our readers that Miss Johnson, being herself an Indian, has a peculiar insight into the lives of the coast tribes and it is natural that they will tell her their legends, when to all others they remain silent." Here, Makovski's assertion of authenticity assumes Johnson's "Indian" heritage as being the same as that of the Capilanos. Although both Sḵwx̱wú7mesh and Haudenosaunee peoples have experienced the impacts of colonialism, this elision dismisses the vast differences in geographic territory, history, language, and culture of Sḵwx̱wú7mesh and Haudenosaunee peoples.

In the published legends, regardless of venue, we gain a clear sense of Johnson's respect and admiration for the Capilanos through her detailed descriptions of both the storytelling context and of Chief Joe and Mary Capilano themselves. According to literary scholar Christine Marshall, "'it is clear that Pauline's handling of the legends includes contextual elements now considered essential to an oral storytelling'. Those elements include 'her detailed descriptions of her relationship to the storyteller, of the occasion of the storytelling, [and] of the language and gestures used.'"[77] Such elements are crucial to positioning both Chief Joe Capilano and Mary Capilano as more than merely disembodied Indigenous voices. And it is here, in what another literary scholar Deena Rymhs describes as the "framing" elements at either end of the legend itself, that we truly get a sense of Johnson's efforts at editorial transparency.[78] In "The Lure in Stanley Park," for example, Johnson acknowledges that although the word "lure" is not what Chief Capilano used in telling this story, she chose the word based on his description: "There is no equivalent for the word in the

Chinook tongue, but the gestures of his voiceful hands so expressed the quality of something between magnetism and charm that I have selected this word 'lure' as best fitting what he wished to convey." A similar editorial admission occurs in many of the stories narrated by Mary Capilano, whereby Johnson acknowledges Mary's "broken English, that, much as I love it, I must leave to the reader's imagination" ("The Legend of Lillooet Falls"). We can consider Johnson's efforts at transparency, rather than accuracy, as perhaps a better goal throughout the collaborative storytelling process.

Through her passage in and out of the narrative margins, we also catch glimpses of Johnson's complicated relationship with her Mohawk identity. For instance, in "The Grey Archway," Johnson includes an affirmation of her Indigeneity from a stranger, as if to placate herself and any readers who may have doubts: "He gave a swift glance at my dark skin, then nodded. 'You are one of us . . . and you will understand.'" Rymhs interestingly points to Johnson's tendency to refer to the Iroquois peoples in quotation marks, "suggest[ing] the narrator's detached stance from the people she here defines as her own."[79] Though part of this narrative uncertainty can be explained by Johnson's position as cultural outsider to the Sḵwx̱wú7mesh Nation, it also reflects the inconsistency of her relationship to her ancestral home at Six Nations. For instance, Mohawk scholar Rick Monture observes that the marriage between Johnson's parents, George Johnson (Onwanonsyshon) and Emily Howells, was unusual for Six Nations at the time; more often, mixed marriages "were between Native women and white men,"[80] a pairing that would, following the Haudenosaunee matrilineal kinship system, pass status onwards to children. Instead, Monture explains, "many people at the time, both Native and non-Native, had some difficulty accepting George and Emily's marriage," and that Johnson's mother, Emily Howells, was "never quite . . . accepted into the social life of the reserve."[81]

When reflecting on Johnson's relationship to Six Nations, Monture notes that "her connection to the reserve was so minimal in the last few years of her life, there wasn't much really to talk about. We're pretty sure that she never did a reading that we know of on the Reserve."[82] And yet, when drawing from her own historical records—as is done in the story, "A Royal Mohawk Chief"—Johnson provides readers with a confident and patriotic retelling of the Duke of Connaught's ceremonial 1869 visit to Six Nations. This story, selected as the concluding story for the *Legends of Vancouver* volume, does not follow the "legend" pattern of the rest of the stories; instead, this story draws on Johnson's own Mohawk history and experiences, referencing a letter, "yellowing with age," addressed from the Duke of Connaught to Johnson's father, Onwanonsyshon.[83] This story also gestures towards the storytelling legacy of her grandfather John "Smoke" Johnson, who was known widely as an orator and shared stories of Iroquois history with Johnson in her youth.[84] However, by placing it at the end of the *Legends* volume (despite being one of the first pieces to appear in the *Province*), following the Sḵwx̱wú7mesh stories that speak to irreparable cultural loss at the hands of the Canadian and British governments, this story's message about everlasting brotherhood between the British and the Mohawk Nation rings somewhat false. These contradictory responses to her own Indigeneity suggest that Johnson was more comfortable drawing from her own experiences and repertoire than in attempting to locate herself within another nation's narrative.

The first version of "A Royal Mohawk Chief," published under the title "A Brother Chief," appeared in the *Weekly Detroit Free Press* on 12 May 1892, nearly twenty years before *Legends* was published. The fact that Johnson penned a version of this story long before her time with the Capilanos in Vancouver suggests that she chose the story for *Legends* as a means of preserving an important part of her own family's legacy; namely, the involvement of her father, George H. M. Johnson (Onwanonsyshon), and grandfather, John "Smoke"

Johnson (Chief Sakayengwaraton), during the Duke of Connaught's visit. In fact, it is likely that the death of Johnson's father in 1884 (eight years before the story's publication) served as motivation to finally put this story to paper. The next version, on which the story in *Legends* is based, was published in *The Vancouver Daily Province* on 2 July 1910 under the title "The Duke of Connaught as Chief of the Iroquois." Another version appeared in *The Boys' World* magazine on 1 October 1910, under the title "A Chieftain Prince." Though these three variations each include distinct opening paragraphs, they share the same key narrative points describing the Duke of Connaught's visit to Six Nations in 1869 and the symbolic conferring of the Duke's title as honorary "Chief of the Six Nations Indians." In his book *We Share Our Matters* (2014) and in our interview, Monture argues that Johnson's story seemingly misinterpreted the symbolic nature of this ceremony: "It is true that her grandfather and father played a role during that time in 1869; but that was essentially a Six Nations response to the recent Confederation of Canada, and they were building relationships, reminding the Crown of our ally-to-ally relationship way back before Confederation."[85] For the Haudenosaunee, the title of Chief conferred to the Duke of Connaught was a gesture of "goodwill"; there was no expectation that he would have any decision-making authority within the Iroquois Confederacy.[86]

The Publication of *Legends* (and Recovering Mary Capilano's Narrative Voice)

About two years after Johnson's breast cancer diagnosis, and with her health rapidly declining, friends and supporters set out to publish a collection of her prose stories to raise funds for her medical treatments. The group, who called themselves the Pauline Johnson Trust Fund, formed in September of 1911 and included Vancouver journalist Isabel McLean (known as "Alexandra"), and the *Vancouver*

Daily Province's Lionel Makovski and Bernard McEvoy. This group of supporters initiated the publication of *Legends of Vancouver*, choosing stories from Johnson's repertoire of "Indian Legends" and arranging them in the collection that would be titled *Legends of Vancouver.*

In the year before the trust became reality, Johnson was hospitalized briefly during the summer of 1910 while still attempting to regularly publish her "legends" in the *Province* and *Mother's*. As she was unable to write anything down, she relied on her editor from the *Daily Province Magazine*, Lionel Makovski, who transcribed her stories from her hospital bed. Makovski explains the process this way: "Over and over again during those times when her health was rapidly deteriorating, I sat with her over a cup of tea and she 'translated' some of Chief Joe's legends for me to transcribe."[87] By using the word "translate," Makovski gestures towards Johnson's process of relaying the legends to him through a combination of memory (recalling the stories as told by the Capilanos in a mixture of English and Chinook) and her own imagination. Friends who were constantly in Johnson's presence during her final years included acquaintances like Isabel McLean and Miss A.M. Ross. In *The Mohawk Princess: Being Some Account of the Life of Tekahion-Wake (E. Pauline Johnson)*, Mrs. W. Garland Foster describes Johnson's friendships during this period as follows: "Could Pauline express herself of those hard times she would probably liken the situation to landing an overloaded canoe in rough water. Everyone about the wharf lent a hand and the landing was made."[88] These examples illustrate the potential of direct intervention throughout the transmission process, adding another layer of mediation between the Capilanos and the published stories.

Several local women's groups became heavily involved in raising money for Johnson's treatment, including the Imperial Order Daughters of the Empire (IODE), Women's Canadian Club, and Canadian Women's Press Club. Members of these groups facilitated nation-wide fundraising efforts, selling copies of Johnson's *Legends* in

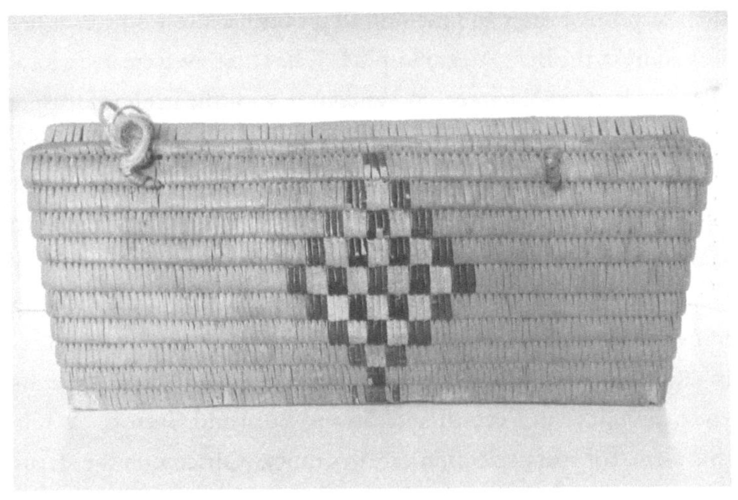

Figure 10: Cedar basket woven by Mary Capilano. Property of the Mathias family. Image by A. Shield, 2018. According to a personal interview with the Mathias family in November 2017, it probably took Mary two years to make this basket: "it takes longer with multicolour."

their respective cities and mailing all profits back to Johnson at her new address: the Bute Street Hospital.[89] The IODE even created a local "Pauline Johnson Chapter" in Vancouver, with the goal of focusing specifically on Johnson's fundraising campaign. And yet despite the involvement of women's groups from across the country, the first edition of *Legends of Vancouver* set a precedent that would ignore and marginalize the contributions of another Indigenous woman, Mary Capilano, for the next century. As the stories selected for publication in *Legends* were chosen only from the *Province* versions, most stories in the volume were narrated by Chief Capilano—and Mary Capilano's voice disappeared. According to Strong-Boag and Gerson, "While this tactic [of story selection] creates unity, it discredits the status originally granted to Lixwelut as a storyteller in her own right."[90] With the help of Mary Capilano in the *Mother's Magazine* versions, Johnson emphasizes themes of motherhood and femininity, often describing the unbreakable bonds between Indigenous women and their children. For instance, in the *Mother's* version of "The Two Sisters" (as "The Legend of the Two Sisters"), the female narrator grounds the story through a gendered metaphor, likening the mountains to Indigenous women: "Yes, the river holds many secrets,' she continued, 'secrets of strong men's battles and many tragedies, but the mountains hold the secrets of an Indian mother's heart, and those are the greatest secrets of all things.'"[91] The version printed in the *Province* one year later dropped this metaphor, and was instead narrated by Chief Capilano and retitled "The True Legend of Vancouver's Lions." Though the "Lions" and the "Two Sisters" both refer to the same North Shore mountains visible across Greater Vancouver, the *Province* opted to use the colonial name (chosen around 1890 by BC Supreme Court Justice John Hamilton Gray[92]) that non-Indigenous readers would recognize. This choice is particularly ironic given that Joe Capilano and a small hunting party accomplished the first recorded ascent of one of the Sisters, the West Lion, in 1889,[93] thereby demonstrating a deeper knowledge and connection to the mountains that preceded the colonial naming.

From the opening lines of the *Mother's* version of the story, we can identify clear differences between this first version and the one that appeared one year later in the *Province.* The legend opens with Johnson's grand description of the mountains, describing "those twin peaks of the twin mountains that lift their pearly summits across the inlet." She then introduces her narrator as the "ancient Klootchman," meaning old "woman" in Chinook; Mary Capilano is never named in the story, nor in any of Johnson's legends.[94] In the framing that precedes the legend, we are introduced to "the handsome chief of the Capilanos," "his slim, silent young daughter," and "the quaint old Indian mother"—and from the outset, the focus of this story remains on the old Klootchman. While the *Mother's Magazine* version begins with an image of the Capilanos as a family, the *Province* version focuses solely on Chief Capilano. Appearing more than a year later in the weekend magazine edition of the *Province* on 16 April 1910, it carries the new title, "The True Legend of Vancouver's Lions." This retitling imparts a sense of ownership of the mountains by the city of Vancouver and privileges non-Indigenous relationships to the land, thus mollifying the *Province*'s majority readership. In addition to opening the *Mother's* legend with a focus on family, Johnson also uses the frame narrative to describe Mary Capilano's highly-regarded basketry—a seemingly minor reference, but one that importantly acknowledges one of Mary's main sources of income, as well as her expression of traditional skills and knowledge: "At our feet were baskets of exquisite weavery, all her handiwork, and that of her young daughter sitting before us. With housewifely care she had stowed these away before starting for the drive, for it was berry time and she had no thought of leaving such precious muck-a-muck [food] for the foxes and birds, when her children and grandchildren had willing mouths to be filled."[95] Beyond acknowledging basketry as a central component of

Table 1: Narrative changes across *Legends of Vancouver*, the *Province*, and *The Mother's Magazine*

LEGENDS OF VANCOUVER (1911)	VANCOUVER DAILY PROVINCE	MOTHER'S MAGAZINE
"The Two Sisters" – JC	"The True Legend of Vancouver's Lions," 16 Apr. 1910 – JC	"The Legend of the Two Sisters," Jan. 1909 – MC
"The Siwash Rock" – JC	"A True Legend of Siwash Rock: A Monument to Clean Fatherhood," 16 Jul. 1910 – JC	"The Legend of Siwash Rock," Oct. 1910 – JC
"The Recluse" – JC	"The Recluse of the Capilano Canyon," 23 Jul. 1910 – JC	"The Legend of the Squamish Twins, or The Call of Kinship," Jul. 1910 – MC & JC
"The Lost Salmon Run" – MC	"The Legend of the Lost Salmon Run," 1 Oct. 1910 – MC	"The Lost Salmon Run: A Legend of the Pacific Coast," Aug. 1910 – MC
"The Deep Waters" – JC	"The Deep Waters: A Rare Squamish Legend," 24 Sept. 1910 – JC	"The Great Deep Water: A Legend of 'The Flood,'" Feb. 1912 – JC
"The Sea-Serpent" – JC	"The Sea-Serpent of Brockton Point," 8 Oct. 1910 – JC	n/a
"The Lost Island" – JC	"A Legend of the Squamish," 9 Jul. 1910 – JC	n/a
"Point Grey" – MJ?**	"A Legend of Point Grey," 10 Dec. 1910 – MJ?**	n/a
"The Tulameen Trail" – EPJ	"The Great Heights above the Tulameen," 17 Dec. 1910 – EPJ	n/a
"The Grey Archway" – Unknown***	"The Grey Archway: A Legend of the Coast," 7 Jan. 1911 – Unknown***	"The Grey Archway: A Legend of the Charlotte Islands," Jun. 1910 – Unknown***
"Deadman's Island" – JC	"The True Legend of Deadman's Island," 22 Oct. 1910 – JC	n/a

LEGENDS OF VANCOUVER (1911)	VANCOUVER DAILY PROVINCE	MOTHER'S MAGAZINE
"A Squamish Legend of Napoleon" – JC	"A Squamish Legend of Napoleon," 29 Oct. 1910 – JC	n/a
"The Lure in Stanley Park" – JC	"The 'Lure' in Stanley Park," 20 Aug. 1910 – JC	n/a
"Deer Lake" – EPJ	"A Legend of Deer Lake," 30 Jul. 1910 – EPJ	n/a
"A Royal Mohawk Chief" – EPJ	"The Duke of Connaught as Chief of the Iroquois," 2 Jul. 1910 – EPJ	"A Chieftain Prince," Oct. 1910 (in The Boys' World) - EPJ
"The Seven Swans" – MC (appears only in Thomson Stationery 1912 edition)	"The Legend of the Seven White Swans," 15 Oct. 1910 – JC	"The Legend of the Seven Swans," Sept. 1911 – MC
"Lillooet Falls" – MC (appears only in Thomson Stationery 1912 edition)	n/a	"The Legend of Lillooet Falls," Jan. 1912 – MC
"The Ice Babies" – MC (appears only in Thomson Stationery 1912 edition)	n/a	"The Legend of the Ice Babies," Nov. 1911 – MC

*Chief Joe Capilano = JC; Mary Agnes Capilano = MC; any stories with Johnson as narrator = EPJ

**MJ – Likely Mathias Joe, son of Mary and Joe Capilano. In the story "Point Grey," first published in December 1910, Johnson introduces a "young Squamish tillicum [Chinook word for friend] of mine who often comes to see me" as the narrator of her story. As Chief Joe Capilano died from tuberculosis in 1910 at the age of about fifty-six, it is unlikely that he would be described in Johnson's stories as a "young" friend; rather, it may have instead been Chief Joe Capilano's son, Mathias Joe, who became chief that same year following his father's passing. In Keller's *Pauline: A Biography*, she likewise acknowledges that Mathias Joe was known to visit Johnson after Chief Capilano's death; Keller writes, "from time to time, young Chief Mathias came to call on Pauline as his father had done" (254).

***Unknown – In this story, Johnson describes the male narrator as "an old tillicum" and member of "the Pacific tribes"; it is possible that the narrator is of the Haida Nation, which would explain his in-depth knowledge of traditional Haida stories.

many twentieth-century Indigenous women's lives and livelihoods, this passage also gestures towards the process of passing these traditional skills on to the next generation—from Mary Capilano to her daughter, Emma. We might also consider the parallels between Mary Capilano's basketry and oral storytelling as another form of weaving, a concept that Stó:lō author and educator Jo-Ann Archibald (Q'um Q'um Xiiem) articulates as "Indigenous storywork." As Mary Capilano wove strips of cedar bark to create baskets (Figure 10), she similarly wove together layers of distinct yet interconnected stories, producing a narrative that has been crafted especially for her listener. This reminder of Mary's lifelong connection to basket weaving echoes Chief Capilano's 1906 visit to King Edward VII when he presented cedar baskets to Queen Alexandra that had been specially crafted by his daughter.[96]

The different narrators in the two versions of "The Two Sisters" and "The True Story of Vancouver's Legends" are not simply the substitution of one name for the other; rather, the stories were changed enough to cause a noticeable shift in each story's tone and theme. For example, in the *Mother's Magazine* version of "The Two Sisters," Mary Capilano passionately conveys the sense of reverence towards women and mothers in Coastal First Nations. She explains: "I say you may not know that when our daughters step from childhood into the great world of womanhood, when the fitness for motherhood crowns them, we coast Indians of the sunset country regard this occasion as one of extreme rejoicing, great honor and unspeakable gladness. The being who possesses the possibility of some day becoming a mother receives much honor in most nations, but to us, the Sunset Tribes of Redmen, she is almost sacred."[97] In the *Vancouver Daily Province* version, Chief Capilano's voice is used to erase Mary's. In the article, Chief Capilano describes the honour of motherhood as culminating in "the possibility of some day mothering a man-child, a warrior, a brave," as if the women are but a means for producing the next generation of men. While the "legend" told in the distant past remains unchanged, we can see from these two versions how each narrator framed the themes of the legend quite differently—with Chief Capilano's celebration of brave warriors overshadowing Mary Capilano's nod to the integral role of matriarchs as a source of strength in Sḵwx̱wú7mesh families, often holding the family together. As Sḵwx̱wú7mesh archaeologist Rudy Reimer explains, we can look at variables such as "who is telling the history, and what they are trying to convey"[98] to the listener to compare different versions of Indigenous oral stories. While the publishers at *Mother's* and the *Province* wanted writing that suited their respective audiences, we can also see how the essence of the story—the focus on "Peace and Brotherhood"[99]—remains consistent across versions.

As these narrative shifts affect the tone and framing of Johnson's stories, they also highlight the differences between Mary and Joe Capilano as storytellers. In the *Mother's* version, Johnson provides readers with a glimpse of Mary Capilano's gentle, kind persona: "I nodded. I could see she liked that wordless reply, for she placed her narrow brown hand on my arm, nor did she remove it during her entire recital."[100] There is a sense of intimacy here, a bond shared between these women. In the *Province* version, Johnson contrastingly describes Chief Capilano's gestures as "strong" and "comprehensive," portraying their encounter as more formal in nature. Thus, it is through these aspects of the "framing" technique that Johnson has memorialized in writing the unique abilities and mannerisms of Joe and Mary Capilano as storytellers.

In addition to the *Mother's* version of "The Two Sisters," which is included in this volume, I have also selected four additional stories narrated by Mary Capilano for this edition to recentre her storytelling contributions: "The Legend of the Squamish Twins," "The Legend of the Seven Swans," "The Legend of Lillooet Falls," and "The Legend of the Ice Babies."[101] In the first version of "The Legend of the Seven Swans," published in the *Province* under a similar title, the story is narrated by Chief Capilano. One year later, a version appeared in *Mother's Magazine* that was narrated by Mary Capilano. "The Legend of Lillooet Falls" and "The Legend of the Ice Babies" were only published in *Mother's Magazine*. That these three stories were selected for the unique Thomson Stationery 1912 edition of *Legends*, which was "specifically marketed in part through the voluntary efforts of women's groups across Canada,"[102] is significant, because it means that the editors deliberately went back to *Mother's Magazine* to select versions narrated by the woman's voice of Mary Capilano, even though in the case of "The Legend of the Seven Swans" a version from the *Province* was more readily available.[103]

As for the Trust's initial decision to exclude these stories from their proposed publication of *Legends*, there is no archival evidence to explain why they made this choice. One may argue that, as these were some of Johnson's last "Indian stories" to be published before her death, they may have missed the publication cut-off for *Legends*—but this doesn't seem likely, as the committee was putting *Legends* together in the fall of 1911 and so could have theoretically selected "The Ice Babies" (Nov. 1911) as well as Chief Capilano's version of "The Seven Swans" (Sept. 1910) for publication. However, it is more likely that those versions published in the American periodical were not selected as they simply weren't on the committee's radar. Given that members of the Trust, namely Bernard McEvoy and Lionel Makovski, were also employed by the *Province*, it seems logical that they would reach for those "legends" already in-house and most recognizable to their loyal Vancouver readers.

Legends of Vancouver, or *Legends of the Capilano*?

Despite being published under the title *Legends of Vancouver* for the past 100 years, Johnson did not want that name for her collection. Documents held in McMaster University's E. Pauline Johnson fonds reveal that the early working title of the monograph was *Indian Legends of the Coast* and that Johnson ultimately wanted the book to be called *Legends of the Capilano*—as a tribute to the Capilano storytellers and their community at Capilano Indian Reserve No. 5.[104] The title that was ultimately chosen by the Pauline Johnson Trust was, as Linda Quirk suggests, misleading: "The legends in this collection are *not* about George Vancouver's explorations of the Pacific coast late in the eighteenth century, nor are they about the founding of the city of Vancouver in the late nineteenth century. They have nothing to do with the city of Vancouver at all."[105]

Also in the Johnson fonds at McMaster are five letters sent from Pauline's sister, Evelyn, to a Mr. James Goulet (of Kent County, Ontario),[106] that reveal the Trust's involvement in selecting the book's colonial title.[107] Though these letters only show Evelyn's side of the correspondence, it becomes clear in the first letter that Mr. Goulet initiated the correspondence to express condolences for Pauline's recent passing. The first letter, dated 8 June 1913, begins with Evelyn stating that she has "received over one hundred letters since [her] sister's death in March." She expresses thanks for Mr. Goulet's "kind letter," and for the many similar "letters of sympathy from friends of [Pauline], or people who had seen and read her, and whom I myself have never met." Evelyn shares some information about Pauline's most recent publications and offers to send Mr. Goulet a copy of *Legends of Vancouver* if he would like one; she notes that the two remaining signed copies are selling for $6.00 apiece. In her next letter, dated 1 July 1913, Evelyn acknowledges receipt of $1.25 (for an unsigned copy of *Legends* plus postage), and hopes that he has received his copy of the book. She elaborates on the history of *Legends of Vancouver*, apologizing for the rather poor binding and explaining that the Pauline Johnson Trust Fund "got out the book very hurriedly" due to Johnson's immediate need for financial support.

Miss
To ~~THE~~ PAULINE JOHNSON ~~TRUST FUND~~
~~BANK OF HAMILTON, VANCOUVER~~

Dear Sirs: Bute St Hospital Vancouver
Enclosed find cheque, M. O. or P. O. order value, $
for the above fund.
Kindly place my name on the list of subscribers to Miss Johnson's works as follows:

INDIAN LEGENDS OF THE COAST, ~~$1.50~~ 2.00 Autographed
~~LEGENDS OF THE COAST~~ . . $5.00
Edition de Luxe—only 500 copies, signed and numbered, to be printed

I include $ 2.00 for the legends, the balance to be used for the purchase of the copyright and expenses of publication.

R. W. Marks Perth, Ont.

Figure 11: Order slip (circulated prior to publication before the book's title was finalized) that was returned by mail from Yorkton, SK, to Johnson at the Bute Street Hospital, requesting one autographed copy of Legends for the price of $2.00. E. Pauline Johnson Fonds, The William Ready Division of Archives and Research Collections, McMaster University Library, Box 1, File 41.

In this same letter, Evelyn explains that the title given to the volume was not what her sister had desired. She writes, "The name 'Legends of Vancouver' was given the book by the Trustees of the Fund in the hope that it would prove a better seller. My sister was greatly disappointed as she had called it 'Legends of the Capilano'—the tribe of Indians on the Coast."

In the next line, Evelyn reveals that she has not shied from sharing this injustice with other correspondents: "I may have written this to you before—I forget, I wrote it to someone." Over the next three letters, dated 12 August, 27 August, and 16 December of that year, Mr. Goulet and Evelyn exchanged newspaper clippings about Pauline and a set of Vancouver postcards.

This is not the first time that Evelyn asserted the provenance of a different title; a similar letter, likely written closer to Evelyn's death

2

that the entire edition was sold out in 3
weeks and they were offering $3.00 a copy
for it and unable to obtain any at that
figure. When she regained more strength
last summer she was enabled to autograph
numbers of copies which sold everywhere
for $2.00 a copy, and the folder I enclosed
was for this last edition.

The pictured head on the cover is merely
a conventional drawing of an Indian's head.
Many persons think it is a picture of Chief
Joe Capilano who related the legends to my
sister. The name "Legends of Vancouver"
was given the book by the trustees of the Fund
in the hope that it would prove a better seller.
My sister was greatly disappointed as she had
called it "Legends of the Capilano" — the
tribe of Indians on the Coast.
I may have written this to you before — I forget
I wrote it to someone.

Thank you for the Globe you so kindly
sent me, and above all thank you for
the clipping of my letter which you have
so kindly said I may keep. I am collecting
everything I can find about my sister to
include in scrap books for reference.

I am so glad you wrote to me, otherwise
I should never have seen my letter.

You may see an article soon in the Globe

Figure 12: Excerpt of a letter from Evelyn H.C. Johnson to Mr. James Goulet, 1 July 1913. E. Pauline Johnson fonds, The William Ready Division of Archives and Research Collections, McMaster University Library, Box 11.

in 1937, exists in the City of Vancouver Archives. That letter states, "Thank you so much for the picture of the house where Pauline lived and thank you for the write up of the Legends of the Capilano, as she always called them." The letter goes on to describe in detail Pauline's dissatisfaction with the chosen title, *Legends of Vancouver*: "When I arrived from New York in Vancouver she was almsot [*sic*] in tears and complained to me, and I said, 'Why didn't you fight them?' She said, 'I was too ill.' But they have gone by the latter name ever since."[108] With Johnson's desired title, *Legends of the Capilano*, it appears that Pauline was describing the people of the Capilano Reserve—those members of the Sḵwx̱wú7mesh Nation, like Chief Joe and Mary Capilano, who called that area of North Vancouver at "Homulcheson" (Capilano Creek) their home. Local newspapers in British Columbia employed similar language during this time, using phrases like "the Capilano village" or "the Capilano" to describe what is now known as Capilano Indian Reserve No. 5.[109] We can consider this intended title an assertion of Indigenous sovereignty, indicative of the Sḵwx̱wú7mesh Nation's inherent rights and responsibilities to the land known colonially as Vancouver and as they are conveyed throughout the *Legends* stories.

Legends of Vancouver: An Overview of Key Editions (1911–2013)

First Edition (Privately Printed, 1911)

The first edition of *Legends of Vancouver*, published privately by Johnson's network of supporters, was released just a few weeks before Christmas 1911. The initial print run of 1000 copies, shoddily bound with paper covers and priced at $1.00 apiece, sold out instantly.[110] In a letter dated 8 December 1911 (a Friday), Pauline writes to her sister: "My book went out in the book stalls on Saturday at noon hour, & by Wednesday, not a copy was left in the publishing house. Spencers (who is like Eatons in Toronto) sold 100 of them last Friday. There never has been such a rush on a holiday book here. Brantford telegraphed for 100 to be sent them, but Mr. Makovski could not let them have *one single copy*. The entire edition is sold out, is it not glorious?"[111] Later, at her friend Walter McRaye's suggestion, Pauline began autographing copies and doubling the price to $2.00.[112] While this edition mentions Chief Capilano in passing, it sets the precedent for recognizing only one author—E. Pauline Johnson—on both the cover and title page of the collection. The cover features an embossed image of a Plains Indian chief, identifiable by the distinct headdress and regalia; this image does not represent Chief Capilano (according to the Mathias family, he only wore fur and cedar hats[113]) nor the Sḵwx̱wú7mesh Nation, and instead constructs a kind of stereotypical or generically "Indian" figure to represent the *Legends* stories. In fact, in the same letter from Evelyn Johnson that reveals the intended title for the collection, Evelyn writes: "The pictured head on the cover is merely a conventional drawing of an Indian's head. Many persons think it is a picture of Chief Joe Capilano who related the legends to my sister."[114]

The only reference to Joe Capilano appears in the brief "Author's Foreword," where Johnson writes of their initial meeting in London and importantly acknowledges her close relationship with the Chief. She writes, "These legends he told me from time to time, just as the mood possessed him, and he frequently remarked that they had never been revealed to any other English-speaking person save myself." This foreword, however, lacks any reference to Mary Capilano, suggesting that Johnson was tasked with writing it based on the stories gathered by the Trust for the collection—stories that were almost all narrated by

Chief Capilano. The "Preface," written by Bernard McEvoy, a Pauline Johnson Trust member and the editor of the *Province*, states that Johnson "has made a most estimable contribution to purely Canadian literature."[115] Under the guise of praise, McEvoy's language in this Preface instead reflects the settler tendency to appropriate Indigeneity when convenient or beneficial to the settler cause.[116]

Thomson Stationery Illustrated Edition (The Thomson Stationery Company, 1912)

The Thomson Stationery Illustrated edition was published in 1912. This edition included three additional stories by Johnson that were published originally in *Mother's Magazine*; these stories, "The Seven Swans," "Lillooet Falls," and "The Ice Babies," were narrated by Mary Capilano, who is referred to in the stories as the "old klootchman."[117] Focusing on themes of love and motherhood, these stories gave Mary Capilano a voice that the previous edition (and all those to follow) had not allowed for. After the successful sale of the first printing of *Legends*, the Trust began promoting the book in earnest; pamphlets were circulated widely to encourage new female subscribers: "It is to be hoped that the Canadian Clubs and Daughters of the Empire will take this opportunity of paying a slight tribute to one of Canada's most patriotic writers."[118] This edition was also heavily advertised in a labour newspaper, the *British Columbia Federationist*, between 1913 and 1914 as a gift book or "a book to mail abroad" and with advertisements often appearing on the same pages as the "Woman Suffrage" column.[119] This edition also incorporated eight photographs, attributed to Vancouver photography company Bishop & Christie, of relevant Vancouver landscapes including "The Lions," "Capilano Canyon," and "Entrance to the Narrows." According to Quirk, the Thomson edition was also available as a leather-bound "deluxe" edition, which sold for $5.00 per copy, a significant increase from the $2.00 cloth binding.[120]

Figure 13: Legends of Vancouver, First edition, privately printed (1911). Image courtesy of SFU Special Collections and Rare Books, PR 9220 O35 L4 1911b.

This edition also includes drawings depicting a selection of Northwest Coast First Nations artwork, each signed with the initials O.B.A.[121] They appear rather haphazardly at the end of some legends, often without a clear connection to the contents of the stories themselves. In contrast to the photographs included in Johnson's books, which were usually attributed to their photographers and cited in a "List of Illustrations," the creator of these drawings was never identified. In a July 2021 article in the online journal *Authorship*, Carole Gerson and I share our recent findings that the artist was Baptist pastor O.B. Anderson.[122] The drawings were taken from Anderson's article "In the Indian Past: Rapidly Vanishing Indian Lore," which appeared in the August 1912 issue of *British Columbia Magazine*. There, Rev. Anderson wrote about his time spent as a missionary among the Tsimshian community at Port Simpson (known today as Lax-Kw'alaams), where he "made a careful study of the Indians and their tribal customs and folklore."[123] Though most of the drawings are not directly relevant to the stories to which they have been added (for example, a drawing of a traditional Tsimshian food dish appears in a story about Sḵwx̱wú7mesh fatherhood), they—although complicated by the circumstances of their production—nonetheless evoke the lives and work of West Coast First Nations peoples. Therefore, these images may have strengthened the connection between Johnson, an outsider to the West Coast, and the contents of her narratives.

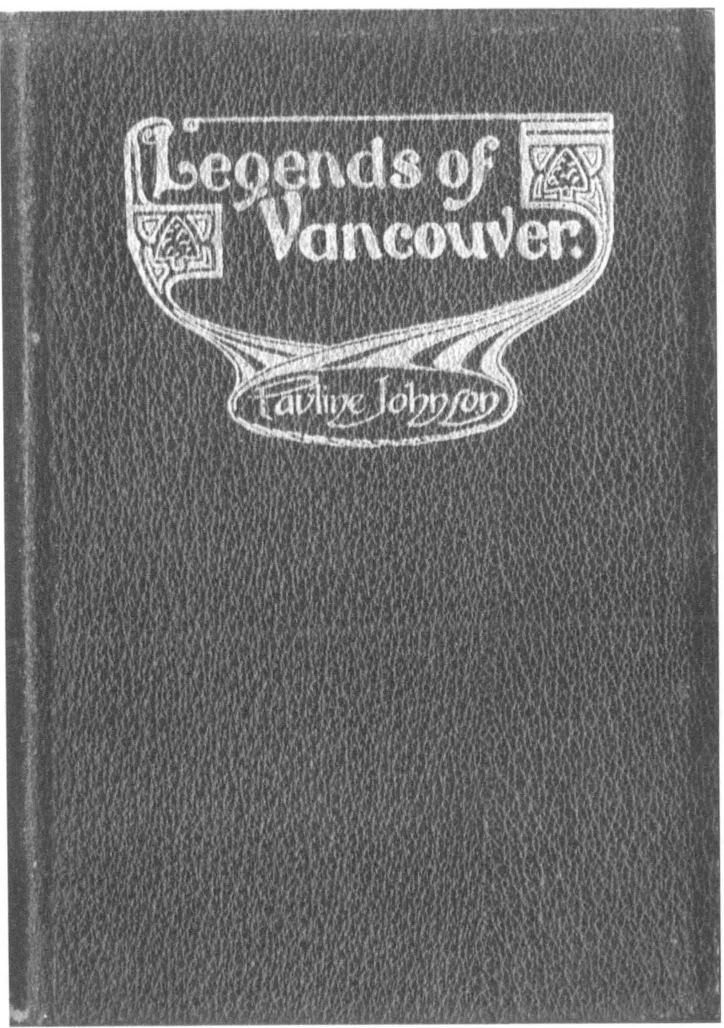

Figure 14: Legends of Vancouver, Thomson Stationery Illustrated edition (1912). Image courtesy of SFU Special Collections and Rare Books, PR 9220 O35 L4 1912d.

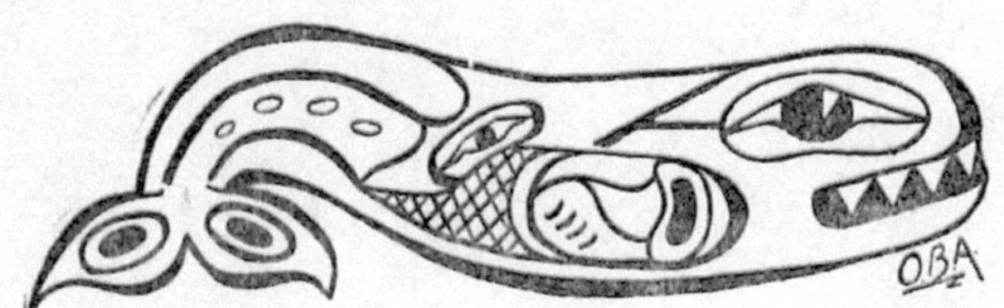

A BOOK TO MAIL ABROAD

The Legends of Vancouver

E. Pauline Johnson

This is a gift that will be appreciated in any part of the world. Tastefully bound in three bindings. Cloth, $1.50; Ooze Calf, $2.50; Burnt Leather, $2.75.

THE ONLY EDITION WITH EIGHT LOCAL ILLUSTRATIONS

Thomson Stationery Co., Ltd.

325 HASTINGS STREET, WEST

Figure 15: Line drawing signed by O.B.A. in Johnson's "The Grey Archway." Image courtesy of SFU Special Collections and Rare Books, PR 9220 O35 L4 1911a [miscatalogued; actually published in 1912].

Figure 16: Advertisement for *Legends of Vancouver* published in the *BC Federationist* newspaper, 12 December 1913, 4.

Saturday Sunset Presses/Geo. S. Forsyth Editions (1913)

In 1913, Vancouver's Saturday Sunset Presses, which was also responsible for publishing the weekly liberal-leaning newspaper, *B.C. Saturday Sunset*, took over publication of *Legends*. The content of this edition (and its subedition distributed by Geo. S. Forsyth) remains largely the same as of those preceding it, with the addition of a posthumous note about Johnson's death and an excerpt from a memorial published in the *Vancouver Daily Province*. In contrast, the only acknowledgement of Chief Capilano's death (1910) appears vaguely within the stories themselves. For example, in the "The Two Sisters" Johnson writes, "This is the Indian legend of 'The Lions of Vancouver' as I had it from one who will tell me no more the traditions of his people."[124] In "The Recluse," Johnson writes, "But I learned this legend from one whose voice was as dulcet as the swirling rapids; but, unlike them, that voice is hushed today, while the river, the river still sings on—sings on."[125] A copy of the Forsyth subedition, held in Simon Fraser University's Special Collections Library, is particularly notable—it has had a hand-painted board glued over top of the original paper binding, giving the volume the new title of *Legends of Capilano*. This one-of-a-kind cover reveals an important gesture by its owner towards the legacy of the Capilanos and suggests that Johnson's wishes for an alternative title were known beyond the personal correspondences of her sister, Evelyn.

McClelland and Stewart Editions (1926, 1961)

In 1914, Johnson's former *Province* editor, Lionel Makovski, transferred copyright of *Legends* over to the Toronto-based publishing house, McClelland, Goodchild and Stewart Limited.[126] They released a redesigned edition of *Legends* that year. In 1920, the publisher ran a second printing under the company's new name, McClelland and Stewart.[127] In 1922, they issued a new edition that featured illustrations by Group of Seven artist J.E.H. MacDonald. The cover included paraphrased content from Johnson's "Author's Foreword," drawing attention to the authorial role of Chief Joe Capilano: "These legends were told to me personally by my honoured friend, the late Chief Joe Capilano of Vancouver." While this is not the same as formally acknowledging Chief Capilano as Johnson's co-author, this edition is notable because his name (but not Mary Capilano's) is placed on the cover for the first time. This is also the first edition to use Tekahionwake, Johnson's Mohawk name, on the cover. Like the editions that preceded it, McClelland and Stewart reprinted the original "Biographical Notice" for Johnson; however, they made no reference to the lives of Chief Joe or Mary Capilano. Imprints of this edition that were published between 1922 and 1949 included additional photographs, such as the "Monument to E. Pauline Johnson" in Stanley Park.

The 1961 redesign of *Legends* coincided with the centennial of Johnson's birth and included new cover art by North Vancouver graphic artist Ben Lim. McClelland and Stewart abridged Johnson's "Foreword" (and removed the earlier indirect acknowledgment of Chief Capilano's co-authorship) to a single sentence and moved it to the back cover, relegating her nod to Capilano as an afterthought. In this location, the reference to Chief Capilano seems to function more like a stamp of authenticity, rather than an acknowledgement of authorship. The movement of Johnson's "Foreword" from its place preceding the stories has the effect of decontextualizing the stories entirely, creating a tangible disconnect between the legends and their Sḵwx̱wú7mesh storytellers (a decision exacerbated further by the removal of Johnson's Mohawk name from the cover, conveying a more general pan-Indigeneity rather than nation specificity). This edition also significantly alters the text's critical framework: the original "Preface," "Author's Foreword," and "Biographical Notice" have been removed and replaced with an introduction written by non-Indigenous journalist Marcus Van Steen. In Van Steen's subsequent biography of

Figures 17 and *18:* Left: *Legends of Vancouver*, Saturday Sunset Presses edition (1913); Right: *Legends of Capilano*, Geo. S. Forsyth subedition (1913). Images courtesy of SFU Special Collections and Rare Books, PR 9220 O35 L4 1913l and PR 9220 O35 L4 1913h.

Johnson, titled *Pauline Johnson: Her Life and Work* and published by Musson a few years later in 1965, he refers to the 1961 edition of *Legends* as "compiled by Marcus Van Steen." This information further clarifies his role as editor of the 1961 edition, and thus responsible for these changes.

In his 1961 Introduction to *Legends*, Van Steen perpetuates a range of pervasive stereotypes relating to Indigenous Peoples, using terms like "folklore" to describe the stories and patronizingly suggesting they are little more than "the simple imaginings of a primitive people."[128] To consider the differences between terms like "folklore" and "legends," we can use the Brian Deer Classification System (BDCS) to understand and classify works of Indigenous literary production. Designed by

Figure 19: Legends of Vancouver, McClelland and Stewart 1926 edition. Image courtesy of SFU Special Collections and Rare Books, PR 9220 O35 L4 1926.

Figure 20: Legends of Vancouver, McClelland and Stewart 1961 edition. Image courtesy of SFU Special Collections and Rare Books, PR 9220 O35 L4 1961.

Kahnawake Mohawk librarian Brian Deer in the 1970s, the BDCS has been implemented by several First Nations libraries in Canada including the Xwi7xwa Library at UBC. Though editors like Van Steen have employed non-Indigenous vocabularies (like "folklore") to describe the *Legends* stories, the BDCS provides a more accurate, Indigenous-centred approach for classifying Indigenous literary legends.[129] Literary scholar Hartmut Lutz's "Canadian Native Literature and the Sixties" similarly critiques Van Steen's Introduction: "In their condescension, Van Steen's words are symptomatic of the early 1960s. More than thirty years later, it seems superfluous to criticize Van Steen in detail, because phrases like '*our* first Canadians [emphasis mine],' or 'simple imaginings of a primitive people' reveal themselves for what they are: as not only racist, but also factually wrong."[130]

Yet Van Steen did accomplish something important for the text: he acknowledged that *Legends of Vancouver* was not Johnson's choice of title. He writes: "Pauline had wanted them called 'Legends of the Capilano' in tribute to her friend, but she was too ill to insist."[131] Prior to this, and other than the 1913 Geo. S. Forsyth subedition located at SFU library, no edition of *Legends* had mentioned Johnson's preferred title.

With regards to both the 1926 and 1961 McClelland and Stewart (M&S) editions, it is unclear from the archives who at M&S was making the editorial decisions noted above. This gap in the archival record can be partially explained by a note on the digital finding aid for the McClelland and Stewart fonds in McMaster University's Archives and Research Collections, which says: "Practically all of the company records prior to 1950 were destroyed by John McClelland. Before this was done, however, George L. Parker examined the records of the company for his doctoral dissertation and made notes. These notes are available to researchers." Unfortunately, the "Parker Notes" collection includes only minimal notations regarding the early sales records of *Legends of Vancouver*;[132] similarly, the only other file for

Figure 21: Legends of Vancouver, Quarry Press edition (1991). Image courtesy of SFU Special Collections and Rare Books, PR 9220 O35 L4 1991.

Legends of Vancouver in the M&S archival holdings is a printing order from October 1973 requesting 1,500 copies.[133]

Quarry Press Edition (1991)

The next significant changes to the book came in 1991, with the edition published by Quarry Press (Kingston, Ontario). Interestingly, this edition was part of the Canadian Children's Classics Series, which highlights books of "exceptional literary and cultural value" written for children. As *Legends* was not explicitly written for this demographic, we might instead consider this edition as a first attempt to market the stories towards a younger readership. However, in a 1994 review published in *Canadian Children's Literature,* this edition was deemed not well-suited for a "children's" reading demographic: "For young readers and listeners, however, Johnson's language may have to be edited or explained."[134] Since the original text of *Legends of Vancouver* was not abbreviated or adapted in any way for this new readership, Johnson's vocabulary (and the context of certain word choices, like the term "savage") was too complex for many child readers; adding a glossary for the mainly Chinook words was not enough to justify a new genre classification.

There have been, however, two recent children's book adaptations of Johnson's *Legends.* An adaptation of "The Two Sisters" was self-published in 2016, with new illustrations by Sandra Butt under her imprint, Waterlea Books (Pender Island, BC). In Butt's abbreviated version of the text, the story begins several paragraphs in from the original: "Many thousands of years ago . . . there were no twin peaks . . . guarding this sunset coast." By omitting the opening "frame" sequence, in which we are introduced to Chief Joe Capilano as the storyteller, this version erases his role in the oral storytelling context.[135] The full text of the story appears at the end of the book, along with a brief introduction to the history of First Nations peoples in the Pacific Northwest and a list of keywords (such as "First Nations," "Pacific

Northwest") for additional research. This edition is recommended for children ages three to five.

The second children's adaptation, of Johnson's "The Lost Island" story, was published in 2004 by children's book publisher Simply Read Books (Vancouver, BC) with illustrations by Bulgarian artist Atanas Matsoureff. In contrast to Butt's adaptation, this book follows Johnson's original story word-for-word; the text is presented in quotation marks to indicate that no editorial changes have been made. The tone of the book, however, takes on a different feeling than the original; the first page of the story depicts an Indigenous storyteller sharing this legend with a non-Indigenous man (rather than with E. Pauline Johnson), as though this new listener better represents the imagined audience and reader of this adaptation. In fact, both adaptations appear to be marketed towards a more generalized, non-Indigenous readership, using language like "Salish" to describe Chief Joe Capilano and removing location-specific words like "Pacific" Coast and "Capilano" Canyon.[136]

The Quarry Press edition, more than any other thus far, also made efforts to reconnect the *Legends* stories with contemporary Indigenous communities—both on the West Coast and in Johnson's ancestral territory at Six Nations. For instance, Johnson's Mohawk name is returned to the front cover, which features original cover art and drawings by Stó:lō artist Laura Wee Láy Láq. Though both the Sḵwx̱wú7mesh and Stó:lō nations are Coast Salish peoples, whose region extends from northern Vancouver Island to western Washington State, they are just two of *many*. Still, while substituting the Stó:lō Nation in place for the Sḵwx̱wú7mesh suggests a generalization of Coast Salish nations, the Quarry Press edition does mark progress for Canadian publishers of Indigenous literatures in efforts to pay attention to the importance of place when publishing Indigenous stories. In fact, that this edition was published in the year following the 1990 land dispute between Kanien'kehá:ka (Mohawk) at Kanesatake and the town of

Oka, Quebec (known as the "Oka Crisis"), we might consider this edition as part of the larger "watershed [moment] for Indigenous literature and literary criticism in Canada"[137]—with key expressions of Indigenous literary nationalism and activism colliding.

This edition also effectively expands the text's critical framework to include an Afterword, Glossary, and Further Reading List, which were all anonymously written. Johnson's original "Foreword" is reinserted at the beginning of the book, emphasizing the importance of framing the legends and Johnson's respect for the Capilanos with her own words. The Glossary provides a resource for readers to understand the Chinook language that had been mostly missing from previous editions. While early editions included several footnoted translations for one or two Chinook words, Quarry's glossary is more complete and attempts to contextualize Johnson's use of language—that is, to emphasize the ways in which language is often "time bound."[138] With *Legends* now in the public domain, Quarry Press opted to donate all royalties from this edition towards the preservation of Chiefswood—Johnson's ancestral home in Brantford, Ontario.[139]

Douglas and McIntyre Edition (1997)

The 1997 edition, published by Douglas and McIntyre (Vancouver, BC), also returns Johnson's "Foreword" to its proper place at the start of the book, and includes a new Introduction by Vancouver writer Robin Laurence. Laurence reminds readers of the text's rootedness in Vancouver, emphasizing Johnson's ever-present legacy, as memorialized in places like Stanley Park, and the importance of her relationship with Joe Capilano. Laurence writes, "These stories are as much about the writer's love of Vancouver's natural setting as they are about her admiration for Chief Joe Capilano and the traditions and oral culture of his people."[140] Though this edition does not include a glossary or further reading resources like the Quarry Press edition, it does include an updated selection of archival images from the Vancouver Public Library and City of Vancouver Archives—five full-page portraits of Johnson, and none of the Capilanos. In her chapter in Janice Fiamengo's *Home Ground and Foreign Territory: Essays on Early Canadian Literature*, Carole Gerson describes the historical absence of photographs of the Capilanos in *Legends* as an "oversight"—one that "has been perpetuated by the current Douglas & McIntyre edition."[141]

Midtown Press 100th Anniversary Edition (2013)

The most recent edition of *Legends* was published in 2013 by Vancouver's Midtown Press; it was issued as the 100th Anniversary edition to commemorate Johnson's death in 1913. This edition interestingly juxtaposes historical photographs of Vancouver with more modern scenes, contrasting the trees and rocks of Stanley Park with the concrete bike-paths and skyscrapers of today's Vancouver.

Johnson's original "Author's Foreword" follows a new Preface, written by Canadian theatre scholar Sheila M.F. Johnston. In the 2017 reprint, or third printing, the publisher added a full-page image of Chief Joe Capilano; this was the first time Capilano's image had been included in any edition of *Legends*.[142] The book's title page features an image of two unidentified Indigenous women paddling a canoe (Figure 24). Though readers might expect an image of E. Pauline Johnson and Mary Capilano, the "List of Photographs" at the end of the book reveals otherwise. Instead, this image is attributed to twentieth-century ethnographer Edward S. Curtis and titled, "Canoeing on Clayquot Sound." Though Curtis's portraits of early-twentieth-century Indigenous peoples were highly regarded at the time, his work has been criticized more recently for contributing to the ideologies of salvage ethnography and the narrative of the "vanishing Indian"; Curtis was known to "dress up" his subjects to better fit his idea of Indigenous peoples as being fixed in the past, rather than reflect their present realities.[143] While this edition does not provide a detailed

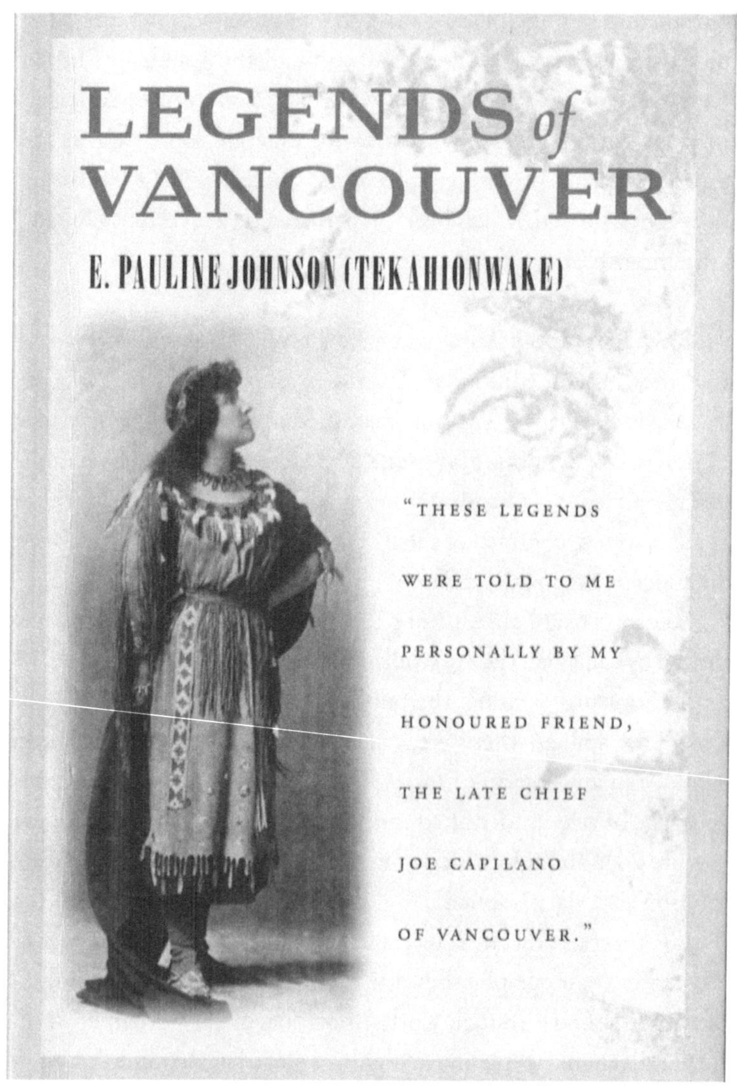

Figure 22: Legends of Vancouver, Douglas & McIntyre edition (1997). Image courtesy of SFU Special Collections and Rare Books, PR 9220 O35 L4 1997.

Figure 23: Legends of Vancouver, Midtown Press edition (2013). Image by A. Shield, scanned from personal collection.

description of the cover image, a Library of Congress database search revealed it to be as follows: "Two Hesquiat women are homeward bound with the product of their day's labor in gathering food, and cedar-bark to be used in making mats."[144] In correspondence with Midtown Press, I learned that the Press opted to use the photograph because it depicted early twentieth-century coastal Indigenous Peoples contemporary with Joe Capilano and because it was aesthetically pleasing, easily accessible, and of no cost to reproduce.[145] Given our current national focus on building and repairing relationships with Indigenous communities, such decisions now would hopefully focus more on incorporating Indigenous editorial protocols,[146] in particular an awareness of the importance of identifying each nation individually rather than grouping them together.

It should also be noted that the cover to this edition features an image titled *Haayiitlik (Sea-serpent)*, created by Musqueam artist Raymond Sim. The decision to highlight Musqueam art rather than Sḵwx̱wú7mesh as the entry-point to the *Legends* text most likely represents another generalization of Coast Salish nations (as in the Quarry Press edition), but it could be read as a gesture towards the borrowing of the Capilano name from the Musqueam Nation and their shared claim, in small part, to the *Legends* stories.

There is a French edition of *Legends*, published in 2012 by Québec publisher Presses de Bras-d'Apic and translated from English by Chantal Ringuet. The design, cover images, and photographs are identical to the Midtown Press edition, with some slight variations in colour to the front/back covers. Unlike the 2013 Midtown Press edition, the French translation was not presented as an anniversary edition; it was released one year prior to the anniversary of Johnson's death. In deciding to publish the first French translation of *Legends*, Midtown Press publisher Louis Anctil explains, "It was important to us that francophones in the BC region and elsewhere in Canada have access to this important work in French."[147]

Figure 24: "Canoeing on Clayquot Sound" by Edward S. Curtis (c1910). Library of Congress, LOT 12328-B.

The French translation includes a Preface written by the translator (Ringuet), titled "Une dame victorienne et une princesse mohawk" ("A Victorian Lady and a Mohawk Princess"), and excludes Johnson's "Foreword"—a necessary component, as I have previously argued, that frames Johnson's relationship to Chief Joe Capilano *in her own words.*

Johnson's Final Will and Other Adaptations of *Legends*

With knowledge of *Legends'* complex publishing history and constant republication over the past 100 years, we might also consider: who profited from the sales of these books after Johnson's death? Though

E. PAULINE JOHNSON

Légendes de Vancouver

Presses de Bras-d'Apic

Figure 25: Presses de Bras-d'Apic *Légendes de Vancouver* French edition (2012). Image by A. Shield, scanned from personal collection.

Legends is now in the public domain, and has been since about 1963, we can look to Johnson's final arrangements for some insights into its stewardship over the last century.

According to Johnson's Last Will and Testament, which was authorized on 26 February 1913—nine days before her death, she bequeathed all profits from the sales of *Legends of Vancouver* to friend and former stage partner Walter McRaye, "my books which he has been instrumental in selling."[148] Johnson left the copyright of *Legends* and any other published materials to her editor Lionel Makovski. In her will, Johnson said that he might, "without imposing any absolute duty," share the profits from any publications "from time to time" with Johnson's remaining siblings, Evelyn and Allen.[149] In 1914, Makovski transferred copyright of *Legends* to the Toronto-based publishing house, McClelland, Goodchild, and Stewart Limited.[150] The publisher controlled publication until the 1991 edition by Quarry Press was produced and the text had entered the public domain. Noticeably absent from Johnson's final will is any reference to the Capilano family, barring them from being entitled to any future monetary profits or copyright to the stories. We do not know why she excluded the Capilanos from her final will. But by leaving them out of her will, Johnson effectively diminished the contributions of the Capilanos, a harbinger of the tone that most subsequent editions of *Legends of Vancouver* followed. Johnson's decision not to assign copyright to the Capilanos could also be a reflection of the misconception that oral stories are not owned (in the Western sense of property ownership) by any one individual and therefore do not require permission or copyright.[151]

In the years following Pauline's death, surviving documents suggest that Makovski was trying to come up with different ways of adapting Johnson's *Legends* stories—perhaps as a form of tribute, or as an attempt to attract new reading audiences. For instance, Makovski wrote to McClelland and Stewart on 15 August 1922, proposing the creation of an educational edition of "Pauline Johnson's book for boys and girls" that would include colour illustrations: "I can imagine an Arthur Rackham [English book illustrator] making an extraordinarily fine edition for children. I think that there might be something in this but instead of the legends being re-written their impression would be stamped by the illustrations. . . . Perhaps for children between eight and twelve the personal touches between Miss Johnson and Chief Capilano and others of her tillicums might be omitted. It may be possible to re-write the stories without losing the poetry and atmosphere, but I am a little doubtful."[152] The proposed table of contents to this edition uses the same titles for each story but adds to each a kind of thematic phrase or "moral" that emphasizes and simplifies the story's main idea. For example, "The Two Sisters" is subtitled "Peace," and "Siwash Rock" becomes "The Rock of Fatherhood." Also included in this letter to John McClelland was a prototype "Foreword" to this new children's edition of *Legends*, which Makovski had retitled *Indian Fairy Tales*. While this proposal for a children's edition was never put into motion, McClelland and Stewart did publish the "New Edition—Illustrated" that year, which featured work by Group of Seven artist J.E.H. MacDonald.[153]

Another adaptation of *Legends* is a limited-edition eight-page pamphlet, measuring only 16 x 12.5 cm, published in the 1920s by Vancouver writer and poet Lionel Haweis (1870–1942), a former UBC librarian and member of the Vancouver Handicrafts Guild. Titled *The Legend of the Salt-Chuck Oluk* and based on Johnson's story "The Sea-Serpent," the pamphlet condenses Johnson's original opening, which introduces concepts of greed or "avarice," but the story is, for the most part, true to the original text. The text is written in calligraphic style, with ornamental designs bordering each page.[154] The back page reads "Published by Special Permission of L.W. Makovski, Copyright Holder," which reaffirms Johnson's designation of all copyright to Makovski as set out in her final will. Haweis also published a series of abbreviated poems, based on the *Legends of Vancouver* stories, between 1913 and 1914 in *British Columbia Magazine*. The poems, which Haweis attributes as being "suggested by the prose of E. Pauline Johnson," include "The Shaman's Sacrifice," based on Johnson's "The Lost Island"; "The Lure of the West," based on Johnson's "The Lure in Stanley Park"; "The Legend of the Siwash Rock," based on Johnson's "The Siwash Rock"; "The Song of the Tulameen River," based on Johnson's "The Tulameen Trail"; and "The Haunted Island or Isle of Dead Men," based on Johnson's "Deadman's Island." That he determined to appropriate so brazenly Johnson's stories shortly after her death, and without her permission, speaks in part to challenges of authority often experienced by Johnson and other Indigenous women writers during the twentieth century: their ideas were not taken seriously, their words were appropriated without permission, and they often struggled to have their ideas expressed in print in ways they intended.[155] These are the very same gender and racial inequalities that shaped Johnson's stories several years earlier for their publication in the *Province* newspaper.

Haweis' poems closely follow the narrative of Johnson's stories but stray occasionally, often to make use of stereotypical or inaccessible language. For example, in "The Legend of Siwash Rock," Haweis repeats Johnson's key phrases like "clean fatherhood" but also invokes terms like "peace-pipe" (line 47) and "squaw" (line 9)—terms that have no relevance to the story as Johnson tells it, but firmly and stereotypically evoke "Indian" for non-Indigenous readers. In "The Legend of Siwash Rock," Haweis describes the moment when the young chief and his wife decide that they must swim:

> "All's one," said he, and smiled. . . . Hand, then, in hand
> They weave the giant woods, the twain in one,
> Now through a mass of green investiture,
> Now 'twixt the bones of naked forests burned,
> Shoreward a path and seaward, questing purity—
> The purity of all the world's unborn.[156]

By using words like "twain" and "investiture," Haweis obscures the original narrative and recasts it for an English-Canadian literary and social elite. Johnson's "The Siwash Rock" depicts the same moment: "He sprang from his couch of wolf-skins and looked out upon the coming day; the promise of what it would bring him seemed breathing through all his forest world. He took her very gently by the hand and led her through the tangle of wilderness down to the water's edge, where the beauty spot we moderns call Stanley Park bends about Prospect Point. 'I must swim,' he told her." This section of Haweis' poem likens nature, and the forests of Stanley Park, to something outside of humanity with words like "investitures," which suggest clothing the land to make it more human and accessible, or as a means of ensuring separation between land and people. In contrast, Johnson's language clearly conveys the young chief's sense of belonging to "his forest world." In addition to rendering the stories inaccessible to most readers, Haweis discards Johnson's use of the frame narrative technique. Traditionally, Johnson utilized the space at the beginning and end of each story to describe for readers the characteristics and mannerisms of Chief Joe and Mary Capilano, her Sḵwx̱wú7mesh storytellers. In the abbreviated poems, however, Haweis jumps right into the "legend"—effectively erasing the presence of multiple narrators and decontextualizing the voices of the Capilanos.

The note "Suggested by the prose of E. Pauline Johnson's 'Legends of Vancouver'" often accompanied Haweis' poems. While importantly acknowledging Johnson's *Legends* as the main source, the attribution also effectively downplays the appropriation of Johnson's writing under the guise of artistic licence. The word "suggested" implies that the words for this poetic rendition somehow came to be of their own volition (and not through Haweis' deliberate, appropriative actions). In his long poem, "The Lure of the West," he similarly writes, "Suggested by the prose of E. Pauline Johnson's 'The Lure in Stanley Park' Vancouver,

The Pale-Faces are stricken with a terrible disease—the love of Gold, now as always. So first they came to us when gold was reported far up the river. With greedy fingers they came—greedy eyes, greedy hearts. They fought, murdered, starved, went mad. Tillicums were tillicums no more, brothers were foes, fathers strove with sons, sons with fathers, for the curse of the disease was upon them—then as now. For we, the Indians, are not greedy. We share and divide among ourselves—food, chickimin, everything. This is not the law, but the fact. It is the custom of our people. It was always so. But there was an Indian—long ago, one Shak-shak, who was greedy. This is the story.

Our young men went as guides to the Pale-Faces. Shak-shak was one of our young men. He went with the others. When they came back—they spoke of many things, but chiefly of greed and of murder, also of Shak-shak, who came not back with them but stayed with the Pale-Faces. Our old people were wise, they shook their heads—No good ever came of murder and greed. Evil will come of it, they said. As for Shak-shak, hawk by name—

Figure 26: The Legend of the Salt-Chuck Oluk (c. 1920). Image courtesy of SFU Special Collections and Rare Books, PR 9220 O35 L3 1902.

B.C. in the book of her Legends." However, to his statement he added: "and by courtesy of the copyright-holder of the original story." As most of these poems appear to have been published during 1914, it is likely that Haweis acquired permission to adapt and publish his poems from Lionel Makovski before the copyright was transferred to McClelland, Goodchild, and Stewart later that year.[157]

Legends of the Capilano: A Collaborative Approach

When contemplating the legacy of *Legends* and Johnson's declining health during its production, we must consider that the book published in 1911, to raise funds for her care, may not have reflected the final wishes of its author—especially given the treatment of Joe and Mary Capilano. In reissuing this text under Johnson's intended title, I hope that this book contributes to and reinvigorates conversations about the Capilanos in both the Mohawk and Sḵwx̱wú7mesh communities.

Within the Mohawk community at Six Nations, Rick Monture asserts that Johnson's "presence is very much around and part of the community,"[158] particularly through the physical embodiment of her legacy at her ancestral home, Chiefswood. However, he also acknowledges the importance of revisiting her work and drawing connections to the lives of Indigenous Peoples today, and in the future. He states, "But 100 years after she's gone, we're still talking about her, and we're seeing a lot of what she was concerned with in her lifetime being talked about today. The roles and importance of Indigenous women, identity issues, non-recognition of history and treaties—all of that. She addressed all those things a hundred and more years ago."[159] For the Sḵwx̱wú7mesh Nation, Rudy Reimer expressed a sense of pride about Johnson's and the Capilano's legacy. *Legends*, suggests Reimer, is a respected text that remains in reader's libraries within the community.[160] Reimer shared with me his version of "The Sea-Serpent," called "Sinulhkai and Xwechtaal," as an example of the many versions of Sḵwx̱wú7mesh stories that can coexist, each with slight differences depending on the location, storyteller, and audience.[161] He considers Johnson's work as presenting "a version of our history,"[162] and as part of the Sḵwx̱wú7mesh historical legacy that ought to be honoured and kept relevant.

For this updated edition, retitled *Legends of the Capilano* as per E. Pauline Johnson's wishes, I've had the privilege of working alongside members of the Mathias family, who are descendants of Chief Joe and Mary Capilano and members of the Sḵwx̱wú7mesh Nation. Our relationship began in 2017, when I reached out to Cody Mathias, great-grandson of the Capilanos and respected carver in the Sḵwx̱wú7mesh community; he invited me to their family's performance of the Sḵwx̱wú7mesh "Daily Welcoming" at Vancouver's The Drum Is Calling Festival. For this first meeting, I came bearing a copy of *Legends of Vancouver* and several bundles of tea. I chose a black tea blend called "London Afternoon," thinking specifically of that fortuitous 1906 meeting between Chief Capilano and E. Pauline Johnson. After their performance, I was invited backstage to meet the family, still dressed in their regalia, where I presented them the gifts and told them about my work on *Legends of Vancouver*.

After the festival, Cody's sister, Rose Seipp, invited me to a Saturday family gathering at her home on the Capilano Reserve. Much to my surprise, the family were enthusiastic about the "Legends of the Capilano" project and welcomed me—a settler scholar and cultural outsider—into their lives; these Saturday visits soon became a regular occurrence. Wanting to follow protocol, I consulted with one of my mentors, Deanna Reder (Cree-Métis), on how to prepare tobacco ties that I would formally present as an offering to each family member before we proceeded. In one of my early meetings with the Mathias family, I explained that I was coming to this work with a good heart and good mind and asked if they would accept the tobacco as a gesture of respect for our collaborative work to come. Since then, I've had the privilege of learning from this family, of sharing with them my archival research and findings, and of better understanding the important role that matriarchs like Mary Capilano maintain within Sḵwxw̱ú7mesh culture.

For the Mathias family, this book represents a tangible expression of pride and reclamation; it connects the past, present, and future generations of their family. The Mathias family grew up on the beach under the Lions Gate Bridge, on what is known officially today as Capilano Indian Reserve No. 5; however, to the many people who grew up there it will always be known as Xwemelch'stn. They are a big family (eleven sisters and five brothers) who grew up taking care of each other; even when six of the siblings were sent to a residential school in Sechelt. The legacy of the Capilanos also lives on in the everyday actions of the Mathias family. Cody, for instance, learned to carve at age ten by watching his grandfather (Chief Mathias Joe) and father (William "Buffalo" Mathias Joe) carve totem poles. Ellan Phyllis Viola Mathias Joe, the youngest of the Mathias siblings, carries today the ancestral name Lixwelut after her great-grandmother, Mary Agnes Capilano. Agi describes Mary Capilano's home being like an orchard; she had five to six types of apples, apricots, salmonberries, and more. Like her great-grandmother, Rose often spent time walking the lands and learning of the traditional foods that were readily available, such as wild rice in the marshy areas, fresh fruit trees and an abundance of fresh seasonal berries and seafood. In recent years, the family began performing their songs and dances publicly, which has brought the family even closer together.

Though the family knew of the book, *Legends of Vancouver*, they never stopped passing the original stories down orally within the family. Katie remembers owning a copy of *Legends of Vancouver* in the 1960s. She recalls, "And it had the Twin Sisters, Siwash Rock, The Sea Serpent, the Lost Island—I keep looking for that Lost Island." For the first time since the 1911 edition of *Legends* was published, the Capilanos' descendants will see their ancestors formally recognized as coauthors of the *Legends* stories. In October 2018, I visited the Capilano Suspension Bridge's "Kia'palano Exhibit" with Agi, which features information on the Capilanos and includes a memorial pole for Mary Capilano that was raised in 1993. As we walked through the outdoor exhibit, Agi pointed up at the picture of Mary Capilano and exclaimed to all the people that walked by, "See, that's my great-grandmother!" It brought her immense pride to stand alongside her ancestor, with the past and present coming together.

With figures like Chief Joe Capilano and Mary Capilano, who continue to mean so much for many people, it's difficult to do these storytellers justice or to fully express the ways they continue to impact the lives of Sḵwx̱wú7mesh peoples. Though this book is written with the consent and cooperation of the Mathias family, I would also like to extend my deepest respect to the Baker family, who are also descendants of the Capilanos and who continue to honour their own stories of Joe and Mary. In gathering information on the lives of Joe and Mary Capilano, I relied often on the autobiography of Chief Simon Baker, Khot-La-Cha; Chief Baker's recollections, particularly of his grandmother, Mary Capilano ("The Princess of Peace"), are respectfully acknowledged throughout this edition.

The Mathias family and I hope that this updated book, with its rightful acknowledgement of the Capilanos as coauthors and additional stories by Mary Capilano included, will spark conversations within the Sḵwx̱wú7mesh community and engage Canadians in necessary conversations about conciliation (and Campbell's notion of "putting things to right") in the context of Indigenous literatures.

I have made no changes to the original *Legends of Vancouver* stories, but I have provided notes with context and additional information where relevant. This new edition also incorporates five additional stories, narrated solely or in part by Mary Capilano, to better reflect Johnson's collaborative relationship with *both* the Capilanos. As per the wishes of the Mathias family, all royalties from the sale of this edition will go to The Chief Joe Mathias BC Aboriginal Scholarship Fund.

LEGENDS *of the* CAPILANO

E. Pauline Johnson (Tekahionwake)
with Chief Joe Capilano (Sahp-luk) and
Mary Agnes Capilano (Lixwelut)

THE TWO SISTERS

THE LIONS

"The sisters mountains—that's where we get our Indian medicine." —CODY MATHIAS

You can see them as you look towards the north and the west, where the dream-hills swim into the sky amid their ever-drifting clouds of pearl and grey. They catch the earliest hint of sunrise, they hold the last colour of sunset. Twin mountains they are, lifting their twin peaks above the fairest city in all Canada, and known throughout the British Empire as "The Lions of Vancouver."

Sometimes the smoke of forest fires blurs them until they gleam like opals in a purple atmosphere, too beautiful for words to paint. Sometimes the slanting rains festoon scarves of mist about their crests, and the peaks fade into shadowy outlines, melting, melting, forever melting into the distances. But for most days in the year the sun circles the twin glories with a sweep of gold. The moon washes them with a torrent of silver. Oftentimes, when the city is shrouded in rain, the sun yellows their snows to a deep orange; but through sun and shadow they stand immovable, smiling westward above the waters of the restless Pacific, eastward above the superb beauty of the Capilano Canyon. But the Indian tribes do not know these peaks as "The Lions." Even the chief whose feet have so recently wandered to the Happy Hunting Grounds[1] never heard the name given them until I mentioned it to him one dreamy August day, as together we followed the trail leading to the canyon. He seemed so surprised at the name that I mentioned the reason it had been applied to them, asking him if he recalled the

Landseer Lions in Trafalgar Square.[2] Yes, he remembered those splendid sculptures, and his quick eye saw the resemblance instantly. It appeared to please him, and his fine face expressed the haunting memories of the far-away roar of Old London. But the "call of the blood" was stronger, and presently he referred to the Indian legend of those peaks—a legend that I have reason to believe is absolutely unknown to thousands of Palefaces who look upon "The Lions" daily, without the love for them that is in the Indian heart, without knowledge of the secret of "The Two Sisters." The legend was intensely fascinating as it left his lips in the quaint broken English that is never so dulcet as when it slips from an Indian tongue. His inimitable gestures, strong, graceful, comprehensive, were like a perfectly chosen frame embracing a delicate painting, and his brooding eyes were as the light in which the picture hung. "Many thousands of years ago," he began, "there were no twin peaks like sentinels guarding the outposts of this sunset coast. They were placed there long after the first creation, when the Sagalie Tyee moulded the mountains, and patterned the mighty rivers where the salmon run, because of His love for His Indian children, and His wisdom for their necessities. In those times there were many and mighty Indian tribes along the Pacific—in the mountain ranges, at the shores and sources of the great Fraser River. Indian law ruled the land. Indian customs prevailed. Indian beliefs were regarded. Those were the legend-making ages when great things occurred to make the traditions we repeat to our children today. Perhaps the greatest of these traditions is the story of 'The Two Sisters,' for they are known to us as 'The Chief's Daughters,' and to them we owe the Great Peace in which we live, and have lived for many countless moons. There is an ancient custom amongst the Coast tribes that, when our daughters step from childhood into the great world of womanhood, the occasion must be made one of extreme rejoicing. The being who possesses the possibility of someday mothering a man-child, a warrior, a brave, receives much consideration in most nations; but to us, the Sunset tribes, she is honoured above all people. The parents usually give a great potlatch, and a feast that lasts many days. The entire tribe and the surrounding tribes are bidden to this festival. More than that, sometimes when a great Tyee celebrates for his daughter, the tribes from far up the coast, from the distant north, from inland, from the island, from the Cariboo country, are gathered as guests to the feast. During these days of rejoicing, the girl is placed in a high seat, an exalted position, for is she not marriageable? And does not marriage mean motherhood? And does not motherhood mean a vaster nation of brave sons and of gentle daughters, who, in their turn, will give us sons and daughters of their own?

"But it was many thousands of years ago that a great Tyee had two daughters that grew to womanhood at the same springtime, when the first great run of salmon thronged the rivers, and the ollallie bushes were heavy with blossoms. These two daughters were young, lovable, and oh! very beautiful. Their father, the great Tyee, prepared to make a feast such as the Coast had never seen. There were to be days and days of rejoicing, the people were to come for many leagues, were to bring gifts to the girls and to receive gifts of great value from the Chief, and hospitality was to reign as long as pleasuring feet could dance, and enjoying lips could laugh, and mouths partake of the excellence of the Chief's fish, game, and ollallies.

"The only shadow on the joy of it all was war, for the tribe of the great Tyee was at war with the Upper Coast Indians, those who lived north, near what is named by the Paleface as the port of Prince Rupert. Giant war canoes slipped along the entire coast, war parties paddled up and down, war songs broke the silences of the nights, hatred, vengeance, strife, horror festered everywhere like sores on the surface of the earth. But the great Tyee, after warring for weeks, turned and laughed at the battle and the bloodshed, for he had been victor in every encounter, and he could well afford to leave the strife for a brief week and feast in his daughters' honour, nor permit any mere enemy to come between him and the traditions of his race and household. So he turned insultingly deaf ears to their war cries; he ignored with arrogant indifference their paddle-dips that encroached within his own coast waters, and he prepared, as a great Tyee should, to royally entertain his tribesmen in honour of his daughters.

"But seven suns before the great feast, these two maidens came before him, hand clasped in hand.

"'Oh! our father,' they said, 'may we speak?'

"'Speak, my daughters, my girls with the eyes of April, the hearts of June'" (early spring and early summer would be the more accurate Indian phrasing).

"'Some day, Oh! our father, we may mother a man-child, who may grow to be just such a powerful Tyee as you are, and for this honour that may some day be ours we have come to crave a favour of you—you, Oh! our father.'

"'It is your privilege at this celebration to receive any favour your hearts may wish,' he replied graciously, placing his fingers beneath their girlish chins. 'The favour is yours before you ask it, my daughters.'

"'Will you, for our sakes, invite the great northern hostile tribe—the tribe you war upon—to this, our feast?' they asked fearlessly.

"'To a peaceful feast, a feast in the honour of women?' he exclaimed incredulously.

"'So we would desire it,' they answered.

"'And so shall it be,' he declared. 'I can deny you nothing this day, and some time you may bear sons to bless this peace you have asked, and to bless their mother's sire for granting it.' Then he turned to all the young men of the tribe and commanded: 'Build fires at sunset on all the coast headlands—fires of welcome. Man your canoes and face the north, greet the enemy, and tell them that I, the Tyee of the Capilanos, ask—no, command—that they join me for a great feast in honour of my two daughters.' And when the northern tribe got this invitation they flocked down the coast to this feast of a Great Peace.

They brought their women and their children; they brought game and fish, gold and white stone beads, baskets and carven ladles, and wonderful woven blankets to lay at the feet of their now acknowledged ruler, the great Tyee. And he, in turn, gave such a potlatch that nothing but tradition can vie with it. There were long, glad days of joyousness, long, pleasurable nights of dancing and camp-fires, and vast quantities of food. The war canoes were emptied of their deadly weapons and filled with the daily catch of salmon. The hostile war songs ceased, and in their place were heard the soft shuffle of dancing feet, the singing voices of women, the play-games of the children of two powerful tribes which had been until now ancient enemies, for a great and lasting brotherhood was sealed between them—their war songs were ended forever.

"Then the Sagalie Tyee smiled on His Indian children: 'I will make these young-eyed maidens immortal,' He said. In the cup of His hands He lifted the Chief's two daughters and set them forever in a high place, for they had borne two offspring—Peace and Brotherhood—each of which is now a great Tyee ruling this land.

"And on the mountain crest the Chief's daughters can be seen wrapped in the suns, the snows, the stars of all seasons, for they have stood in this high place for thousands of years, and will stand for thousands of years to come, guarding the peace of the Pacific Coast and the quiet of the Capilano Canyon."

This is the Indian legend of "The Lions of Vancouver" as I had it from one who will tell me no more the traditions of his people.

THE SIWASH ROCK

Unique, and so distinct from its surroundings as to suggest rather the handicraft of man than a whim of Nature, it looms up at the entrance to the Narrows, a symmetrical column of solid grey stone. There are no similar formations within the range of vision, or indeed within many a day's paddle up and down the coast. Amongst all the wonders, the natural beauties that encircle Vancouver, the marvels of mountains shaped into crouching lions and brooding beavers, the yawning canyons, the stupendous forest firs and cedars, Siwash Rock stands as distinct, as individual, as if dropped from another sphere.

I saw it first in the slanting light of a redly setting August sun; the little tuft of green shrubbery that crests its summit was black against the crimson of sea and sky, and its colossal base of grey stone gleamed like flaming polished granite.

My old tillicum lifted his paddle-blade to point towards it. "You know the story?" he asked. I shook my head (experience has taught me his love of silent replies, his moods of legend-telling). For a time we paddled slowly; the rock detached itself from its background of forest and shore, and it stood forth like a sentinel—erect, enduring, eternal.

"Do you think it stands straight—like a man?" he asked.

"Yes, like some noble-spirited, upright warrior," I replied.

"It is a man," he said, "and a warrior man, too; a man who fought for everything that was noble and upright."

"What do you regard as everything that is noble and upright, Chief?" I asked, curious as to his ideas. I shall not forget the reply; it was but two words—astounding, amazing words. He said simply:

"Clean fatherhood."

Through my mind raced tumultuous recollections of numberless articles in yet numberless magazines, all dealing with the recent "fad" of motherhood, but I had to hear from the lip of a Squamish Indian Chief the only treatise on the nobility of "clean fatherhood" that I have yet unearthed. And this treatise has been an Indian legend for centuries; and, lest they forget how all-important those two little words must ever be, Siwash Rock stands to remind them, set there by the Deity as a monument to one who kept his own life clean, that cleanliness might be the heritage of the generations to come.

It was "thousands of years ago" (all Indian legends begin in extremely remote times) that a handsome boy chief journeyed in his canoe to the upper coast for the shy little northern girl whom he brought home as his wife. Boy though he was, the young chief had proved himself to be an excellent warrior, a fearless hunter, and an upright, courageous man among men. His tribe loved him, his enemies respected him, and the base and mean and cowardly feared him.

The customs and traditions of his ancestors were a positive religion to him, the sayings and the advices of the old people were his creed. He was conservative in every rite and ritual of his race. He fought his tribal enemies like the savage that he was. He sang his war songs, danced his war dances, slew his foes, but the little girl-wife from the north he treated with the deference that he gave his own mother, for was she not to be the mother of his warrior son?

The year rolled round, weeks merged into months, winter into spring, and one glorious summer at daybreak he wakened to her voice calling him. She stood beside him, smiling.

"It will be to-day," she said proudly.

He sprang from his couch of wolf-skins and looked out upon the coming day: the promise of what it would bring him seemed breathing through all his forest world. He took her very gently by the hand and led her through the tangle of wilderness down to the water's edge, where the beauty spot we moderns call Stanley Park bends about Prospect Point. "I must swim," he told her.

"I must swim, too," she smiled, with the perfect understanding of two beings who are mated. For, to them, the old Indian custom was law—the custom that the parents of a coming child must swim until their flesh is so clear and clean that a wild animal cannot scent their proximity. If the wild creatures of the forests have no fear of them, then, and only then, are they fit to become parents, and to scent a human is in itself a fearsome thing to all wild creatures.

So those two plunged into the waters of the Narrows as the grey dawn slipped up the eastern skies and all the forest awoke to the life of a new, glad day. Presently he took her ashore, and smilingly she crept away under the giant trees. "I must be alone," she said, "but come to me at sunrise: you will not find me alone then." He smiled also, and plunged back into the sea. He must swim, swim, swim through this hour when his fatherhood was coming upon him. It was the law that he must be clean, spotlessly clean, so that when his child looked out upon the world it would have the chance to live its own life clean. If he did not swim hour upon hour his child would come to an unclean father. He must give his child a chance in life; he must not hamper it by his own uncleanliness at its birth. It was the tribal law—the law of vicarious purity.

As he swam joyously to and fro, a canoe bearing four men headed up the Narrows. These men were giants in stature, and the stroke of their paddles made huge eddies that boiled like the seething tides.

"Out from our course!" they cried as his lithe, copper-coloured body arose and fell with his splendid stroke. He laughed at them, giants though they were, and answered that he could not cease his swimming at their demand.

"But you shall cease!" they commanded. "We are the men (agents) of the Sagalie Tyee (God), and we command you ashore out of our way!" (I find in all these Coast Indian legends that the Deity is represented by four men, usually paddling an immense canoe.)

He ceased swimming, and, lifting his head, defied them. "I shall not stop, nor yet go ashore," he declared, striking out once more to the middle of the channel.

"Do you dare disobey us," they cried—"we, the men of the Sagalie Tyee? We can turn you into a fish, or a tree, or a stone for this; do you dare disobey the Great Tyee?"

"I dare anything for the cleanliness and purity of my coming child. I dare even the Sagalie Tyee Himself, but my child must be born to a spotless life."

The four men were astounded. They consulted together, lighted their pipes, and sat in council. Never had they, the men of the Sagalie Tyee, been defied before. Now, for the sake of a little unborn child, they were ignored, disobeyed, almost despised. The lithe young copper-coloured body still disported itself in the cool waters; superstition held that should their canoe, or even their paddle-blades, touch a human being, their marvellous power would be lost. The handsome young chief swam directly in their course. They dared not run him down; if so, they would become as other men. While they yet counselled what to do, there floated from out the forest a faint, strange, compelling sound. They listened, and the young chief ceased his stroke as he listened also. The faint sound drifted out across the waters once more. It was the cry of a little, little child. Then one of the four men, he that steered the canoe, the strongest and tallest of them all, arose and, standing erect, stretched out his arms towards the rising sun and chanted, not a curse on the young chief's disobedience, but a promise of everlasting days and freedom from death.

"Because you have defied all things that come in your path we promise this to you," he chanted: "you have defied what interferes with your child's chance for a clean life, you have lived as you wish your son to live, you have defied us when we would have stopped your swimming and hampered your child's future. You have placed that child's future before all things, and for this the Sagalie Tyee commands us to make you forever a pattern for your tribe. You shall never die, but you shall stand through all the thousands of years to come, where all eyes can see you. You shall live, live, live as an indestructible monument to Clean Fatherhood."

The four men lifted their paddles and the handsome young chief swam inshore; as his feet touched the line where sea and land met, he was transformed into stone.

Then the four men said, "His wife and child must ever be near him; they shall not die, but live also." And they, too, were turned into stone. If you penetrate the hollows in the woods near Siwash Rock you will find a large rock and a smaller one beside it. They are the shy little bride-wife from the north, with her hour-old baby beside her. And from the uttermost parts of the world vessels come daily throbbing and sailing up the Narrows. From far trans-Pacific ports, from the frozen North, from the lands of the Southern Cross,[3] they pass and repass the living rock that was there before their hulls were shaped, that will be there when their very names are forgotten, when their crews and their captains have taken their long last voyage, when their merchandise has rotted, and their owners are known no more. But the tall, grey column of stone will still be there—a monument to one man's fidelity to a generation yet unborn—and will endure from everlasting to everlasting.

THE RECLUSE

Journeying toward the upper course of the Capilano River, about a mile citywards from the dam, you will pass a disused logger's shack. Leave the trail at this point and strike through the undergrowth for a few hundred yards to the left, and you will be on the rocky borders of that purest, most restless river in all Canada. The stream is haunted with tradition, teeming with a score of romances that vie with its grandeur and loveliness, and of which its waters are perpetually whispering. But I learned this legend from one whose voice was as dulcet as the swirling rapids; but, unlike them, that voice is hushed today, while the river, the river still sings on—sings on.

It was singing in very melodious tones through the long August afternoon two summers ago, while we, the chief, his happy-hearted wife and bright, young daughter,[4] all lounged amongst the boulders and watched the lazy clouds drift from peak to peak far above us. It was one of his inspired days; legends crowded to his lips as a whistle teases the mouth of a happy boy; his heart was brimming with tales of the bygones, his eyes were dark with dreams and that strange mournfulness that always haunted them when he spoke of long-ago romances. There was not a tree, a boulder, a dash of rapid upon which his glance fell which he could not link with some ancient poetic superstition. Then abruptly, in the very midst of his verbal reveries, he turned and asked me if I were superstitious. Of course I replied that I was.

"Do you think some happenings will bring trouble later on—will foretell evil?" he asked.

I made some evasive answer, which, however, seemed to satisfy him, for he plunged into the strange tale of the recluse of the canyon with more vigour than dreaminess; but first he asked me the question:

"What do your own tribes, those east of the great mountains, think of twin children?"

I shook my head.

"That is enough," he said before I could reply. "I see, your people do not like them."

"Twin children are almost unknown with us," I hastened. "They are rare, very rare; but it is true we do not welcome them."

"Why?" he asked abruptly.

I was a little uncertain about telling him. If I said the wrong thing, the coming tale might die on his lips before it was born to speech, but we understood each other so well that I finally ventured the truth:

"We Iroquois say that twin children are as rabbits," I explained. "The nation always nicknames the parents 'Tow-wan-da-na-ga.' That is the Mohawk for rabbit."

"Is that all?" he asked curiously.

"That is all. Is it not enough to render twin children unwelcome?" I questioned.

He thought awhile, then, with evident desire to learn how all races regarded this occurrence, he said, "You have been much among the Palefaces; what do they say of twins?"

"Oh! the Palefaces like them. They are—they are—oh! well, they say they are very proud of having twins," I stammered. Once again I was hardly sure of my ground. He looked most incredulous, and I was led to enquire what his own people of the Squamish thought of this discussed problem.

"It is no pride to us," he said decidedly, "nor yet is it disgrace of rabbits, but it is a fearsome thing—a sign of coming evil to the father, and, worse than that, of coming disaster to the tribe."

Then I knew he held in his heart some strange incident that gave substance to the superstition. "Won't you tell it to me?" I begged.

He leaned a little backward against a giant boulder, clasping his thin, brown hands about his knees; his eyes roved up the galloping river, then swept down the singing waters to where they crowded past the sudden bend, and during the entire recital of the strange legend his eyes never left that spot where the stream disappeared in its hurrying journey to the sea. Without preamble he began:

"It was a grey morning when they told him of this disaster that had befallen him. He was a great chief, and he ruled many tribes on the North Pacific Coast; but what was his greatness now? His young wife had borne him twins, and was sobbing out her anguish in the little fir-bark lodge near the tidewater.

"Beyond the doorway gathered many old men and women—old in years, old in wisdom, old in the lore and learning of their nations. Some of them wept, some chanted solemnly the dirge of their lost hopes and happiness, which would never return because of this calamity; others discussed in hushed voices this awesome thing, and for hours their grave council was broken only by the infant cries of the two boy-babies in the bark lodge, the hopeless sobs of the young mother, the agonized moans of the stricken chief—their father.

"'Something dire will happen to the tribe,' said the old men in council.

"'Something dire will happen to him, my husband,' wept the afflicted young mother.

"'Something dire will happen to us all,' echoed the unhappy father.

"Then an ancient medicine man arose, lifting his arms, outstretching his palms to hush the lamenting throng. His voice shook with the weight of many winters, but his eyes were yet keen and mirrored the clear thought and brain behind them, as the still trout-pools in the Capilano mirror the mountain-tops. His words were masterful, his gestures commanding, his shoulders erect and kindly. His was a personality and an inspiration that no one dared dispute, and his judgment was accepted as the words fell slowly, like a doom.

"'It is the olden law of the Squamish that, lest evil befall the tribe, the sire of twin children must go afar and alone into the mountain fastnesses, there by his isolation and his loneliness to prove himself stronger than the threatened evil, and thus to beat back the shadow that would otherwise follow him and all his people. I, therefore, name for him the length of days that he must spend alone fighting his invisible enemy. He will know by some great sign in Nature the hour that the evil is conquered, the hour that his race is saved. He must leave before this sun sets, taking with him only his strongest bow, his fleetest arrows, and, going up into the mountain wilderness, remain there ten days—alone, alone.'

"The masterful voice ceased, the tribe wailed their assent, the father arose speechless, his drawn face revealing great agony over this seemingly brief banishment. He took leave of his sobbing wife, of the two tiny souls that were his sons, grasped his favourite bow and arrows, and faced the forest like a warrior. But at the end of the ten days he did not return, nor yet ten weeks, nor yet ten months.

"'He is dead,' wept the mother into the baby ears of her two boys. 'He could not battle against the evil that threatened; it was stronger than he—he, so strong, so proud, so brave.'

"'He is dead,' echoed the tribesmen and the tribeswomen. 'Our strong, brave chief, he is dead.' So they mourned the long year through, but their chants and their tears but renewed their grief; he did not return to them.

"Meanwhile, far up the Capilano the banished chief had built his solitary home; for who can tell what fatal trick of sound, what current of air, what faltering note in the voice of the Medicine Man had deceived his alert Indian ears? But some unhappy fate had led him to understand that his solitude must be of ten years' duration, not ten days, and he had accepted the mandate with the heroism of a stoic. For if he had refused to do so his belief was that, although the threatened disaster would be spared him, the evil would fall upon his tribe. Thus was one more added to the long list of self-forgetting souls whose creed has been, 'It is fitting that one should suffer for the people.' It was the world-old heroism of vicarious sacrifice.

"With his hunting-knife the banished Squamish chief stripped the bark from the firs and cedars, building for himself a lodge beside the Capilano River, where leaping trout and salmon could be speared by arrow-heads fastened to deftly shaped, long handles. All through the salmon run he smoked and dried the fish with the care of a housewife. The mountain sheep and goats, and even huge black and cinnamon bears, fell before his unerring arrows; the fleet-footed deer never returned to their haunts from their evening drinking at the edge of the stream—their wild hearts, their agile bodies were stilled when he took aim. Smoked hams and saddles hung in rows from the cross-poles of his bark lodge, and the magnificent pelts of animals carpeted his floors, padded his couch, and clothed his body. He tanned the soft doe-hides, making leggings, moccasins, and shirts, stitching them together with deer-sinew as he had seen his mother do in the long-ago. He gathered the juicy salmon-berries, their acid a sylvan, healthful change from meat and fish. Month by month and year by year he sat beside his lonely camp-fire, waiting for his long term of solitude to end. One comfort alone was his—he was enduring the disaster, fighting the evil, that his tribe might go unscathed, that his people be saved from calamity. Slowly, laboriously the tenth year dawned; day by day it dragged its long weeks across his waiting heart, for Nature had not yet given the sign that his long probation was over.

"Then, one hot summer day, the Thunder Bird[5] came crashing through the mountains about him. Up from the arms of the Pacific rolled the storm-cloud, and the Thunder Bird, with its eyes of flashing light, beat its huge vibrating wings on crag and canyon.

"Up-stream, a tall shaft of granite rears its needle-like length. It is named 'Thunder Rock,' and wise men of the Paleface people say it is rich in ore—copper, silver, and gold. At the base of this shaft the Squamish chief crouched when the storm-cloud broke and bellowed through the ranges, and on its summit the Thunder Bird perched, its gigantic wings threshing the air into booming sounds, into splitting terrors, like the crash of a giant cedar hurtling down the mountain-side.

"But when the beating of those black pinions ceased and the echo of their thunder-waves died down the depths of the canyon, the Squamish chief arose as a new man. The shadow on his soul had lifted, the fears of evil were cowed and conquered. In his brain, his blood, his veins, his sinews, he felt that the poison of melancholy dwelt no more. He had redeemed his fault of fathering twin children; he had fulfilled the demands of the law of his tribe.

"As he heard the last beat of the Thunder Bird's wings dying slowly, faintly, faintly, among the crags, he knew that the bird, too, was dying, for its soul was leaving its monster black body, and presently that soul appeared in the sky. He could see it arching overhead, before it took its long journey to the Happy Hunting Grounds, for the soul of the Thunder Bird was a radiant half-circle of glorious colour spanning from peak to peak. He lifted his head then, for he knew it was the sign the ancient Medicine Man had told him to wait for—the sign that his long banishment was ended.

"And all these years, down in the tidewater country, the little brown-faced twins were asking childwise, 'Where is our father? Why have we no father, like other boys?' To be met only with the oft-repeated reply, 'Your father is no more. Your father, the great chief, is dead.'

"But some strange filial intuition told the boys that their sire would some day return. Often they voiced this feeling to their mother, but she would only weep and say that not even the witchcraft of the great Medicine Man could bring him to them. But when they were ten years old the two children came to their mother, hand within hand. They were armed with their little hunting-knives, their salmon-spears, their tiny bows and arrows.

"'We go to find our father,' they said.

"'Oh! useless quest,' wailed the mother.

"'Oh! useless quest,' echoed the tribes-people.

"But the great Medicine Man said, 'The heart of a child has invisible eyes; perhaps the child-eyes see him. The heart of a child has invisible ears; perhaps the child-ears hear him call. Let them go.' So the little children went forth into the forest; their young feet flew as though shod with wings, their young hearts pointed to the north as does the white man's compass. Day after day they journeyed up-stream, until rounding a sudden bend they beheld a bark lodge with a thin blue curl of smoke drifting from its roof.

"'It is our father's lodge,' they told each other, for their childish hearts were unerring in response to the call of kinship. Hand in hand they approached, and, entering the lodge, said the one word, 'Come.'

"The great Squamish chief outstretched his arms towards them, then towards the laughing river, then towards the mountains.

"'Welcome, my sons!' he said. 'And good-bye, my mountains, my brothers, my crags, and my canyons!' And with a child clinging to each hand he faced once more the country of the tidewater."

The legend was ended.

For a long time he sat in silence. He had removed his gaze from the bend in the river, around which the two children had come and where the eyes of the recluse had first rested on them after ten years of solitude.

The chief spoke again: "It was here, on this spot we are sitting, that he built his lodge: here he dwelt those ten years alone, alone."

I nodded silently. The legend was too beautiful to mar with comments, and as the twilight fell we threaded our way through the underbrush, past the disused logger's camp, and into the trail that leads citywards.

THE LOST SALMON RUN

Great had been the "run," and the sockeye season was almost over. For that reason I wondered many times why my old friend, the klootchman, had failed to make one of the fishing fleet. She was an indefatigable work-woman, rivalling her husband as an expert catcher, and all the year through she talked of little else but the coming run. But this especial season she had not appeared amongst her fellow-kind. The fleet and the canneries knew nothing of her, and when I enquired of her tribes-people they would reply without explanation, "She not here this year."

But one russet September afternoon I found her. I had idled down the trail from the swans' basin in Stanley Park to the rim that skirts the Narrows, and I saw her graceful, high-bowed canoe heading for the beach that is the favourite landing-place of the "tillicums" from the Mission. Her canoe looked like a dream-craft, for the water was very still, and everywhere a blue film hung like a fragrant veil, for the peat on Lulu Island[6] had been smouldering for days and its pungent odours and blue-grey haze made a dream-world of sea and shore and sky.

I hurried upshore, hailing her in the Chinook, and as she caught my voice she lifted her paddle directly above her head in the Indian signal of greeting.

As she beached, I greeted her with extended eager hands to assist her ashore, for the klootchman is getting to be an old woman; albeit she paddles against tide-water like a boy in his teens.

"No," she said, as I begged her to come ashore. "I not wait—me. I just come to fetch Maarda; she been city; she soon come—now." But she left her "working" attitude and curled like a school-girl in the bow of the canoe, her elbows resting on her paddle which she had flung across the gunwales.

"I have missed you, klootchman; you have not been to see me for three moons, and you have not fished or been at the canneries," I remarked.

"No," she said. "I stay home this year." Then, leaning towards me with grave import in her manner, her eyes, her voice, she added, "I have a grandchild, born first week July, so—I stay."

So this explained her absence. I, of course, offered congratulations and enquired all about the great event, for this was her first grandchild, and the little person was of importance.

"And are you going to make a fisherman of him?" I asked.

"No, no, not boy-child, it is girl-child," she answered with some indescribable trick of expression that led me to know she preferred it so.

"You are pleased it is a girl?" I questioned in surprise.

"Very pleased," she replied emphatically. "Very good luck to have girl for first grandchild. Our tribe not like yours; we want girl-children first; we not always wish boy-child born just for fight. Your people, they care only for war-path; our tribe more peaceful. Very good sign first grandchild to be girl. I tell you why: girl-child may be some time mother herself; very grand thing to be mother."

I felt I had caught the secret of her meaning. She was rejoicing that this little one should some time become one of the mothers of her race. We chatted over it a little longer and she gave me several playful "digs" about my own tribe thinking so much less of motherhood than hers, and so much more of battle and bloodshed. Then we drifted into talk of the sockeye run and of the hyiu chickimin the Indians would get.

"Yes, hyiu chickimin," she repeated with a sigh of satisfaction. "Always; and hyiu muck-a-muck when big salmon run. No more ever come that bad year when not any fish."

"When was that?" I asked.

"Before you born, or I, or"—pointing across the park to the distant city of Vancouver that breathed its wealth and beauty across the September afternoon—"before that place born, before white man came here—oh! long before."

Dear old klootchman! I knew by the dusk in her eyes that she was back in her Land of Legends, and that soon I would be the richer in my hoard of Indian lore. She sat, still leaning on her paddle; her eyes, half closed, rested on the distant outline of the blurred heights across the Inlet. I shall not further attempt her broken English, for this is but the shadow of her story, and without her unique personality the legend is as a flower that lacks both colour and fragrance. She called it "The Lost Salmon Run."

"The wife of the Great Tyee was but a wisp of a girl, but all the world was young in those days; even the Fraser River was young and small, not the mighty water it is today; but the pink salmon crowded its throat just as they do now, and the tillicums caught and salted and smoked the fish just as they have done this year, just as they will always do. But it was yet winter, and the rains were slanting and the fogs drifting, when the wife of the Great Tyee stood before him and said:

"'Before the salmon run I shall give to you a great gift. Will you honour me most if it is the gift of a boy-child or a girl-child?' The Great Tyee loved the woman. He was stern with his people, hard with his tribe; he ruled his council-fires with a will of stone. His medicine men said he had no human heart in his body; his warriors said he had no human blood in his veins. But he clasped this woman's hands, and his eyes, his lips, his voice, were gentle as her own, as he replied:

"'Give to me a girl-child—a little girl-child—that she may grow to be like you, and, in her turn, give to her husband children.'

"But when the tribes-people heard of his choice they arose in great anger. They surrounded him in a deep, indignant circle. 'You are a slave to the woman,' they declared, 'and now you desire to make yourself a slave to a woman-baby. We want an heir—a man-child to be our Great

Tyee in years to come. When you are old and weary of tribal affairs, when you sit wrapped in your blanket in the hot summer sunshine, because your blood is old and thin, what can a girl-child do, to help either you or us? Who, then, will be our Great Tyee?'

"He stood in the centre of the menacing circle, his arms folded, his chin raised, his eyes hard as flint. His voice, cold as stone, replied:

"'Perhaps she will give you such a man-child, and, if so, the child is yours; he will belong to you, not to me; he will become the possession of the people. But if the child is a girl she will belong to me—she will be mine. You cannot take her from me as you took me from my mother's side and forced me to forget my aged father in my service to the tribe; she will belong to me, will be the mother of my grandchildren, and her husband will be my son.'

"'You do not care for the good of your tribe. You care only for your own wishes and desires,' they rebelled. 'Suppose the salmon run is small, we will have no food; suppose there is no man-child, we will have no Great Tyee to show us how to get food from other tribes, and we shall starve.'

"'Your hearts are black and bloodless,' thundered the Great Tyee, turning upon them fiercely, 'and your eyes are blinded. Do you wish the tribe to forget how great is the importance of a child that will some day be a mother herself, and give to your children and grandchildren a Great Tyee? Are the people to live, to thrive, to increase, to become more powerful with no mother-women to bear future sons and daughters? Your minds are dead, your brains are chilled. Still, even in your ignorance, you are my people: you and your wishes must be considered. I call together the great medicine men, the men of witchcraft, the men of magic. They shall decide the laws which will follow the bearing of either boy or girl-child. What say you, oh! mighty men?'

"Messengers were then sent up and down the coast, sent far up the Fraser River, and to the valley lands inland for many leagues, gathering as they journeyed, all the men of magic that could be found. Never were so many medicine men in council before. They built fires and danced and chanted for many days. They spoke with the gods of the mountains, with the gods of the sea; then 'the power' of decision came to them. They were inspired with a choice to lay before the tribes-people, and the most ancient medicine man in all the coast region arose and spoke their resolution:

"'The people of the tribe cannot be allowed to have all things. They want a boy-child and they want a great salmon-run also. They cannot have both. The Sagalie Tyee has revealed to us, the great men of magic, that both these things will make the people arrogant and selfish. They must choose between the two.'

"'Choose, oh! you ignorant tribes-people,' commanded the Great Tyee. 'The wise men of our coast have said that the girl-child who will some day bear children of her own will also bring abundance of salmon at her birth; but the boy-child brings to you but himself.'

"'Let the salmon go,' shouted the people, 'but give us a future Great Tyee. Give us the boy-child.'

"And when the child was born it was a boy.

"'Evil will fall upon you,' wailed the Great Tyee. 'You have despised a mother-woman. You will suffer evil and starvation and hunger and poverty, oh! foolish tribes-people. Did you not know how great a girl-child is?'

"That spring, people from a score of tribes came up to the Fraser for the salmon-run. They came great distances—from the mountains, the lakes, the far-off dry lands, but not one fish entered the vast rivers of the Pacific Coast. The people had made their choice. They had forgotten the honour that a mother-child would have brought them. They were bereft of their food. They were stricken with poverty. Through the long winter that followed they endured hunger and starvation. Since then our tribe has always welcomed girl-children—we want no more lost runs."

The klootchman lifted her arms from her paddle as she concluded; her eyes left the irregular outline of the violet mountains. She had come back to this year of grace—her Legend Land had vanished.

"So," she added, "you see now, maybe, why I am glad my grandchild is girl; it means big salmon-run next year."

"It is a beautiful story, klootchman," I said, "and I feel a cruel delight that your men of magic punished the people for their ill choice."

"That because you girl-child yourself," she laughed.

There was the slightest whisper of a step behind me. I turned to find Maarda almost at my elbow. The rising tide was unbeaching the canoe, and as Maarda stepped in and the klootchman slipped astern, it drifted afloat.

"Kla-how-ya," nodded the klootchman as she dipped her paddle-blade in exquisite silence.

"Kla-how-ya," smiled Maarda.

"Kla-how-ya, tillicums," I replied, and watched for many moments as they slipped away into the blurred distance, until the canoe merged into the violet and grey of the farther shore.

THE DEEP WATERS

Far over your left shoulder as your boat leaves the Narrows to thread the beautiful waterways that lead to Vancouver Island, you will see the summit of Mount Baker robed in its everlasting whiteness and always reflecting some wonderful glory from the rising sun, the golden noontide, or the violet and amber sunset. This is the Mount Ararat[7] of the Pacific Coast peoples; for those readers who are familiar with the ways and beliefs and faiths of primitive races will agree that it is difficult to discover anywhere in the world a race that has not some story of the Deluge, which they have chronicled and localized to fit the understanding and the conditions of the nation that composes their own immediate world.

Amongst the red nations of America I doubt if any two tribes have the same ideas regarding the Flood. Some of the traditions concerning this vast whim of Nature are grotesque in the extreme; some are impressive; some even profound; but of all the stories of the Deluge that I have been able to collect I know of not a single one that can even begin to equal in beauty of conception, let alone rival in possible reality and truth, the Squamish legend of "The Deep Waters."

I here quote the legend of "mine own people," the Iroquois tribes of Ontario, regarding the Deluge. I do this to paint the colour of contrast in richer shades, for I am bound to admit that we who pride ourselves on ancient intellectuality have but a childish tale of the Flood when compared with the jealously preserved annals of the Squamish, which savour more of history than tradition. With "mine own people," animals always play a much more important part, and are endowed with a finer intelligence, than humans. I do not find amid my notes a single tradition of the Iroquois wherein animals do not figure, and our story of the Deluge rests entirely with the intelligence of sea-going and river-going creatures. With us, animals in olden times were greater than man; but it is not so with the Coast Indians, except in rare instances.

When a Coast Indian consents to tell you a legend he will, without variation, begin it with, "It was before the white people came."

The natural thing for you, then, to ask is, "But who were here then?"

He will reply, "Indians, and just the trees, and animals, and fishes, and a few birds."

So you are prepared to accept the animal world as intelligent co-habitants of the Pacific slope; but he will not lead you to think he regards them as equals, much less superiors. But to revert to "mine own people": they hold the intelligence of wild animals far above that of man, for perhaps the one reason that when an animal is sick it effects its own cure; it knows what grasses and herbs to eat, what to avoid, while the sick human calls the medicine man, whose wisdom is not only the result of years of study, but also heredity; consequently any great natural event, such as the Deluge, has much to do with the wisdom of the creatures of the forests and the rivers.

Iroquois tradition tells us that once this earth was entirely submerged in water, and during this period for many days a busy little muskrat swam about vainly looking for a foothold of earth wherein to build his house. In his search he encountered a turtle also leisurely swimming; so they had speech together, and the muskrat complained of weariness; he could find no foothold; he was tired of incessant swimming, and longed for land such as his ancestors enjoyed. The turtle suggested that the muskrat should dive and endeavour to find earth at the bottom of the sea. Acting on this advice the muskrat plunged down, then arose with his two little forepaws grasping some earth he had found beneath the waters.

"Place it on my shell and dive again for more," directed the turtle. The muskrat did so; but when he returned with his paws filled with earth he discovered the small quantity he had first deposited on the turtle's shell had doubled in size. The return from the third trip found the turtle's load again doubled. So the building went on at double compound increase, and the world grew its continents and its islands with great rapidity, and now rests on the shell of a turtle.

If you ask an Iroquois, "And did no men survive this flood?" he will reply, "Why should men survive? The animals are wiser than men; let the wisest live."

How, then, was the earth repeopled?

The Iroquois will tell you that the otter was a medicine man; that in swimming and diving about he found corpses of men and women; he sang his medicine-songs and they came to life, and the otter brought them fish for food until they were strong enough to provide for themselves. Then the Iroquois will conclude his tale with, "You know well that the otter has greater wisdom than a man."

So much for "mine own people" and our profound respect for the superior intelligence of our little brothers of the animal world.

But the Squamish tribe hold other ideas. It was on a February day that I first listened to this beautiful, humane story of the Deluge. My royal old tillicum had come to see me through the rains and mists of late winter days. The gateways of my wigwam always stood open—very widely open—for his feet to enter, and this especial day he came with the worst downpour of the season.

Woman-like, I protested with a thousand contradictions in my voice that he should venture out to see me on such a day. It was, "Oh! Chief, I am so glad to see you!" and it was "Oh! Chief, why didn't you stay at home on such a wet day your poor throat will suffer." But I soon had quantities of hot tea for him, and the huge cup my own father always used was his as long as the Sagalie Tyee allowed his dear feet to wander my way. The immense cup stands idle and empty now for the second time.

Helping him off with his great-coat, I chatted on about the deluge of rain, and he remarked it was not so very bad, as one could yet walk.

"Fortunately, yes, for I cannot swim," I told him.

He laughed, replying, "Well, it is not so bad as when the Great Deep Waters covered the world."

Immediately I foresaw the coming legend, so crept into the shell of monosyllables.

"No?" I questioned.

"No," he replied. "For, one time, there was no land here at all; everywhere there was just water."

"I can quite believe it," I remarked caustically.

He laughed—that irresistible, though silent, David Warfield[8] laugh of his that always brought a responsive smile from his listeners. Then he plunged directly into the tradition, with no preface save a comprehensive sweep of his wonderful hands towards my wide window, against which the rains were beating.

"It was after a long, long time of this—this rain. The mountain-streams were swollen, the rivers choked, the sea began to rise—and yet it rained; for weeks and weeks it rained." He ceased speaking, while the shadows of centuries gone crept into his eyes. Tales of the misty past always inspired him.

"Yes," he continued. "It rained for weeks and weeks, while the mountain torrents roared thunderingly down, and the sea crept silently up. The level lands were first to float in sea-water, then to disappear. The slopes were next to slip into the sea. The world was slowly being flooded. Hurriedly the Indian tribes gathered in one spot, a place of safety far above the reach of the on-creeping sea. The spot was the circling shore of Lake Beautiful, up the North Arm. They held a Great Council and decided at once upon a plan of action. A giant canoe should be built, and some means contrived to anchor it in case the waters mounted to the heights. The men undertook the canoe, the women the anchorage.

"A giant tree was felled, and day and night the men toiled over its construction into the most stupendous canoe the world has ever known. Not an hour, not a moment, but many worked, while the toil-wearied ones slept, only to awake to renewed toil. Meanwhile, the women also worked at a cable—the largest, the longest, the strongest that Indian hands and teeth had ever made. Scores of them gathered and prepared the cedar-fibre; scores of them plaited, rolled, and seasoned it; scores of them chewed upon it inch by inch to make it pliable; scores of them oiled and worked, oiled and worked, oiled and worked it into a sea-resisting fabric. And still the sea crept up, and up, and up. It was the last day; hope of life for the tribes, of land for the world, was doomed. Strong hands, self-sacrificing hands, fastened the cable the women had made—one end to the giant canoe, the other about an enormous boulder, a vast immovable rock as firm as the foundations of the world—for might not the canoe, with its priceless freight, drift out, far out, to sea, and when the water subsided might not this ship of safety be leagues and leagues beyond the sight of land on the storm-driven Pacific?

"Then, with the bravest hearts that ever beat, noble hands lifted every child of the tribes into this vast canoe; not one single baby was overlooked. The canoe was stocked with food and fresh water, and, lastly, the ancient men and women of the race selected as guardians to these children the bravest, most stalwart, handsomest young man of the tribes and the mother of the youngest baby in the camp—she was but a girl of sixteen, her child but two weeks old; but she, too, was brave and very beautiful. These two were placed, she at the bow of the canoe to watch, he at the stern to guide, and all the little children crowded between.

"And still the sea crept up, and up, and up. At the crest of the bluffs about Lake Beautiful the doomed tribes crowded. Not a single person attempted to enter the canoe. There was no wailing, no crying out for safety. 'Let the little children, the young mother, and the bravest and best of our young men live,' was all the farewell those in the canoe heard as the waters reached the summit, and—the canoe floated. Last of all to be seen was the top of the tallest tree, then—all was a world of water.

"For days and days there was no land—just the rush of swirling, snarling sea; but the canoe rode safely at anchor, the cable those scores of dead, faithful women had made held true as the hearts that beat behind the toil and labour of it all.

"But one morning at sunrise, far to the south, a speck floated on the breast of the waters; at midday it was larger; at evening it was yet larger. The moon arose, and in its magic light the man at the stern saw it was a patch of land. All night he watched it grow, and at daybreak looked with glad eyes upon the summit of Mount Baker. He cut the cable, grasped his paddle in his strong young hands, and steered for the south. When they landed, the waters were sunken half down the mountain-side. The children were lifted out; the beautiful young mother, the stalwart young brave, turned to each other, clasped hands, looked into each other's eyes—and smiled.

"And down in the vast country that lies between Mount Baker and the Fraser River they made a new camp, built new lodges, where the little children grew and thrived, and lived and loved, and the earth was repeopled by them.

"The Squamish say that in a gigantic crevice half-way to the crest of Mount Baker may yet be seen the outlines of an enormous canoe, but I have never seen it myself."

He ceased speaking with that far-off cadence in his voice with which he always ended a legend, and for a long time we both sat in silence listening to the rains that were still beating against the window.

THE SEA-SERPENT

There is one vice that is absolutely unknown to the red man; he was born without it, and amongst all the deplorable things he has learned from the white races, this, at least, he has never acquired. That is the vice of avarice. That the Indian looks upon greed of gain, miserliness, avariciousness, and wealth accumulated above the head of his poorer neighbour as one of the lowest degradations he can fall to, is perhaps more aptly illustrated in this legend than anything I could quote to demonstrate his horror of what he calls "the white man's unkindness." In a very wide and varied experience with many tribes, I have yet to find even one instance of avarice, and I have encountered but one single case of a "stingy Indian," and this man was so marked amongst his fellows that at mention of his name his tribes-people jeered and would remark contemptuously that he was like a white man—hated to share his money and his possessions. All red races are born Socialists, and most tribes carry out their communistic ideas to the letter. Amongst the Iroquois it is considered disgraceful to have food if your neighbour has none. To be a creditable member of the nation you must divide your possessions with your less fortunate fellows. I find it much the same amongst the Coast Indians, though they are less bitter in their hatred of the extremes of wealth and poverty than are the Eastern tribes. Still, the very fact that they have preserved this legend, in which they liken avarice to a slimy sea-serpent, shows the trend of their ideas; shows, too, that an Indian is an Indian, no matter what his tribe; shows that he cannot, or will not, hoard money; shows that his native morals demand that the spirit of greed must be strangled at all cost.

The Chief and I had sat long over our luncheon. He had been talking of his trip to England and of the many curious things he had seen. At last, in an outburst of enthusiasm, he said: "I saw everything in the world—everything but a sea-serpent!"

"But there is no such thing as a sea-serpent," I laughed, "so you must have really seen everything in the world."

His face clouded; for a moment he sat in silence; then, looking directly at me, said, "Maybe none now, but long ago there was one here—in the Inlet."

"How long ago?" I asked.

"When first the white gold-hunters came," he replied. "Came with greedy, clutching fingers, greedy eyes, greedy hearts. The white men fought, murdered, starved, went mad with love of that gold far up the Fraser River. Tillicums were tillicums no more, brothers were foes, fathers and sons were enemies. Their love of the gold was a curse."

"Was it then the sea-serpent was seen?" I asked, perplexed with the problem of trying to connect the gold-seekers with such a monster.

"Yes, it was then, but—" he hesitated, then plunged into the assertion, "but you will not believe the story if you think there is no such thing as a sea-serpent."

"I shall believe whatever you tell me, Chief," I answered. "I am only too ready to believe. You know I come of a superstitious race, and all my association with the Palefaces has never yet robbed me of my birthright to believe strange traditions."

"You always understand," he said after a pause.

"It's my heart that understands," I remarked quietly.

He glanced up quickly, and with one of his all too few radiant smiles, he laughed.

"Yes, skookum tum-tum." Then without further hesitation he told the tradition, which, although not of ancient happening, is held in great reverence by his tribe. During its recital he sat with folded arms, leaning on the table, his head and shoulders bending eagerly towards me as I sat at the opposite side. It was the only time he ever talked to me when he did not use emphasizing gesticulations, but his hands never once lifted: his wonderful eyes alone gave expression to what he called "The Legend of the 'Salt-Chuck Oluk'" (sea-serpent).[9]

"Yes, it was during the first gold craze, and many of our young men went as guides to the whites far up the Fraser. When they returned they brought these tales of greed and murder back with them, and our old people and our women shook their heads and said evil would come of it. But all our young men, except one, returned as they went—kind to the poor, kind to those who were foodless, sharing whatever they had with their tillicums. But one, by name Shak-shak (The Hawk), came back with hoards of gold nuggets, chickimin, everything; he was rich like the white men, and, like them, he kept it. He would count his chickimin, count his nuggets, gloat over them, toss them in his palms. He rested his head on them as he slept, he packed them about with him through the day. He loved them better than food, better than his tillicums, better than his life. The entire tribe arose. They said Shak-shak had the disease of greed; that to cure it he must give a great potlatch, divide his riches with the poorer ones, share them with the old, the sick, the foodless. But he jeered and laughed and told them No, and went on loving and gloating over his gold.

"Then the Sagalie Tyee spoke out of the sky and said, 'Shak-shak, you have made of yourself a loathsome thing; you will not listen to the cry of the hungry, to the call of the old and sick; you will not share your possessions; you have made of yourself an outcast from your tribe and disobeyed the ancient laws of your people. Now I will make of you a thing loathed and hated by all men, both white and red. You will have two heads, for your greed has two mouths to bite. One bites the poor, and one bites your own evil heart; and the fangs in these mouths are poison—poison that kills the hungry, and poison that kills your own manhood. Your evil heart will beat in the very centre of your foul body, and he that pierces it will kill the disease of greed forever from amongst his people.' And when the sun arose above the North Arm the next morning the tribes-people saw a gigantic sea-serpent stretched across the surface of the waters. One hideous head rested on the bluffs at Brockton Point, the other rested on a group of rocks just below the Mission, at the western edge of North Vancouver. If you care to go there some day I will show you the hollow in one great stone where that head lay. The tribes-people were stunned with horror. They loathed the creature, they hated it, they feared it. Day after day it lay there, its monstrous heads lifted out of the waters, its mile-long body blocking all entrance from the Narrows, all outlet from the North Arm. The chiefs made council, the medicine men danced and chanted, but the salt-chuck oluk never moved. It could not move, for it was the hated totem of what now rules the white man's world—greed and love of chickimin. No one can ever move the love of chickimin from the white man's heart, no one can ever make him divide all with the poor. But after the chiefs and medicine men had done all in their power and still the salt-chuck oluk lay across the waters, a handsome boy of sixteen approached them and reminded them of the words of the Sagalie Tyee, 'that he that pierced the monster's heart would kill the disease of greed forever amongst his people.'

"'Let me try to find this evil heart, oh! great men of my tribe,' he cried. 'Let me war upon this creature; let me try to rid my people of this pestilence.'

"The boy was brave and very beautiful. His tribes-people called him the Tenas Tyee (Little Chief) and they loved him. Of all his wealth of fish and furs, of game and hykwa (large shell money) he gave to the boys who had none; he hunted food for the old people; he tanned skins and furs for those whose feet were feeble, whose eyes were fading, whose blood ran thin with age.

"'Let him go!' cried the tribes-people. 'This unclean monster can only be overcome by cleanliness, this creature of greed can only be overthrown by generosity. Let him go!' The chiefs and the medicine men listened, then consented. 'Go,' they commanded, 'and fight this thing with your strongest weapons—cleanliness and generosity.'

"The Tenas Tyee turned to his mother. 'I shall be gone four days,' he told her, 'and I shall swim all that time. I have tried all my life to be generous, but the people say I must be clean also to fight this unclean thing. While I am gone put fresh furs on my bed every day, even if I am not here to lie on them; if I know my bed, my body, and my heart are all clean I can overcome this serpent.'

"'Your bed shall have fresh furs every morning,' his mother said simply.

"The Tenas Tyee then stripped himself, and, with no clothing save a buckskin belt into which he thrust his hunting-knife, he flung his lithe young body into the sea. But at the end of four days he did not return. Sometimes his people could see him swimming far out in mid-channel, endeavouring to find the exact centre of the serpent, where lay its evil, selfish heart; but on the fifth morning they saw him rise out of the sea, climb to the summit of Brockton Point, and greet the rising sun with outstretched arms. Weeks and months went by, still the Tenas Tyee would swim daily searching for that heart of greed; and each morning the sunrise glinted on his slender young copper-coloured body as he stood with outstretched arms at the tip of Brockton Point, greeting the coming day and then plunging from the summit into the sea.

"And at his home on the north shore his mother dressed his bed with fresh furs each morning. The seasons drifted by; winter followed summer, summer followed winter. But it was four years before the Tenas Tyee found the centre of the great salt-chuck oluk and plunged his hunting-knife into its evil heart. In its death-agony it writhed through the Narrows, leaving a trail of blackness on the waters. Its huge body began to shrink, to shrivel; it became dwarfed and withered, until nothing but the bones of its back remained, and they, sea-bleached and lifeless, soon sank to the bed of the ocean leagues off from the rim of land. But as the Tenas Tyee swam homeward and his clean young body crossed through the black stain left by the serpent, the waters became clear and blue and sparkling. He had overcome even the trail of the salt-chuck oluk.

"When at last he stood in the doorway of his home he said, 'My mother, I could not have killed the monster of greed amongst my people had you not helped me by keeping one place for me at home fresh and clean for my return.'

"She looked at him as only mothers look. 'Each day, these four years, fresh furs have I laid for your bed. Sleep now, and rest, oh! my Tenas Tyee,' she said."

The Chief unfolded his arms, and his voice took another tone as he said, "What do you call that story—a legend?"

"The white people would call it an allegory," I answered. He shook his head.

"No savvy," he smiled.

I explained as simply as possible, and with his customary alertness he immediately understood. "That's right," he said. "That's what we say it means, we Squamish, that greed is evil and not clean, like the salt-chuck oluk. That it must be stamped out amongst our people, killed by cleanliness and generosity. The boy that overcame the serpent was both these things."

"What became of this splendid boy?" I asked.

"The Tenas Tyee? Oh! some of our old, old people say they sometimes see him now, standing on Brockton Point, his bare young arms outstretched to the rising sun," he replied.

"Have you ever seen him, Chief?" I questioned.

"No," he answered simply. But I have never heard such poignant regret as his wonderful voice crowded into that single word.

THE LOST ISLAND

"Yes," said my old tillicum, "we Indians have lost many things. We have lost our lands, our forests, our game, our fish; we have lost our ancient religion, our ancient dress; some of the younger people have even lost their fathers' language and the legends and traditions of their ancestors. We cannot call those old things back to us; they will never come again. We may travel many days up the mountain-trails, and look in the silent places for them. They are not there. We may paddle many moons on the sea, but our canoes will never enter the channel that leads to the yesterdays of the Indian people. These things are lost, just like 'The Island of the North Arm.' They may be somewhere nearby, but no one can ever find them."

"But there are many islands up the North Arm," I asserted.

"Not the island we Indian people have sought for many tens of summers," he replied sorrowfully.

"Was it ever there?" I questioned.

"Yes, it was there," he said. "My grandsires and my great-grandsires saw it; but that was long ago. My father never saw it, though he spent many days in many years searching, always searching for it. I am an old man myself, and I have never seen it, though from my youth I, too, have searched. Sometimes in the stillness of the nights I have paddled up in my canoe." Then, lowering his voice: "Twice I have seen its shadow: high rocky shores, reaching as high as the tree-tops on the mainland, then tall pines and firs on its summit like a king's crown. As I paddled up the Arm one summer night, long ago, the shadow of these rocks and firs fell across my canoe, across my face, and across the waters beyond. I turned rapidly to look. There was no island there, nothing but a wide stretch of waters on both sides of me, and the moon almost directly overhead. Don't say it was the shore that shadowed me," he hastened, catching my thought. "The moon was above me; my canoe scarce made a shadow on the still waters. No, it was not the shore."

"Why do you search for it?" I lamented, thinking of the old dreams in my own life whose realization I have never attained.

"There is something on that island that I want. I shall look for it until I die, for it is there," he affirmed.

There was a long silence between us after that. I had learned to love silences when with my old tillicum, for they always led to a legend. After a time he began voluntarily:

"It was more than one hundred years ago. This great city of Vancouver was but the dream of the Sagalie Tyee (God) at that time. The dream had not yet come to the white man; only one great Indian medicine man knew that some day a great camp for Palefaces would lie between False Creek and the Inlet. This dream haunted him; it came to him night and day—when he was amid his people laughing and feasting, or when he was alone in the forest chanting his strange songs, beating his hollow drum, or shaking his wooden witch-rattle to gain more power to cure the sick and the dying of his tribe. For years this dream followed him. He grew to be an old, old man, yet always he could hear voices, strong and loud, as when they first spoke to him in his youth, and they would say: 'Between the two narrow strips of salt water the white men will camp—many hundreds of them, many thousands of them. The Indians will learn their ways, will live as they do, will become as they are. There will be no more great war dances, no more fights with other powerful tribes; it will be as if the Indians had lost all bravery, all courage, all confidence.' He hated the voices, he hated the dream; but all his power, all his big medicine, could not drive them away. He was the strongest man on all the North Pacific Coast. He was mighty and very tall, and his muscles were as those of Leloo, the timber-wolf, when he is strongest to kill his prey. He could go for many days without food; he could fight the largest mountain lion; he could overthrow the fiercest grizzly bear; he could paddle against the wildest winds and ride the highest waves. He could meet his enemies and kill whole tribes single-handed. His strength, his courage, his power, his bravery, were those of a giant. He knew no fear; nothing in the sea, or in the forest, nothing in the earth or the sky, could conquer him. He was fearless, fearless. Only this haunting dream of the coming white man's camp he could not drive away; it was the only thing in life he had tried to kill and failed. It drove him from the feasting, drove him from the pleasant lodges, the fires, the dancing, the story-telling of his people in their camp by the water's edge, where the salmon thronged and the deer came down to drink of the mountain-streams. He left the Indian village, chanting his wild songs as he went. Up through the mighty forests he climbed, through the trail-less deep mosses and matted vines, up to the summit of what the white men call Grouse Mountain. For many days he camped there. He ate no food, he drank no water, but sat and sang his medicine songs through the dark hours and through the day. Before him—far beneath his feet—lay the narrow strip of land between the two salt waters. Then the Sagalie Tyee gave him the power to see far into the future. He looked across a hundred years, just as he looked across what you call the Inlet, and he saw mighty lodges built close together, hundreds and thousands of them—lodges of stone and wood, and long straight trails to divide them. He saw these trails thronging with Palefaces; he heard the sound of the white man's paddle-dip on the waters, for it is not silent like the Indian's; he saw the white man's trading posts, saw the fishing-nets, heard his speech. Then the vision faded as gradually as it came. The narrow strip of land was his own forest once more.

"'I am old,' he called, in his sorrow and his trouble for his people. 'I am old, oh, Sagalie Tyee! Soon I shall die and go to the Happy Hunting Grounds of my fathers. Let not my strength die with me. Keep living for all time my courage, my bravery, my fearlessness. Keep them for my people that they may be strong enough to endure the white man's rule. Keep my strength living for them; hide it so that the Paleface may never find or see it.'

"Then he came down from the summit of Grouse Mountain. Still chanting his medicine songs, he entered his canoe and paddled through the colours of the setting sun far up the North Arm. When night fell he came to an island with misty shores of great grey rock; on its summit tall pines and firs encircled like a king's crown. As he neared it he felt all his strength, his courage, his fearlessness, leaving him; he could see these things drift from him on to the island. They were as the clouds that rest on the mountains, grey-white and half transparent. Weak as a woman, he paddled back to the Indian village; he told them to go and search for 'The Island,' where they would find all his courage, his fearlessness and his strength, living, living forever. He slept then, but—in the morning he did not awake. Since then our young men and our old have searched for 'The Island.' It is there somewhere, up some lost channel, but we cannot find it. When we do, we will get back all the courage and bravery we had before the white man came, for the great medicine man said those things never die—they live for one's children and grandchildren."

His voice ceased. My whole heart went out to him in his longing for the lost island. I thought of all the splendid courage I knew him to possess, so made answer: "But you say that the shadow of this island has fallen upon you; is it not so, tillicum?"

"Yes," he said half mournfully. "But only the shadow."

POINT GREY

"Have you ever sailed around Point Grey?" asked a young Squamish tillicum of mine who often comes to see me, to share a cup of tea and a taste of muck-a-muck that otherwise I should eat in solitude.

"No," I admitted, I had not had that pleasure, for I did not know the uncertain waters of English Bay sufficiently well to venture about its headlands in my frail canoe.

"Some day, perhaps next summer, I'll take you there in a sail-boat, and show you the big rock at the south-west of the Point. It is a strange rock; we Indian people call it Homolsom."

"What an odd name!" I commented. "Is it a Squamish word?—it does not sound to me like one."

"It is not altogether Squamish, but half Fraser River language. The Point was the dividing-line between the grounds and waters of the two tribes, so they agreed to make the name 'Homolsom' from the two languages."

I suggested more tea, and, as he sipped it, he told me the legend that few of the younger Indians know. That he believes the story himself is beyond question, for many times he admitted having tested the virtues of this rock, and it had never once failed him. All people that have to do with water-craft are superstitious about some things, and I freely acknowledge that times innumerable I have "whistled up" a wind when dead calm threatened, or stuck a jack-knife in the mast, and afterwards watched with great contentment the idle sail fill, and the canoe pull out to a light breeze. So, perhaps, I am prejudiced in favour of this legend of Homolsom Rock, for it strikes a very responsive chord in that portion of my heart that has always throbbed for the sea.

"You know," began my young tillicum, "that only waters unspoiled by human hands can be of any benefit. One gains no strength by swimming in any waters heated or boiled by fires that men build. To grow strong and wise one must swim in the natural rivers, the mountain torrents, the sea, just as the Sagalie Tyee made them. Their virtues die when human beings try to improve them by heating or distilling, or placing even tea in them, and so—what makes Homolsom Rock so full of 'good medicine' is that the waters that wash up about it are straight from the sea, made by the hand of the Great Tyee, and unspoiled by the hand of man.

"It was not always there, that great rock, drawing its strength and its wonderful power from the seas, for it, too, was once a Great Tyee, who ruled a mighty tract of waters. He was god of all the waters that wash the coast, of the Gulf of Georgia, of Puget Sound, of the Straits of Juan de Fuca, of the waters that beat against even the west coast of Vancouver Island, and of all the channels that cut between the Charlotte Islands. He was Tyee of the West Wind, and his storms and tempests were so mighty that the Sagalie Tyee Himself could not control the havoc that he created. He warred upon all fishing craft, he demolished canoes, and sent men to graves in the sea. He uprooted forests and drove the surf on shore heavy with wreckage of despoiled trees and with beaten and bruised fish. He did all this to reveal his powers, for he was cruel and hard of heart, and he would laugh and defy the Sagalie Tyee, and, looking up to the sky, he would call, 'See how powerful I am, how mighty, how strong; I am as great as you.'

"It was at this time that the Sagalie Tyee in the persons of the Four Men came in the great canoe up over the rim of the Pacific, in that age thousands of years ago when they turned the evil into stone, and the kindly into trees.

"'Now,' said the god of the West Wind, 'I can show how great I am. I shall blow a tempest that these men may not land on my coast. They shall not ride my seas and sounds and channels in safety. I shall wreck them and send their bodies into the great deeps, and I shall be Sagalie Tyee in their place and ruler of all the world.' So the god of the West Wind blew forth his tempests. The waves arose mountain high, the seas lashed and thundered along the shores. The roar of his mighty breath could be heard wrenching giant limbs from the forest trees, whistling down the canyons and dealing death and destruction for leagues and leagues along the coast. But the canoe containing the Four Men rode upright through all the heights and hollows of the seething ocean. No curling crest or sullen depth could wreck that magic craft, for the hearts it bore were filled with kindness for the human race, and kindness cannot die.

"It was all rock and dense forest, and unpeopled; only wild animals and seabirds sought the shelter it provided from the terrors of the West Wind; but he drove them out in sullen anger, and made on this strip of land his last stand against the Four Men. The Paleface calls the place Point Grey, but the Indians yet speak of it as 'The Battle Ground of the West Wind.' All his mighty forces he now brought to bear against the oncoming canoe; he swept great hurricanes about the stony ledges; he caused the sea to beat and swirl in tempestuous fury along its narrow fastnesses, but the canoe came nearer and nearer, invincible as those shores, and stronger than death itself. As the bow touched the land the Four Men arose and commanded the West Wind to cease his war-cry, and, mighty though he had been, his voice trembled and sobbed itself into a gentle breeze, then fell to a whispering note, then faded into exquisite silence.

"'Oh, you evil one with the unkind heart,' cried the Four Men, 'you have been too great a god for even the Sagalie Tyee to obliterate you forever, but you shall live on, live now to serve, not to hinder mankind. You shall turn into stone where you now stand, and you shall rise only as men wish you to. Your life from this day shall be for the good of man, for when the fisherman's sails are idle and his lodge is leagues away you shall fill those sails and blow his craft free, in whatever direction he desires. You shall stand where you are through all the thousands upon thousands of years to come, and he who touches you with his paddle-blade shall have his desire of a breeze to carry him home.'"

My young tillicum had finished his tradition, and his great, solemn eyes regarded me half-wistfully.

"I wish you could see Homolsom Rock," he said. "For that is he who was once the Tyee of the West Wind."

"Were you ever becalmed around Point Grey?" I asked irrelevantly.

"Often," he replied. "But I paddle up to the rock and touch it with the tip of my paddle-blade, and, no matter which way I want to go, the wind will blow free for me, if I wait a little while."

"I suppose your people all do this?" I replied.

"Yes, all of them," he answered. "They have done it for hundreds of years. You see the power in it is just as great now as at first, for the rock feeds every day on the unspoiled sea that the Sagalie Tyee made."

THE TULAMEEN TRAIL

Did you ever "holiday" through the valley lands of the Dry Belt?[10] Ever spend days and days in a swinging, swaying coach, behind a four-in-hand, when "Curly" or "Nicola Ned" held the ribbons, and tooled his knowing little leaders and wheelers down those horrifying mountain trails that wind like russet skeins of cobweb through the heights and depths of the Okanagan, the Nicola, and the Similkameen countries? If so, you have listened to the call of the Skookum Chuck, as the Chinook speakers call the rollicking, tumbling streams that sing their way through the canyons with a music so dulcet, so insistent, that for many moons the echo of it lingers in your listening ears, and you will, through all the years to come, hear the voices of those mountain-rivers calling you to return.

But the most haunting of all the melodies is the warbling laughter of the Tulameen; its delicate note is far more powerful, more far-reaching than the throaty thunders of Niagara. That is why the Indians of the Nicola country still cling to their old-time story that the Tulameen carries the spirit of a young girl enmeshed in the wonders of its winding course; a spirit that can never free itself from the canyons, to rise above the heights and follow its fellows to the Happy Hunting Grounds, but which is contented to entwine its laughter, its sobs, its lonely whispers, its still lonelier call for companionship, with the wild music of the waters that sing forever beneath the western stars.

As your horses plod up and up the almost perpendicular trail that leads out of the Nicola Valley to the summit, a paradise of beauty outspreads at your feet; the colour is indescribable in words, the atmosphere thrills you. Youth and the pulse of rioting blood are yours again, until, as you near the heights, you become strangely calmed by the voiceless silence of it all—a silence so holy that it seems the whole world about you is swinging its censer before an altar in some dim remote cathedral! The choir voices of the Tulameen are yet very far away across the summit, but the heights of the Nicola are the silent prayer that holds the human soul before the first great chords swell down from the organ-loft. In this first long climb up miles and miles of trail, even the staccato of the drivers' long blacksnake whip is hushed. He lets his animals pick their own sure-footed way, but once across the summit he gathers the reins in his steely fingers, gives a low, quick whistle, the whiplash curls about the ears of the leaders, and the plunge down the dip of the mountain begins. Every foot of the way is done at a gallop. The coach rocks and swings as it dashes through a trail rough-hewn from the heart of the forest; at times the angles are so abrupt that you cannot see the heads of the leaders as they swing around the grey crags that almost scrape the tires on the left, while within a foot of the rim of the trail the right wheels whirl along the edge of a yawning canyon. The rhythm of the hoof-beats, the recurrent low whistle and crack of the whiplash, the occasional rattle of pebbles showering down to the depths, loosened by rioting wheels, have broken the sacred silence. Yet above all those nearby sounds there seems to be an indistinct murmur, which grows sweeter, more musical, as you gain the base of the mountains, where it rises above all harsher notes. It is the voice of the restless Tulameen as it dances and laughs through the rocky throat of the canyon, three hundred feet below. Then, following the song, comes a glimpse of the river itself—white-garmented in the film of its countless rapids, its showers of waterfalls. It is as beautiful to look at as to listen to, and it is here, where the trail winds about and above it for leagues, that the Indians say it caught the spirit of the maiden that is still interlaced in its loveliness.

It was in one of the terrible battles that raged between the valley tribes before the white man's footprints were seen along these trails.

None can now tell the cause of this warfare, but the supposition is that it was merely for tribal supremacy—that primeval instinct that assails the savage in both man and beast, that drives the hill-men to bloodshed and the leaders of buffalo herds to conflict. It is the greed to rule; the one barbarous instinct that civilization has never yet been able to eradicate from armed nations. This war of the tribes of the valley lands was of years in duration; men fought, and women mourned, and children wept, as all have done since time began. It seemed an unequal battle, for the old, experienced, war-tried chief and his two astute sons were pitted against a single young Tulameen brave. Both factors had their loyal followers, both were indomitable as to courage and bravery, both were determined and ambitious, both were skilled fighters.

But on the older man's side were experience and two other wary, strategic brains to help him, while on the younger was but the advantage of splendid youth and unconquerable persistence. But at every pitched battle, at every skirmish, at every single-handed conflict the younger man gained little by little, the older man lost step by step. The experience of age was gradually but inevitably giving way to the strength and enthusiasm of youth. Then, one day, they met face to face and alone—the old, war-scarred chief, the young battle-inspired brave. It was an unequal combat, and at the close of a brief but violent struggle the younger had brought the older to his knees. Standing over him with up-poised knife the Tulameen brave laughed sneeringly, and said:

"Would you, my enemy, have this victory as your own? If so, I give it to you; but in return for my submission I demand of you—your daughter."

For an instant the old chief looked in wonderment at his conqueror; he thought of his daughter only as a child who played about the forest trails or sat obediently beside her mother in the lodge, stitching her little moccasins or weaving her little baskets.

"My daughter!" he answered sternly. "My daughter—who is barely out of her own cradle-basket—give her to you, whose hands are blood-dyed with the killing of a score of my tribe? You ask for this thing?"

"I do not ask it," replied the young brave. "I demand it; I have seen the girl and I shall have her."

The old chief sprang to his feet and spat out his refusal. "Keep your victory, and I keep my girl-child," though he knew he was not only defying his enemy, but defying death as well.

The Tulameen laughed lightly, easily. "I shall not kill the sire of my wife," he taunted. "One more battle must we have, but your girl-child will come to me."

Then he took his victorious way up the trail, while the old chief walked with slow and springless step down into the canyon.

The next morning the chief's daughter was loitering along the heights, listening to the singing river, and sometimes leaning over the precipice to watch its curling eddies and dancing waterfalls. Suddenly she heard a slight rustle, as though some passing bird's wing had clipt the air. Then at her feet there fell a slender, delicately shaped arrow. It fell with spent force, and her Indian woodcraft told her it had been shot to her, not at her. She started like a wild animal. Then her quick eye caught the outline of a handsome, erect figure that stood on the heights across the river. She did not know him as her father's enemy. She only saw him to be young, stalwart, and of extraordinary manly beauty. The spirit of youth and of a certain savage coquetry awoke within her. Quickly she fitted one of her own dainty arrows to the bow-string and sent it winging across the narrow canyon; it fell, spent, at his feet, and he knew she had shot it to him, not at him.

Next morning, woman-like, she crept noiselessly to the brink of the heights. Would she see him again—that handsome brave? Would he speed another arrow to her? She had not yet emerged from the tangle of forest before it fell, its faint-winged flight heralding its coming. Near the feathered end was tied a tassel of beautiful ermine tails. She took from her wrist a string of shell beads, fastened it to one of her little arrows and winged it across the canyon, as yesterday.

The following morning, before leaving the lodge, she fastened the tassel of ermine-tails in her straight black hair. Would he see them? But no arrow fell at her feet that day, but a dearer message was there on the brink of the precipice. He himself awaited her coming—he who had never left her thoughts since that first arrow came to her from his bow-string. His eyes burned with warm fires, as she approached, but his lips said simply: "I have crossed the Tulameen River." Together they stood, side by side, and looked down at the depths before them, watching in silence the little torrent rollicking and roystering over its boulders and crags.

"That is my country," he said, looking across the river. "This is the country of your father, and of your brothers; they are my enemies. I return to my own shore tonight. Will you come with me?"

She looked up into his handsome young face. So this was her father's foe—the dreaded Tulameen!

"Will you come?" he repeated.

"I will come," she whispered.

It was in the dark of the moon and through the kindly night he led her far up the rocky shores to the narrow belt of quiet waters, where they crossed in silence into his own country. A week, a month, a long golden summer, slipped by, but the insulted old chief and his enraged sons failed to find her.

Then one morning as the lovers walked together on the heights above the far upper reaches of the river, even the ever-watchful eyes of the Tulameen failed to detect the lurking enemy. Across the narrow canyon crouched and crept the two outwitted brothers of the girl-wife at his side; their arrows were on their bow-strings, their hearts on fire with hatred and vengeance. Like two evil-winged birds of prey those arrows sped across the laughing river, but before they found their mark in the breast of the victorious Tulameen the girl had unconsciously stepped before him. With a little sigh, she slipped into his arms, her brothers' arrows buried into her soft, brown flesh.

It was many a moon before his avenging hand succeeded in slaying the old chief and those two hated sons of his. But when this was finally done the handsome young Tulameen left his people, his tribe, his country, and went into the far north. "For," he said, as he sang his farewell war song, "my heart lies dead in the Tulameen River."

But the spirit of his girl-wife still sings through the canyon, its song blending with the music of that sweetest-voiced river in all the great valleys of the Dry Belt. That is why this laughter, the sobbing murmur of the beautiful Tulameen, will haunt for evermore the ear that has once listened to its song.

THE GREY ARCHWAY

The steamer, like a huge shuttle, wove in and out among the countless small islands; its long trailing scarf of grey smoke hung heavily along the uncertain shores, casting a shadow over the pearly waters of the Pacific, which swung lazily from rock to rock in indescribable beauty.

After dinner I wandered astern with the traveller's ever-present hope of seeing the beauties of a typical Northern sunset, and by some happy chance I placed my deck-stool near an old tillicum, who was leaning on the rail, his pipe between his thin, curved lips, his brown hands clasped idly, his sombre eyes looking far out to sea, as though they searched the future—or was it that they were seeing the past?

"Kla-how-ya, tillicum!" I greeted.

He glanced round, and half smiled.

"Kla-how-ya, tillicum!" he replied, with the warmth of friendliness I have always met with among the Pacific tribes.

I drew my deck-stool nearer to him, and he acknowledged the action with another half smile, but did not stir from his entrenchment, remaining as if hedged about with an inviolable fortress of exclusiveness. Yet I knew that my Chinook salutation would be a drawbridge by which I might hope to cross the moat into his castle of silence.

Indian-like, he took his time before continuing the acquaintance. Then he began in most excellent English:

"You do not know these northern waters?"

I shook my head.

After many moments he leaned forward, looking along the curve of the deck, up the channels and narrows we were threading, to a broad strip of waters off the port bow. Then he pointed with that peculiar, thoroughly Indian gesture of the palm uppermost.

"Do you see it—over there? The small island? It rests on the edge of the water, like a grey gull."

It took my unaccustomed eyes some moments to discern it; then all at once I caught its outline, veiled in the mists of distance—grey, cobwebby, dreamy.

"Yes," I replied, "I see it now. You will tell me of it—tillicum?"

He gave a swift glance at my dark skin, then nodded. "You are one of us," he said, with evidently no thought of a possible contradiction. "And you will understand, or I should not tell you. You will not smile at the story, for you are one of us."

"I am one of you, and I shall understand," I answered.

It was a full half-hour before we neared the island, yet neither of us spoke during that time; then, as the "grey gull" shaped itself into rock and tree and crag, I noticed in the very centre a stupendous pile of stone lifting itself skyward, without fissure or cleft; but a peculiar haziness about the base made me peer narrowly to catch the perfect outline.

"It is the 'Grey Archway,'" he explained simply.

Only then did I grasp the singular formation before us: the rock was a perfect archway, through which we could see the placid Pacific shimmering in the growing colours of the coming sunset at the opposite rim of the island.

"What a remarkable whim of Nature!" I exclaimed, but his brown hand was laid in a contradictory grasp on my arm, and he snatched up my comment almost with impatience.

"No, it was not Nature," he said. "That is the reason I say you will understand—you are one of us—you will know what I tell you is true. The Great Tyee did not make that archway, it was—" here his voice lowered—"it was magic, red man's medicine and magic—you savvy?"

"Yes," I said. "Tell me, for I—savvy."

"Long time ago," he began, stumbling into a half-broken English language, because, I think, of the atmosphere and environment, "long before you were born, or your father, or grandfather, or even his father, this strange thing happened. It is a story for women to hear, to remember. Women are the future mothers of the tribe, and we of the Pacific Coast hold such in high regard, in great reverence. The women who are mothers—o-ho!—they are the important ones, we say. Warriors, fighters, brave men, fearless daughters, owe their qualities to these mothers—eh, is it not always so?"

I nodded silently. The island was swinging nearer to us, the "Grey Archway" loomed almost above us, the mysticism crowded close; it enveloped me, caressed me, appealed to me.

"And?" I hinted.

"And," he proceeded, "this 'Grey Archway' is a story of mothers, of magic, of witchcraft, of warriors, of—love."

An Indian rarely uses the word "love," and when he does it expresses every quality, every attribute, every intensity, emotion, and passion embraced in those four little letters. Surely this was an exceptional story I was to hear.

I did not answer, only looked across the pulsing waters toward the "Grey Archway," which the sinking sun was touching with soft pastels, tints one could give no name to, beauties impossible to describe.

"You have not heard of Yaada?" he questioned. Then, fortunately, he continued without waiting for a reply. He well knew that I had never heard of Yaada, so why not begin without preliminary to tell me of her?—so—

"Yaada was the loveliest daughter of the Haida tribe. Young braves from all the islands, from the mainland, from the upper Skeena country came, hoping to carry her to their far-off lodges, but they always returned alone. She was the most desired of all the island maidens, beautiful, brave, modest, the daughter of her own mother.

"But there was a great man, a very great man—a medicine man, skilful, powerful, influential, old, deplorably old, and very, very rich; he said, 'Yaada shall be my wife.' And there was a young fisherman, handsome, loyal, boyish, poor, oh! very poor, and gloriously young, and he, too, said, 'Yaada shall be my wife.'

"But Yaada's mother sat apart and thought and dreamed, as mothers will. She said to herself, 'The great medicine man has power, has vast riches, and wonderful magic, why not give her to him? But Ulka has the boy's heart, the boy's beauty; he is very brave, very strong; why not give her to him?'

"But the laws of the great Haida tribe prevailed. Its wise men said, 'Give the girl to the greatest man, give her to the most powerful, the richest. The man of magic must have his choice.'

"But at this the mother's heart grew as wax in the summer sunshine—it is a strange quality that mothers' hearts are made of! 'Give her to the best man—the man her heart holds highest,' said this Haida mother.

"Then Yaada spoke: 'I am the daughter of my tribe; I would judge of men by their excellence. He who proves most worthy I shall marry; it is not riches that make a good husband; it is not beauty that makes a good father for one's children. Let me and my tribe see some proof of the excellence of these two men—then, only, shall I choose who is to be the father of my children. Let us have a trial of their skill; let them show me how evil or how beautiful is the inside of their hearts. Let each of them throw a stone with some intent, some purpose in their hearts. He who makes the noblest mark may call me wife.'

"'Alas! Alas!' wailed the Haida mother. 'This casting of stones does not show worth. It but shows prowess.'

"'But I have implored the Sagalie Tyee of my father, and of his fathers before him, to help me to judge between them by this means,' said the girl. 'So they must cast the stones. In this way only shall I see their innermost hearts.'

"The medicine man never looked so old as at that moment; so hopelessly old, so wrinkled, so palsied: he was no mate for Yaada. Ulka never looked so godlike in his young beauty, so gloriously young, so courageous. The girl, looking at him, loved him—almost was she placing her hand in his, but the spirit of her forefathers halted her. She had spoken the word—she must abide by it. 'Throw!' she commanded.

"Into his shrivelled fingers the great medicine man took a small, round stone, chanting strange words of magic all the while; his greedy eyes were on the girl, his greedy thoughts about her.

"Into his strong young fingers Ulka took a smooth, flat stone; his handsome eyes were lowered in boyish modesty, his thoughts were worshipping her. The great medicine man cast his missile first; it swept through the air like a shaft of lightning, striking the great rock with a force that shattered it. At the touch of that stone the 'Grey Archway' opened and has remained open to this day.

"'Oh, wonderful power and magic!' clamoured the entire tribe. 'The very rocks do his bidding.'

"But Yaada stood with eyes that burned in agony. Ulka could never command such magic—she knew it. But at her side Ulka was standing erect, tall, slender, and beautiful, but just as he cast his missile the evil voice of the old medicine man began a still more evil incantation. He fixed his poisonous eyes on the younger man, eyes with hideous magic in their depths—ill-omened and enchanted with 'bad medicine.' The stone left Ulka's fingers; for a second it flew forth in a straight line, then, as the evil voice of the old man grew louder in its incantations, the stone curved. Magic had waylaid the strong arm of the young brave. The stone poised an instant above the forehead of Yaada's mother, then dropped with the weight of many mountains, and the last long sleep fell upon her.

"'Slayer of my mother!' stormed the girl, her suffering eyes fixed upon the medicine man. 'Oh, I now see your black heart through your black magic. Through good magic you cut the 'Great Archway,' but your evil magic you used upon young Ulka. I saw your wicked eyes upon him; I heard your wicked incantations; I know your wicked heart. You used your heartless magic in hope of winning me—in hope of making him an outcast of the tribe. You cared not for my sorrowing heart, my motherless life to come.' Then, turning to the tribe, she demanded: 'Who of you saw his evil eyes fixed on Ulka? Who of you heard his evil song?'

"'I,' and 'I,' and 'I,' came voice after voice.

"'The very air is poisoned that we breathe about him,' they shouted. 'The young man is blameless, his heart is as the sun; but the man who has used his evil magic has a heart black and cold as the hours before the dawn.'

"Then Yaada's voice arose in a strange, sweet, sorrowful chant:

My feet shall walk no more upon this island,
With its great, Grey Archway.
My mother sleeps forever on this island,
With its great, Grey Archway.
My heart would break without her on this island,
With its great, Grey Archway.
My life was of her life upon this island,
With its great, Grey Archway.
My mother's soul has wandered from this island,
With its great, Grey Archway.
My feet must follow hers beyond this island,
With its great, Grey Archway.

"As Yaada chanted and wailed her farewell she moved slowly towards the edge of the cliff. On its brink she hovered a moment with outstretched arms, as a seagull poises on its weight—then she called:

"'Ulka, my Ulka! Your hand is innocent of wrong; it was the evil magic of your rival that slew my mother. I must go to her; even you cannot keep me here; will you stay, or come with me? Oh! my Ulka!'

"The slender, gloriously young boy sprang toward her; their hands closed one within the other; for a second they poised on the brink of the rocks, radiant as stars; then together they plunged into the sea."

The legend was ended. Long ago we had passed the island with its "Grey Archway"; it was melting into the twilight, far astern.

As I brooded over this strange tale of a daughter's devotion I watched the sea and sky for something that would give me a clue to the inevitable sequel that the tillicum, like all his race, was surely withholding until the opportune moment.

Something flashed through the darkening waters not a stone's throw from the steamer. I leaned forward, watching it intently. Two silvery fish were making a succession of little leaps and plunges along the surface of the sea, their bodies catching the last tints of sunset, like flashing jewels. I looked at the tillicum quickly. He was watching me—a world of anxiety in his half-mournful eyes.

"And those two silvery fish?" I questioned.

He smiled. The anxious look vanished. "I was right," he said; "you do know us and our ways, for you are one of us. Yes, those fish are seen only in these waters; there are never but two of them. They are Yaada and her mate, seeking for the soul of the Haida woman—her mother."

DEADMAN'S ISLAND

It is dusk on the Lost Lagoon,
And we two dreaming the dusk away,
Beneath the drift of a twilight grey—
Beneath the drowse of an ending day
And the curve of a golden moon.

It is dark in the Lost Lagoon,
And gone are the depths of haunting blue,
The grouping gulls, and the old canoe,
The singing firs, and the dusk and—you,
And gone is the golden moon.

O! lure of the Lost Lagoon—
I dream tonight that my paddle blurs
The purple shade where the seaweed stirs—
I hear the call of the singing firs
In the hush of the golden moon.

For many minutes we stood silently, leaning on the western rail of the bridge as we watched the sun set across that beautiful little basin of water known as Coal Harbour. I have always resented that jarring, unattractive name, for years ago, when I first plied paddle across the gunwale of a light little canoe, and idled about its margin, I named the sheltered little cove the Lost Lagoon. This was just to please my own fancy, for as that perfect summer month drifted on, the ever-restless tides left the harbour devoid of water at my favourite canoeing hour, and my pet idling-place was lost for many days—hence my fancy to call it the Lost Lagoon. But the chief, Indian-like, immediately adopted the name, at least when he spoke of the place to me, and, as we watched the sun slip behind the rim of firs, he expressed the wish that his dugout were here instead of lying beached at the farther side of the park.

"If canoe was here, you and I we paddle close to shores all 'round your Lost Lagoon: we make track just like half-moon. Then we paddle under this bridge, and go channel between Deadman's Island and park. Then 'round where cannon speak time at nine o'clock. Then 'cross Inlet to Indian side of Narrows."

I turned to look eastward, following in fancy the course he had sketched. The waters were still as the footsteps of the oncoming twilight, and, floating in a pool of soft purple, Deadman's Island rested like a large circle of candle moss.

"Have you ever been on it?" he asked as he caught my gaze centering on the irregular outline of the island pines.

"I have prowled the length and depth of it," I told him. "Climbed over every rock on its shores, crept under every tangled growth of its interior, explored its overgrown trails, and more than once nearly got lost in its very heart."

"Yes," he half laughed, "it pretty wild; not much good for anything."

"People seem to think it valuable," I said. "There is a lot of litigation—of fighting going on now about it."[11]

"Oh! that the way always," he said, as though speaking of a long accepted fact. "Always fight over that place. Hundreds of years ago they fight about it; Indian people; they say hundreds of years to come everybody will still fight—never be settled what that place is, who it belong to, who has right to it. No, never settle. Deadman's Island always mean fight for someone."

"So the Indians fought amongst themselves about it?" I remarked, seemingly without guile, although my ears tingled for the legend I knew was coming.

"Fought like lynx at close quarters," he answered. "Fought, killed each other, until the island ran with blood redder than that sunset, and the sea-water about it was stained flame colour—it was then, my people say, that the scarlet fire-flower was first seen growing along this coast."

"It is a beautiful colour—the fire-flower," I said.

"It should be fine colour, for it was born and grew from the hearts of fine tribes-people—very fine people," he emphasized.

We crossed to the eastern rail of the bridge, and stood watching the deep shadows that gathered slowly and silently about the island; I have seldom looked upon anything more peaceful.

The chief sighed. "We have no such men now, no fighters like those men, no hearts, no courage like theirs. But I tell you the story; you understand it then. Now all peace; to-night all good tillicums; even dead man's spirit does not fight now, but long time after it happen those spirits fought."

"And the legend?" I ventured.

"Oh! yes," he replied, as if suddenly returning to the present from out a far country in the realm of time. "Indian people, they call it the 'Legend of the Island of Dead Men.'

"There was war everywhere. Fierce tribes from the northern coast, savage tribes from the south, all met here and battled and raided, burned and captured, tortured and killed their enemies. The forests smoked with camp-fires, the Narrows were choked with war canoes, and the Sagalie Tyee—He who is a man of peace—turned His face away from His Indian children. About this island there was dispute and contention. The medicine men from the North claimed it as their chanting-ground. The medicine men from the South laid equal claim to it. Each wanted it as the stronghold of their witchcraft, their magic. Great bands of these medicine men met on the small space, using every sorcery in their power to drive their opponents away. The witch-doctors of the North made their camp on the northern rim of the island; those from the South settled along the southern edge, looking towards what is now the great city of Vancouver. Both factions danced, chanted, burned their magic powders, built their magic fires, beat their magic rattles, but neither would give way, yet neither conquered. About them, on the waters, on the mainlands, raged the warfare of their respective tribes—the Sagalie Tyee had forgotten His Indian children.

"After many months, the warriors on both sides weakened. They said the incantations of the rival medicine men were bewitching them, were making their hearts like children's, and their arms nerveless as women's. So friend and foe arose as one man and drove the medicine men from the island, hounded them down the Inlet, herded them through the Narrows, and banished them out to sea, where they took refuge on one of the outer islands of the gulf. Then the tribes once more fell upon each other in battle.

"The warrior blood of the North will always conquer. They are the stronger, bolder, more alert, more keen. The snows and the ice of their country make swifter pulse than the sleepy suns of the South can awake in a man; their muscles are of sterner stuff, their endurance greater. Yes, the northern tribes will always be victors.*[12] But the craft and the strategy of the southern tribes are hard things to battle against. While those of the North followed the medicine men farther out to sea to make sure of their banishment, those from the South returned under cover of night and seized the women and children and the old, enfeebled men in their enemy's camp, transported them all to the Island of Dead Men, and there held them as captives. Their war canoes circled the island like a fortification, through which drifted the sobs of the imprisoned women, the mutterings of the aged men, the wail of little children.

"Again and again the men of the North assailed that circle of canoes, and again and again were repulsed. The air was thick with poisoned arrows, the water stained with blood. But day by day the circle of southern canoes grew thinner and thinner; the northern arrows were telling, and truer of aim. Canoes drifted everywhere, empty, or, worse still, manned only by dead men. The pick of the southern warriors had already fallen, when their greatest Tyee mounted a large rock on the eastern shore. Brave and unmindful of a thousand weapons aimed at his heart, he uplifted his hand, palm outward—the signal for conference. Instantly every northern arrow was lowered, and every northern ear listened for his words.

"'Oh! men of the upper coast,' he said, 'you are more numerous than we are; your tribe is larger, your endurance greater. We are growing hungry, we are growing less in numbers. Our captives—your women and children and old men—have lessened, too, our stores of food. If you refuse our terms we will yet fight to the finish. Tomorrow we will kill all our captives before your eyes, for we can feed them no longer, or you can have your wives, your mothers, your fathers, your children, by giving us for each and every one of them one of your best and bravest young warriors, who will consent to suffer death in their stead. Speak! You have your choice.'

"In the northern canoes scores and scores of young warriors leapt to their feet. The air was filled with glad cries, with exultant shouts. The whole world seemed to ring with the voices of those young men who called loudly, with glorious courage:

"'Take me, but give me back my old father.'

"'Take me, but spare to my tribe my little sister.'

"'Take me, but release my wife and boy-baby.'

"So the compact was made. Two hundred heroic, magnificent young men paddled up to the island, broke through the fortifying circle of canoes, and stepped ashore. They flaunted their eagle plumes with the spirit and boldness of young gods. Their shoulders were erect, their step was firm, their hearts strong. Into their canoes they crowded the two hundred captives. Once more their women sobbed, their old men muttered, their children wailed, but those young copper-coloured gods never flinched, never faltered. Their weak and their feeble were saved. What mattered to them such a little thing as death?

"The released captives were quickly surrounded by their own people, but the flower of their splendid nation was in the hands of their enemies, those valorous young men who thought so little of life that they willingly, gladly laid it down to serve and to save those they loved and cared for. Amongst them were war-tried warriors who had fought fifty battles, and boys not yet full grown, who were drawing a bow-string for the first time; but their hearts, their courage, their self-sacrifice were as one.

"Out before a long file of southern warriors they stood. Their chins uplifted, their eyes defiant, their breasts bared. Each leaned forward and laid his weapons at his feet, then stood erect, with empty hands, and laughed forth his challenge to death. A thousand arrows ripped the air, two hundred gallant northern throats flung forth a death-cry exultant, triumphant as conquering kings—then two hundred fearless northern hearts ceased to beat.

"But in the morning the southern tribes found the spot where they fell peopled with flaming fire-flowers. Dread terror seized upon them. They abandoned the island, and when night again shrouded them they manned their canoes and noiselessly slipped through the Narrows, turned their bows southward, and this coastline knew them no more."

"What glorious men," I half whispered as the chief concluded the strange legend.

"Yes, men!" he echoed. "The white people call it Deadman's Island. That is their way; but we of the Squamish call it The Island of Dead Men."

The clustering pines and the outlines of the island's margin were now dusky and indistinct. Peace, peace lay over the waters, and the purple of the summer twilight had turned to grey, but I knew that in the depths of the undergrowth on Deadman's Island there blossomed a flower of flaming beauty; its colours were veiled in the coming night-fall, but somewhere down in the sanctuary of its petals pulsed the heart's blood of many and valiant men.

A SQUAMISH LEGEND OF NAPOLEON

Holding an important place among the majority of curious tales held in veneration by the coast tribes are those of the sea-serpent. The monster appears and reappears with almost monotonous frequency in connection with history, traditions, legends and superstitions; but perhaps the most wonderful part it ever played was in the great drama that held the stage of Europe, and incidentally all the world during the stormy days of the first Napoleon.

Throughout Canada I have never failed to find an amazing knowledge of Napoleon Bonaparte amongst the very old and "uncivilized" Indians. Perhaps they may be unfamiliar with every other historical character from Adam down, but they will all tell you they have heard of the "Great French Fighter," as they call the wonderful little Corsican.

Whether this knowledge was obtained through the fact that our earliest settlers and pioneers were French, or whether Napoleon's almost magical fighting career attracted the Indian mind to the exclusion of lesser warriors, I have never yet decided. But the fact remains that the Indians of our generation are not as familiar with Bonaparte's name as were their fathers and grandfathers, so either the predominance of English-speaking settlers or the thinning of their ancient war-loving blood by modern civilization and peaceful times must, one or the other, account for the younger Indian's ignorance of the Emperor of the French.

In telling me the legend of "The Lost Talisman," my good tillicum, the late Chief Capilano, began the story with the almost amazing question, Had I ever heard of Napoleon Bonaparte? It was some moments before I just caught the name, for his English, always quaint and beautiful, was at times a little halting; but when he said, by way of explanation, "You know big fighter, Frenchman. The English they beat him in big battle," I grasped immediately of whom he spoke.

"What do you know of him?" I asked.

His voice lowered, almost as if he spoke a state secret. "I know how it is that English they beat him."

I have read many historians on this event, but to hear the Squamish version was a novel and absorbing thing. "Yes?" I said—my usual "leading" word to lure him into channels of tradition.

"Yes," he affirmed. Then, still in a half-whisper, he proceeded to tell me that it all happened through the agency of a single joint from the vertebra of a sea-serpent.

In telling me the story of Brockton Point and the valiant boy who killed the monster, he dwelt lightly on the fact that all people who approach the vicinity of the creature are palsied, both mentally and physically—bewitched, in fact—so that their bones become disjointed and their brains incapable; but to-day he elaborated upon this peculiarity until I harked back to the boy of Brockton Point and asked how it was that his body and brain escaped this affliction.

"He was all good, and had no greed," he replied. "He was proof against all bad things."

I nodded understandingly, and he proceeded to tell me that all successful Indian fighters and warriors carried somewhere about their person a joint of a sea-serpent's vertebra; that the medicine men threw "the power" about them so that they were not personally affected by this little "charm," but that immediately they approached an enemy the "charm" worked disaster, and victory was assured to the fortunate possessor of the talisman. There was one particularly effective joint that had been treasured and carried by the warriors of a great Squamish family for a century. These warriors had conquered every foe they encountered, until the talisman had become so renowned that the totem pole of their entire "clan" was remodelled, and the new one crested by the figure of a single joint of a sea-serpent's vertebra.

About this time stories of Napoleon's first great achievements drifted across the seas; not across the land—and just here may be a clue to buried Coast-Indian history, which those who are cleverer at research than I can puzzle over. The chief was most emphatic about the source of Indian knowledge of Napoleon.

"I suppose you heard of him from Quebec, through, perhaps, some of the French priests," I remarked.

"No, no," he contradicted hurriedly. "Not from East; we hear it from over the Pacific, from the place they call Russia." But who conveyed the news or by what means it came he could not further enlighten me. But a strange thing happened to the Squamish family about this time. There was a large blood connection, but the only male member living was a very old warrior, the hero of many battles and the possessor of the talisman. On his death-bed his women of three generations gathered about him; his wife, his sisters, his daughters, his granddaughters, but not one man, nor yet a boy of his own blood, stood by to speed his departing warrior spirit to the land of peace and plenty.

"The charm cannot rest in the hands of women," he murmured almost with his last breath. "Women may not war and fight other nations or other tribes; women are for the peaceful lodge and for the leading of little children. They are for holding baby hands, teaching baby feet to walk. No, the charm cannot rest with you, women. I have no brother, no cousin, no son, no grandson, and the charm must not go to a lesser warrior than I. None of our tribe, nor of any tribe on the coast, ever conquered me. The charm must go to one as unconquerable as I have been. When I am dead send it across the great salt chuck, to the victorious 'Frenchman'; they call him Napoleon Bonaparte." They were his last words.

The older women wished to bury the charm with him, but the younger women, inspired with the spirit of their generation, were determined to send it overseas. "In the grave it will be dead," they argued. "Let it still live on. Let it help some other fighter to greatness and victory."

As if to confirm their decision, the next day a small sealing-vessel anchored in the Inlet. All the men aboard spoke Russian, save two thin, dark, agile sailors, who kept aloof from the crew and conversed in another language. These two came ashore with part of the crew and talked in French with a wandering Hudson's Bay trapper, who often lodged with the Squamish people. Thus the women, who yet mourned over their dead warrior, knew these two strangers to be from the land where the great "Frenchman" was fighting against the world.

Here I interrupted the chief. "How came the Frenchmen in a Russian sealer?" I asked.

"Captives," he replied. "Almost slaves, and hated by their captors, as the majority always hate the few. So the women drew those two Frenchmen apart from the rest and told them the story of the bone of the sea-serpent, urging them to carry it back to their own country and give it to the great 'Frenchman' who was as courageous and as brave as their dead leader.

"The Frenchmen hesitated; the talisman might affect them, they said; might jangle their own brains, so that on their return to Russia they would not have the sagacity to plan an escape to their own country; might disjoint their bodies, so that their feet and hands would be useless, and they would become as weak as children. But the women assured them that the charm only worked its magical powers over a man's enemies, that the ancient medicine men had 'bewitched' it with this quality. So the Frenchmen took it and promised that if it were in the power of man they would convey it to 'the Emperor.'

"As the crew boarded the sealer, the women watching from the shore observed strange contortions seize many of the men; some fell on the deck; some crouched, shaking as with palsy; some writhed for a moment, then fell limp and seemingly boneless; only the two Frenchmen stood erect and strong and vital—the Squamish talisman had already overcome their foes. As the little sealer set sail up the gulf she was commanded by a crew of two Frenchmen—men who had entered these waters as captives, who were leaving them as conquerors. The palsied Russians were worse than useless, and what became of them the chief could not state; presumably they were flung overboard, and by some trick of a kindly fate the Frenchmen at last reached the coast of France.

"Tradition is so indefinite about their movements subsequent to sailing out of the Inlet that even the ever-romantic and vividly coloured imaginations of the Squamish people have never supplied the details of this beautifully childish, yet strangely historical, fairy-tale. But the voices of the trumpets of war, the beat of drums throughout Europe heralded back to the wilds of the Pacific Coast forests the intelligence that the great Squamish 'charm' eventually reached the person of Napoleon; that from this time onward his career was one vast victory, that he won battle after battle, conquered nation after nation, and, but for the direst calamity that could befall a warrior, would eventually have been master of the world."

"What was this calamity, Chief?" I asked, amazed at his knowledge of the great historical soldier and strategist.

The chief's voice again lowered to a whisper—his face was almost rigid with intentness as he replied:

"He lost the Squamish charm—lost it just before one great fight with the English people."

I looked at him curiously; he had been telling me the oddest mixture of history and superstition, of intelligence and ignorance, the most whimsically absurd, yet impressive, tale I ever heard from Indian lips.

"What was the name of the great fight—did you ever hear it?" I asked, wondering how much he knew of events which took place at the other side of the world a century agone.

"Yes," he said, carefully, thoughtfully; "I hear the name sometime in London when I there. Railroad station there—same name."

"Was it Waterloo?" I asked.

He nodded quickly, without a shadow of hesitation. "That the one," he replied. "That's it, Waterloo."[13]

THE LURE IN STANLEY PARK

There is a well-known trail in Stanley Park that leads to what I always love to call the "Cathedral Trees"—that group of some half-dozen forest giants that arch overhead with such superb loftiness. But in all the world there is no cathedral whose marble or onyx columns can vie with those straight, clean, brown tree-boles that teem with the sap and blood of life. There is no fresco that can rival the delicacy of lace-work they have festooned between you and the far skies. No tiles, no mosaic or inlaid marbles, are as fascinating as the bare, russet, fragrant floor outspreading about their feet. They are the acme of Nature's architecture, and in building them she has outrivalled all her erstwhile conceptions. She will never originate a more faultless design, never erect a more perfect edifice. But the divinely moulded trees and the man-made cathedral have one exquisite characteristic in common. It is the atmosphere of holiness. Most of us have better impulses after viewing a stately cathedral, and none of us can stand amid that majestic forest group without experiencing some elevating thoughts, some refinement of our coarser nature. Perhaps those who read this little legend will never again look at those cathedral trees without thinking of the glorious souls they contain, for according to the Coast Indians they do harbour human souls, and the world is better because they once had the speech and the hearts of mighty men.

My tillicum did not use the word "lure" in telling me this legend. There is no equivalent for the word in the Chinook tongue, but the gestures of his voiceful hands so expressed the quality of something between magnetism and charm that I have selected this word "lure" as best fitting what he wished to convey. Some few yards beyond the cathedral trees, an overgrown disused trail turns into the dense wilderness to the right. Only Indian eyes could discern that trail, and the Indians do not willingly go to that part of the park to the right of the great group. Nothing in this, nor yet the next world, would tempt a Coast Indian into the compact centres of the wild portions of the park, for therein, concealed cunningly, is the "lure" they all believe in. There is not a tribe in the entire district that does not know of this strange legend. You will hear the tale from those that gather at Eagle Harbour for the fishing, from the Fraser River tribes, from the Squamish at the Narrows, from the Mission, from up the Inlet, even from the tribes at North Bend, but no one will volunteer to be your guide, for having once come within the "aura" of the lure it is a human impossibility to leave it. Your will-power is dwarfed, your intelligence blighted, your feet will refuse to lead you out by a straight trail, you will circle, circle forevermore about this magnet, for if death kindly comes to your aid your immortal spirit will go on in that endless circling that will bar it from entering the Happy Hunting Grounds.

And, like the cathedral trees, the lure once lived, a human soul, but in this instance it was a soul depraved, not sanctified. The Indian belief is very beautiful concerning the results of good and evil in the human body. The Sagalie Tyee (God) has His own way of immortalizing each. People who are wilfully evil, who have no kindness in their hearts, who are bloodthirsty, cruel, vengeful, unsympathetic, the Sagalie Tyee turns to solid stone that will harbour no growth, even that of moss or lichen, for these stones contain no moisture, just as their wicked hearts lacked the milk of human kindness. The one famed exception, wherein a good man was transformed into stone, was in the instance of Siwash Rock, but as the Indian tells you of it he smiles with gratification as he calls your attention to the tiny tree cresting that imperial monument. He says the tree was always there to show the nations that the good in this man's heart kept on growing even when his body had ceased to be. On the other hand, the Sagalie Tyee transforms the kindly people, the humane, sympathetic, charitable, loving people into trees, so that after death they may go on forever benefiting all mankind; they may yield fruit, give shade and shelter, afford unending service to the living by their usefulness as building material and as firewood. Their saps and gums, their fibres, their leaves, their blossoms, enrich, nourish, and sustain the human form; no evil is produced by trees—all, all is goodness, is hearty, is helpfulness and growth. They give refuge to the birds, they give music to the winds, and from them are carved the bows and arrows, the canoes and paddles, bowls, spoons, and baskets. Their service to mankind is priceless; the Indian that tells you this tale will enumerate all these attributes and virtues of the trees. No wonder the Sagalie Tyee chose them to be the abode of souls good and great.

But the lure in Stanley Park is that most dreaded of all things, an evil soul. It is embodied in a bare, white stone, which is shunned by moss and vine and lichen, but over which are splashed innumerable jet-black spots that have eaten into the surface like an acid.

This condemned soul once animated the body of a witch-woman, who went up and down the coast, over seas and far inland, casting her evil eye on innocent people, and bringing them untold evils and diseases. About her person she carried the renowned "Bad Medicine" that every Indian believes in—medicine that weakened the arm of the warrior in battle, that caused deformities, that poisoned minds and characters, that engendered madness, that bred plagues and epidemics; in short, that was the seed of every evil that could befall mankind. This witch-woman herself was immune from death; generations were born and grew to old age, and died, and other generations arose in their stead, but the witch-woman went about, her heart set against her kind. Her acts were evil, her purposes wicked. She broke hearts and bodies and souls; she gloried in tears, and revelled in unhappiness, and sent them broadcast wherever she wandered. And in His high heaven the Sagalie Tyee wept with sorrow for His afflicted human children. He dared not let her die, for her spirit would still go on with its evil doing. In mighty anger He gave command to His Four Men (always representing the Deity) that they should turn this witch-woman into a stone and enchain her spirit in its centre, that the curse of her might be lifted from the unhappy race.

So the Four Men entered their giant canoe, and headed, as was their custom, up the Narrows. As they neared what is now known as Prospect Point they heard from the heights above them a laugh, and, looking up, they beheld the witch-woman jeering defiantly at them. They landed and, scaling the rocks, pursued her as she danced away, eluding them like a will-o'-the-wisp as she called out to them sneeringly:

"Care for yourselves, oh! men of the Sagalie Tyee, or I shall blight you with my evil eye. Care for yourselves and do not follow me." On and on she danced through the thickest of the wilderness, on and on they followed until they reached the very heart of the sea-girt neck of land we know as Stanley Park. Then the tallest, the mightiest of the Four Men, lifted his hand and cried out: "Oh! woman of the stony heart, be stone for evermore, and bear forever a black stain for each one of your evil deeds." And as he spoke the witch-woman was transformed into this stone that tradition says is in the centre of the park.

Such is the "Legend of the Lure." Whether or not this stone is really in existence—who knows? One thing is positive, however: no Indian will ever help to discover it.

Three different Indians have told me that fifteen or eighteen years ago, two tourists—a man and a woman—were lost in Stanley Park. When found a week later the man was dead, the woman mad, and each of my informants firmly believed they had, in their wanderings, encountered "the stone" and were compelled to circle around it, because of its powerful lure.

But this wild tale, fortunately, has a most beautiful conclusion. The Four Men, fearing that the evil heart imprisoned in the stone would still work destruction, said: "At the end of the trail we must place so good and great a thing that it will be mightier, stronger, more powerful than this evil." So they chose from the nations the kindliest, most benevolent men, men whose hearts were filled with the love of their fellow-beings, and transformed these merciful souls into the stately group of "Cathedral Trees."

How well the purpose of the Sagalie Tyee has wrought its effect through time! The good has predominated, as He planned it to, for is not the stone hidden in some unknown part of the park where eyes do not see it and feet do not follow—and do not the thousands who come to us from the uttermost parts of the world seek that wondrous beauty spot, and stand awed by the majestic silence, the almost holiness of that group of giants?

More than any other legend that the Indians about Vancouver have told me does this tale reveal the love of the Coast native for kindness, and his hatred of cruelty. If these tribes really have ever been a warlike race I cannot think they pride themselves much on the occupation. If you talk with any of them, and they mention some man they particularly like or admire, their first qualification of him is: "He's a kind man." They never say he is brave, or rich, or successful, or even strong, that characteristic so loved by the red man. To these Coast tribes if a man is "kind" he is everything. And almost without exception their legends deal with rewards for tenderness and self-abnegation, and personal and mental cleanliness.

Call them fairy-tales if you wish to,[14] they all have a reasonableness that must have originated in some mighty mind, and, better than that, they all tell of the Indian's faith in the survival of the best impulses of the human heart, and the ultimate extinction of the worst.

In talking with my many good tillicums, I find this witch-woman legend is the most universally known and thoroughly believed in of all traditions they have honoured me by revealing to me.

DEER LAKE

Few white men ventured inland, a century ago, in the days of the first Chief Capilano,[15] when the spoils of the mighty Fraser River poured into copper-coloured hands, but did not find their way to the remotest corners of the earth, as in our times, when the gold from its sources, the salmon from its mouth, the timber from its shores are world-known riches.

The fisherman's craft, the hunter's cunning, were plied where now cities and industries, trade and commerce, buying and selling, hold sway. In those days the moccasined foot awoke no echo in the forest trails. Primitive weapons, arms, implements, and utensils were the only means of the Indian's food-getting. His livelihood depended upon his own personal prowess, his skill in woodcraft and water lore. And, as this is a story of an elk-bone spear, the reader must first be in sympathy with the fact that this rude instrument, most deftly fashioned, was of priceless value to the first Capilano, to whom it had come through three generations of ancestors, all of whom had been experienced hunters and dexterous fishermen.

Capilano himself was without a rival as a spearman. He knew the moods of the Fraser River, the habits of its thronging tenants, as no other man has ever known them before or since. He knew every isle and inlet along the coast, every boulder, the sand-bars, the still pools, the temper of the tides. He knew the spawning grounds, the secret streams that fed the larger rivers, the outlets of rock-bound lakes, the turns and tricks of swirling rapids. He knew the haunts of bird and beast and fish and fowl, and was master of the arts and artifice that man must use when matching his brain against the eluding wiles of the untamed creatures of the wilderness.

Once only did his cunning fail him, once only did Nature baffle him with her mysterious fabric of waterways and land-lures. It was when he was led to the mouth of the unknown river, which has evaded discovery through all the centuries, but which—so say the Indians—still sings on its way through some buried channel that leads from the lake to the sea.

He had been sealing along the shores of what is now known as Point Grey. His canoe had gradually crept inland, skirting up the coast to the mouth of False Creek. Here he encountered a very king of seals, a colossal creature that gladdened the hunter's eyes as game worthy of his skill. For this particular prize he would cast the elk-bone spear. It had never failed his sire, his grandsire, his great-grandsire. He knew it would not fail him now. A long, pliable, cedar-fibre rope lay in his canoe. Many expert fingers had woven and plaited the rope, had beaten and oiled it until it was soft and flexible as a serpent. This he attached to the spearhead, and with deft, unerring aim cast it at the king seal. The weapon struck home. The gigantic creature shuddered, and, with a cry like a hurt child, it plunged down into the sea. With the rapidity and strength of a giant fish it scudded inland with the rising tide, while Capilano paid out the rope its entire length, and, as it stretched taut, felt the canoe leap forward, propelled by the mighty strength of the creature which lashed the waters into whirlpools, as though it was possessed with the power and properties of a whale.

Up the stretch of False Creek the man and monster drove their course, where a century hence great city bridges were to over-arch the waters. They strove and struggled each for the mastery; neither of them weakened, neither of them faltered—the one dragging, the other driving. In the end it was to be a matching of brute and human wits, not forces. As they neared the point where now Main Street bridge flings its shadow across the waters, the brute leaped high into the air, then plunged headlong into the depths. The impact ripped the rope from Capilano's hands. It rattled across the gunwale. He stood staring at the spot where it had disappeared—the brute had been victorious. At low tide the Indian made search. No trace of his game, of his precious elk-bone spear, of his cedar-fibre rope, could be found. With the loss of the latter he firmly believed his luck as a hunter would be gone. So he patrolled the mouth of False Creek for many moons. His graceful, high-bowed canoe rarely touched other waters, but the seal king had disappeared. Often he thought long strands of drifting sea grasses were his lost cedar-fibre rope. With other spears, with other cedar-fibres, with paddle blade and cunning traps he dislodged the weeds from their moorings, but they slipped their slimy lengths through his eager hands: his best spear with its attendant coil was gone.

The following year he was sealing again off the coast of Point Grey, and one night, after sunset, he observed the red reflection from the west, which seemed to transfer itself to the eastern skies. Far into the night dashes of flaming scarlet pulsed far beyond the head of False Creek. The colour rose and fell like a beckoning hand, and, Indian-like, he immediately attached some portentous meaning to the unusual sight. That it was some omen he never doubted, so he paddled inland, beached his canoe, and took the trail towards the little group of lakes that crowd themselves into the area that lies between the present cities of Vancouver and New Westminster. But long before he reached the shores of Deer Lake he discovered that the beckoning hand was in reality flame. The little body of water was surrounded by forest fires. One avenue alone stood open. It was a group of giant trees that as yet the flames had not reached. As he neared the point he saw a great moving mass of living things leaving the lake and hurrying northward through this one egress. He stood, listening, intently watching with alert eyes; the swirr of myriads of little travelling feet caught his quick ear—the moving mass was an immense colony of beaver. Thousands upon thousands of them. Scores of baby beavers staggered along, following their mothers; scores of older beavers that had felled trees and built dams through many seasons; a countless army of trekking fur-bearers, all under the generalship of a wise old leader, who, as king of the colony, advanced some few yards ahead of his battalions. Out of the waters through the forest towards the country to the north they journeyed. Wandering hunters said they saw them cross Burrard Inlet at the Second Narrows, heading inland as they reached the farther shore. But where that mighty army of royal little Canadians set up their new colony, no man knows. Not even the astuteness of the first Capilano ever discovered their destination. Only one thing was certain: Deer Lake knew them no more.

After their passing, the Indian retraced their trail to the water's edge. In the red glare of the encircling fires he saw what he at first thought was some dead and dethroned king beaver on the shore. A huge carcass lay half in, half out, of the lake. Approaching it, he saw the wasted body of a giant seal. There could never be two seals of that marvellous size. His intuition now grasped the meaning of the omen of the beckoning flame that had called him from the far coasts of Point Grey. He stooped above his dead conqueror and found, embedded in its decaying flesh, the elk-bone spear of his forefathers, and, trailing away at the water's rim, was a long, flexible cedar-fibre rope.

As he extracted this treasured heirloom he felt the "power," that men of magic possess, creep up his sinewy arms. It entered his heart, his blood, his brain. For a long time he sat and chanted songs that only great medicine men may sing, and, as the hours drifted by, the heat of the forest fires subsided, the flames diminished into smouldering blackness. At daybreak the forest fire was dead, but its beckoning fingers had served their purpose. The magic elk-bone spear had come back to its own.

Until the day of his death the first Capilano searched for the unknown river up which the seal travelled from False Creek to Deer Lake, but its channel is a secret that even Indian eyes have not seen.

But although those of the Squamish tribe tell and believe that the river still sings through its hidden trail that leads from Deer Lake to the sea, its course is as unknown, its channel is as hopelessly lost as the brave little army of beavers that a century ago marshalled their forces and travelled up into the great lone north.

A ROYAL MOHAWK CHIEF

How many Canadians are aware that in Prince Arthur,[16] Duke of Connaught, and only surviving son of Queen Victoria, who has been appointed to represent King George V. in Canada, they undoubtedly have what many wish for—one bearing an ancient Canadian title as Governor-General of all the Dominion? It would be difficult to find a man more Canadian than any one of the fifty chiefs who compose the parliament of the ancient Iroquois nation, that loyal race of Redskins that has fought for the British Crown against all of the enemies thereof, adhering to the British flag through the wars against both the French and the colonists.

Arthur, Duke of Connaught, is the only living white man who to-day has an undisputed right to the title of "Chief of the Six Nations Indians" (known collectively as the Iroquois). He possesses the privilege of sitting in their councils, of casting his vote on all matters relative to the governing of the tribes, the disposal of reservation lands, the appropriation of both the principal and interest of the more than half a million dollars these tribes hold in Government bonds at Ottawa, accumulated from the sales of their lands. In short, were every drop of blood in his royal veins red, instead of blue, he could not be more fully qualified as an Indian chief than he now is, not even were his title one of the fifty hereditary ones whose illustrious names composed the Iroquois confederacy before the Paleface ever set foot in America.

It was on the occasion of his first visit to Canada in 1869, when he was little more than a boy, that Prince Arthur received, upon his arrival at Quebec, an address of welcome from his royal mother's "Indian Children" on the Grand River Reserve, in Brant county, Ontario. In addition to this welcome they had a request to make of him: would he accept the title of Chief and visit their reserve to give them the opportunity of conferring it?

One of the great secrets of England's success with savage races has been her consideration, her respect, her almost reverence of native customs, ceremonies, and potentates. She wishes her own customs and kings to be honoured, so she freely accords like honour to her subjects—it matters not whether they be white, black, or red.

Young Arthur was delighted—royal lads are pretty much like all other boys; the unique ceremony would be a break in the endless round of state receptions, banquets, and addresses. So he accepted the Red Indians' compliment, knowing well that it was the loftiest honour these people could confer upon a white man.

It was the morning of October first when the royal train steamed into the little city of Brantford, where carriages awaited to take the Prince and his suite to the "Old Mohawk Church," in the vicinity of which the ceremony was to take place. As the Prince's especial escort, Onwanonsyshon,[17] head chief of the Mohawks, rode on a jet-black pony beside the carriage. The chief was garmented in full native costume—a buckskin suit, beaded moccasins, headband of owl's and eagle's feathers, and ornaments hammered from coin silver that literally covered his coat and leggings. About his shoulders was flung a scarlet blanket, consisting of the identical broadcloth from which the British army tunics are made; this he "hunched" with his shoulders from time to time in true Indian fashion. As they drove along the Prince chatted boyishly with his Mohawk escort, and once leaned forward to pat the black pony on its shining neck and speak admiringly of it. It was a warm autumn day: the roads were dry and dusty, and, after a mile or so, the boy-prince brought from beneath the carriage seat a basket of grapes. With his handkerchief he flicked the dust from them, handed a bunch to the chief, and took one himself. An odd spectacle to be traversing a country road: an English prince and an Indian chief, riding amicably side by side, enjoying a banquet of grapes like two schoolboys.

On reaching the church, Arthur leapt lightly to the greensward. For a moment he stood, rigid, gazing before him at his future brother-chiefs. His escort had given him a faint idea of what he was to see, but he certainly never expected to be completely surrounded by three hundred full-blooded Iroquois braves and warriors, such as now encircled him on every side. Every Indian was in war-paint and feathers, some stripped to the waist, their copper-coloured skins brilliant with paints, dyes, and "patterns"; all carried tomahawks, scalping-knives, and bows and arrows. Every red throat gave a tremendous war-whoop as he alighted, which was repeated again and again, as for that half moment he stood silent, a slim, boyish figure, clad in light grey tweeds—a singular contrast to the stalwarts in gorgeous costumes who crowded about him. His young face paled to ashy whiteness, then with true British grit he extended his right hand and raised his black "billy-cock" hat with his left. At the same time he took one step forward. Then the war-cries broke forth anew, deafening, savage, terrible cries, as one by one the entire three hundred filed past, the Prince shaking hands with each one, and removing his glove to do so. This strange reception over, Onwanonsyshon rode up, and, flinging his scarlet blanket on the grass, dismounted, and asked the Prince to stand on it.

Then stepped forward an ancient chief, father of Onwanonsyshon, and Speaker of the Council.[18] He was old in inherited and personal loyalty to the British Crown. He had fought under Sir Isaac Brock at Queenston Heights in 1812, while yet a mere boy, and upon him was laid the honour of making his Queen's son a chief. Taking Arthur by the hand, this venerable warrior walked slowly to and fro across the blanket, chanting as he went the strange, wild formula of induction. From time to time he was interrupted by loud expressions of approval and assent from the vast throng of encircling braves, but apart from this no sound was heard but the low, weird monotone of a ritual older than the white man's foot-prints in North America.

It is necessary that a chief of each of the three "clans" of the Mohawks shall assist in this ceremony. The veteran chief, who sang the formula, was of the Bear clan. His son, Onwanonsyshon, was of the Wolf (the clanship descends through the mother's side of the family). Then one other chief, of the Turtle clan, and in whose veins coursed the blood of the historic Brant,[19] now stepped to the edge of the scarlet blanket. The chant ended, these two young chiefs received the Prince into the Mohawk tribe, conferring upon him the name of "Kavakoudge," which means "the sun flying from East to West under the guidance of the Great Spirit."

Onwanonsyshon then took from his waist a brilliant deep-red sash, heavily embroidered with beads, porcupine quills, and dyed moose-hair, placing it over the Prince's left shoulder and knotting it beneath his right arm. The ceremony was ended. The constitution that Hiawatha had founded centuries ago, a constitution wherein fifty chiefs, no more, no less, should form the parliament of the "Six Nations," had been shattered and broken, because this race of loyal red men desired to do honour to a slender young boy-prince, who now bears the fifty-first title of the Iroquois.[20]

Many white men have received from these same people honorary titles, but none has been bestowed through the ancient ritual, with the imperative members of the three clans assisting, save that borne by Arthur of Connaught.

After the ceremony the Prince entered the church to autograph his name in the ancient Bible, which, with a silver Holy Communion service, a bell, two tablets inscribed with the Ten Commandments, and a bronze British coat of arms, had been presented to the Mohawks by Queen Anne. He inscribed "Arthur" just below the "Albert Edward," which, as Prince of Wales, the late King wrote when he visited Canada in 1860.

When he returned to England Chief Kavakoudge sent his portrait, together with one of Queen Victoria and the Prince Consort,[21] to be placed in the Council House of the "Six Nations," where they decorate the walls today.

As I write, I glance up to see, in a corner of my room, a draping scarlet blanket, made of British army broadcloth, for the chief who rode the jet-black pony so long ago was the writer's father. He was not here to wear it when Arthur of Connaught again set foot on Canadian shores.[22]

Many of these facts I have culled from a paper that lies on my desk; it is yellowing with age, and bears the date, "Toronto, October 2, 1869," and on the margin is written, in a clear, half-boyish hand, "Onwanonsyshon, with kind regards from your brother-chief, Arthur."

STORIES *of* MARY AGNES CAPILANO

Mary Agnes Capilano (Lixwelut)

THE LEGEND OF THE TWO SISTERS[1]

You can see them from the heights, from the pleasure grounds, from the gay thoroughfares, from the great hotel windows—those twin peaks of the twin mountains that lift their pearly summits across the inlet which washes with its ceaseless tides the margins of Vancouver, the beautiful city which is called "The Sunset Gateway" of the Dominion of Canada.

Sometimes the smoke of forest fires blurs these twin peaks, until they swim in a purple atmosphere too beautiful for words to paint. Sometimes the slanting rains festoon their grey and gauzy veils about the crests, and the peaks fade into inadequate outlines of soft shadows, melting, melting, forever melting, into the distances. But for most days of the year, the sun circles the twin glories with a sweep of gold, the moon washes them with a torrent of silver, and they stand immovable through sun and shadow, smiling on one side above the waters of the restless Pacific, on the other, above the depths and eternal silence of the Capilano Canyon.[2]

Throughout the British Empire these peaks are known as "The Lions of Vancouver." Their striking resemblance to Landseer's Lions at the base of Nelson's Monument[3] in Trafalgar Square, London, has won them this name. But the Indians of the coast know nothing of the white man's appellation, and you must indeed get near to the heart of some ancient Klootchman*[4] before she will consent to tell you the Legend of the Twin Sisters.

We had been driving for some time, the handsome chief of the Capilanos sitting in the front seat of the light surrey, his slim, silent young daughter beside him, I in the back seat, and at my side the quaint old Indian mother, who, from time to time, told me the traditions of her people, in the half-halting broken English that is never so beautiful as when it slips from an Indian tongue. At our feet were baskets of exquisite weavery, all her handiwork, and that of her young daughter sitting before us. With housewifely care she had stowed these away before starting for the drive, for it was berry time, and she had no thought of leaving such precious muck-a-muck for the foxes and birds, when her children and grandchildren had willing mouths to be filled. The chief was an excellent provider, but "Why not add to the store?" she remarked simply. "One must not be wasteful of these precious, God-given wild things." So the baskets reposed nearby, ready to be filled when opportunity afforded.

The trail wound about the foot of a cluster of mountains, following a riotous stream called the Capilano River, which brawled and quarrelled, whispered and laughed among its rocks and boulders, tumbling head-long one moment, the next circling into a deep, transparent pool where leaping salmon and shy mountain trout glinted in the sunshine.

"So many things belong to this river," said the Klootchman in her pretty, stammering English, which I must eliminate if I am to make this story lucid. So I must keep to the everyday phrases, and my readers must be the losers of her fascinating expressions; but after all, it was her wonderful eyes and gestures that really made the tale, and what use to attempt a description of these? It is impossible.

"Yes, the river holds many secrets," she continued, "secrets of strong men's battles and many tragedies, but the mountains hold the secrets of an Indian mother's heart, and those are the greatest secrets of all things."

Her voice fell to a whisper, but her speaking eyes swept the distant summits with an understanding far subtler than sight. I did not offer a reply, for I knew that in her own good time the Klootchman would catch the mood of the mountains and impart to me some of their lore. The silence was long. Once or twice she swept effective gestures that were filled with meaning. She wishes me to notice the crags and ledges, haunts of the mountain sheep and wild goats, a winging hawk, a leaping trout, the crimsoning o-lil-lies (Chinook for berries). Then as if from dreams she suddenly awoke.

"You will want to know the secret that is held in the mountains, the secret of the Indian mother's heart?" she asked.

I nodded. I could see she liked that wordless reply, for she placed her narrow brown hand on my arm, nor did she remove it during her entire recital of

THE LEGEND OF THE TWO SISTERS

"You see them—those two peaks—towering forever and ever in that high place? Those are the Chief's Daughters, that every Indian mother loves. You see them, but you may not know—you who have come from the Land of Morning, the Land of Sunrise—for you have different customs, different traditions, from those of our people in the Sunset Land. I say you may not know that when our daughters step from childhood into the great world of womanhood, when the fitness for motherhood crowns them, we coast Indians of the sunset country regard this occasion as one of extreme rejoicing, great honour and unspeakable gladness. The being who possesses the possibility of some day becoming a mother receives much honour in most nations, but to us, the Sunset Tribes of Redmen, she is almost sacred. So, when our girls reach womanhood, we make it a great occasion. The parents usually give a feast that lasts many days. The entire tribe is bidden to this festival. More than that, when a great Tyee (Chinook for chief) celebrates for his daughter, sometimes the tribes from far up the coast, from the far North, from inland, from the mountain passes, and the Cariboo Country, are bidden as guests to the feast. During these feast days the girl is placed in a high seat, an exalted position, for is she not marriageable? and does not marriage mean motherhood? and is not motherhood the most exalted position in the world? So we place the girl on a high elevation, for she must know and realize her responsibility, she must recognize that she is the greatest factor in the world, and she must sit in a high place as becomes her heritage as a woman, therefore as a possible mother, for this is the law of our people—we of the Sunset Tribes.

"It was years ago, hundreds of years—yes, thousands of years (the sweet old Klootchman pronounced it 'Tousen off yea-rs.' It was the only sentence of her quaint, broken English I was ever able to actually capture)—yes, more than thousands of years ago that the great Tyee of our tribe had two daughters, young, lovable, and oh! very beautiful. They grew to womanhood the same time, and a mighty feast was to be given, such a feast as the Coast had never yet seen. The only shadow on the joy of it all was *war*, for the tribe of the great Tyee was at war with the Upper Coast Indians—those who lived north of what is now named by the white men the Port of Prince Rupert.

"Giant war canoes fretted the entire coast line, war parties paddled their way up and down, war songs broke the silences of the nights, strife, hatred, vengeance festered everywhere, like sores on the surface of the earth. But the great Tyee snatched a week away from the bloodshed and battle, for he must make this feast in his daughter's honour, nor permit any mere enemy to come between him and the traditions of his race and household. So he turned deaf ears to their war songs, he ignored their insulting paddle-dips, which encroached within his own coast waters, and he prepared, as a great Tyee should, to celebrate in honour of his daughters.

"But five suns before the feast these two maidens came to him, hand within hand. 'Some day we may mother a man-child,' they said, 'a man-child who may grow to be just such a great Tyee as you are, oh, our father, and for this honour that may some day be ours, we have come to crave a favour of you.'

"'What favour, children of mine, and of your mother? It is yours for the asking, this day,' he answered.

"'Will you, for our sakes, invite the hostile tribe, the tribe you war upon, to our feast?' they asked.

"'To a peaceful feast, a feast in the honour of women?' he exclaimed.

"'So we would have it,' they replied.

"'And so shall it be,' he declared. 'I can deny you nothing this day, and sometime your sons may be born to bless this peace you have asked, and to bless their mothers' sire for giving it.'

"Then he turned to the young men of the tribe and said, 'Build fires this night on all the coast headlines, fires of welcome. Go forth in your canoes, face the north, and greet the enemy, and tell them that I, the Tyee of the Capilanos, bid them join me for a feast in honour of my two daughters.'

"And when the Northern tribes got the invitation they flocked down the coast to this feast of a great Peace. They brought their women and their children, they brought game and fish and o-lil-lie, as gifts. Never was such a Potlatch (a gift feast), never was such joyousness, such long, glad days, such soft, sweet nights. The war canoes were emptied of deadly weapons and filled with the daily catch of salmon. The hostile war songs ceased, and in their place were heard laughter and singing, and the play-games of the children of two tribes which had been until now ancient enemies, and a great and lasting brotherhood was sealed between them. The war songs were ended forever."

The Klootchman's voice fell very low, and the last words were almost whispered.

"And what of the two sweet daughters of the great Tyee?" I asked, slipping my hand in hers.

"They are there," she said, pointing to the twin peaks which rose far above us. "The Great Spirit made them immortal. They will always be there in that high place. Their offspring now rule these tribes, for were not Peace and Brotherhood born of them? And there the two Sisters have stood these thousands of years, and will stand for thousands of years to come, guarding the Peace of the Pacific coast, and the serenity of the Capilano Canyon."[5]

THE LEGEND OF THE SQUAMISH TWINS[6]

The most dulcet of all music was lulling me into drowsiness—the liquid, lovely cadence of mountain waters purling and singing about sand reaches and innumerable rocks and boulders. Beyond the shade of the clustering, boughless firs wherein I stretched to dream and listen, the yellow August sunshine fell in a shower of gold, and circling all were the purple peaks of that majestic range of mountains that sweeps down the Pacific Coast like an imperial army outflung to guard the western portals of the continent. The handsome Squamish chief had sat in silence for a full hour, a few feet from where I lounged. His wife was amusing herself casting for salmon in the rollicking stream, and had been rewarded with some success; several gleaming beauties lay up shore, their iridescent scales flashing back [the sunlight], their firm bodies promising a delicious supper hours hence.

"What is it that you see, Chief?" I asked, for his usually shrewd and twinkling eyes had grown broodingly melancholy.

"I see dead faces, hear dead voices, listen to dead legends," he replied, dreamily.

"The legends at least will live again if you tell them—to me," I suggested, with some craft.

"You shall hear them, then," he answered graciously, for he ever loved my desire to know of his people; for we are of the same color, this Squamish chief and I, though not of the same tribe or race. But the copper color? Ah, it makes us cousins in heart!

He broke abruptly into his subject. "You have been much among the palefaces; what do they say of twin children?" he asked.

"Oh, twins," I said, rather startled at the odd question. "Why, the palefaces like them; they are—they are—well, very proud of having twins," I stammered, hardly sure of my ground.

He laughed derisively. "And the people of the East—of the land beyond the Great Lakes—do they ever give welcome to twins?"

His tones were half mocking, half fearful of my reply. I smiled, shaking my head. "No [red race] ever does," I answered.

"Now we understand each other," he said, with evident relief. "But what say your tribe to this—this twins?"

"Not good," I admitted, dropping into his own fashion of broken English. "We Iroquois count twins undesirable, almost a disgrace. We say they are as rabbits—'Tow-wen-da-na-ga,' their parents are called. That is the Mohawk of 'rabbit.'"

"Is that all?" he asked, his eyes and voice very solemn.

"That is all," I replied. "Is it not enough?"

He shook his head. "Not so with us of the Sunset Tribes," he said. "Twins no disgrace here, only a fearsome thing, and a warning of coming evil to the father [of the] tribe; but not disgrace."

"Won't you tell me of it—both of you?" I added, for Mrs. Chief began to put up her fishing rod. At the word "twins" her eyes lost their interest in the stream, her hand went lax and inert in holding the rod; she forthwith climbed across the boulders and seated herself close to me wordlessly, but I knew she had much to tell.

So from them both I extracted this tale. I cannot hope to repeat it in the fascinating dialect they uttered, but I always hear mingled with their dulcet voices the rippling of that mountain stream when I think of the Squamish Legend.

"It was a gray morning when they told him of this disaster that had fallen upon him. He was a great chief; he ruled over many a tribe on the north Pacific Coast, but what now availed his greatness? His young wife had borne him twins, and was sobbing out her anguish in the little fir bark tepee near the tide-water.

"Beyond the doorway gathered many old men and women, old in years, in wisdom and the lore of their nations. Their hushed voices discussed the awesome thing, and for hours their grave council was broken only by the infant sobs of the two boy babies in the tepee.

"'Something dire will happen to him,' grieved the young mother. 'To him, my husband, the father of my boys.' And outside the men and women echoed, 'Something dire will happen to him.' Then an ancient medicine man arose, lifting his outstretched palms to hush the lamenting throng. His voice shook with the weight of many winters, but his eyes were yet keen, and mirrored the clear thought and brain behind them, and his words rolled forth with a certain mastery that no one essayed to dispute. 'It is the olden law of the Squamish that, lest evil befall the father because of his being the sire of twins, he go afar and alone into the mountain fastnesses, there, by his isolation and his loneliness, to prove himself stronger than the threatened evil, and thus to beat back the shadow that would otherwise follow him. I therefore name for him the length of days which he must spend alone fighting his invisible enemy. He must leave this hour, taking with him only his trustworthy bows and fleetest arrows, and, going up into the mountain wildernesses, remain there ten days—alone.'

"The masterful voice ceased. The tribe wailed their assent. The father arose, speechless, his drawn face revealing great agony over this seemingly brief banishment. He took leave of his sobbing wife, of the two tiny souls that were his sons, grasped his favorite bows and arrows, and faced the forest like a warrior. But at the end of ten days he did not return. Nor yet ten weeks, nor ten months.

"'He is dead!' wept the mother into the baby ears of her tiny boys. 'He could not battle against the evil that threatened. It was stronger than he—he so strong, and proud, and brave; he is dead.'

"'He is dead!' echoed the tribesmen and the tribeswomen. 'Our strong, proud, brave chief! He is dead.' So they mourned the long year through, but their chants and their tears were unanswered.

"Meanwhile, far up the Capilano Canyon, the banished chief had made his solitary home—for who can tell what fatal trick of sound, what current of air, what faltering expression had deceived his alert Indian ears? But some unhappy fate had made him understand that his solitude must be of *ten years'* duration, not ten days, and he had accepted the mandate with the heroism of a stoic. For had he refused to do so, his belief was that the threatened evil would be spared him, but would fall upon his tribe. Thus was one more added to the long list of souls whose creed has been: 'It is fitting that one should suffer for the people.'

"With his hunting knife the banished Squamish chief stripped the bark from the gigantic firs and cedars, building for himself a lodge beside the Capilano River, where leaping salmon could be speared by arrowheads fastened to deftly-shaped, long handles. All through the fishing season he 'laid by' for the winter, smoking and drying the firm, pink salmon with the care of a housewife. The mountain sheep and goats, and even great cinnamon and grizzly bears, fell before his unerring arrows, until their smoked hams and saddles hung in rows from the crosspoles of his bark lodge, and their magnificent pelts carpeted his floor, hung on his walls, padded his bed, and clothes his body. He made leggings, moccasins and shirts by stitching them together with deer sinews. He gathered the brilliant scarlet salmon berries, their acid flavor being a grateful change from meat and fish. Month by month and year by year he sat beside his lonely campfire, waiting, waiting for his long term of solitude to end. And then one hot summer day the Thunder Bird came crashing through the mountains about him. Up from the arms of the Pacific rolled the storm cloud, and the Thunder Bird, with its eyes of flashing light, beat its huge, vibrating wings on crag and canyon.

"Upstream a tall shaft of granite reared its needle-like length. It is named Thunder Rock, and wise men of the paleface people say it is rich in ore, copper, silver and gold. At the base of this shaft the Squamish chief crouched when the storm cloud broke and bellowed through the range, and on its summit the Thunder Bird perched, its gigantic wings threshing the air into booming sounds, into splitting terrors, like a Douglas pine crashing down the mountain side. But when the beating of those black pinions ceased, and the echoes of their thunder waves died down in the depths of the canyon, the Squamish chief arose, a new man. The shadow on his soul had lifted, the fears of threatening evil were cowed and conquered. In his brain, his blood, his veins, his sinews, he felt that the poison of melancholy dwelt no more—he had fulfilled the demands of the law of Red Nations.

"As he heard the last beat of the Thunder Bird's wings dying slowly, slowly, faintly, faintly among the crags, he knew that the Bird, too, was dying, for its soul was leaving its monster black body, and presently appeared in the sky; he could see it arching overhead before it took its long journey to the Happy Hunting Grounds, for the soul of the Thunder Bird was a radiant half circle of glorious color, spanning from peak to peak.

"He lifted his head then, for his long banishment was ended.

"But down in the tide-water country the little, brown-faced twins were growing towards the questioning age that most children, whether red or white, are sure to reach with the widening intelligence of big boyhood. All through the years they asked, 'Have we no father, as other boys have?' and were met with silent lips and shaking heads, and the oft-repeated reply, 'Your father is no more; your father, the great chief, is dead.' But some filial intuition told the twins that their sire would yet return, but when they would say this to their sad-eyed mother, she would only weep and reply that not even the witchcraft of the old medicine man could restore him to them. Then came the time when they would be ten years old, and one week before their birthday the two children stood hand-in-hand before their mother; upon their slender shoulders they had strapped food for a long journey, their bows and arrows, their little hunting knives, their salmon spears.

"'We go to find our father,' they said simply.

"What use to protest? They were as young gods, and in their eyes was the fire of purpose.

"'Oh, useless quest!' wailed the mother.

"'Oh, useless quest!' wailed all the men and women.

"But the two children went forth into the forest, following upstream to its source the lapping, laughing Capilano River. For many days their young feet flew as though shod with wings; no rocks, no boulders, no heights, no depths, discouraged them, and when the sun arose on the morning of their tenth birthday, they, too, arose from a brief night's sleep, and far upstream they beheld a thin, blue curl of smoke drifting above a fir-bark roof. 'It is our father's lodge,' they told each other; for their little Indian hearts were unerring in response to the call of kinship. Hand-in-hand, they approached, and, entering the lodge, said but one word: 'Come.' The great Squamish chief outstretched his arms towards them, then towards the laughing river, then towards the mountains.

"'Welcome, my sons!' he said. 'And good-by, my mountains, my brothers, my crags and canyons.' And with a child clinging to each hand he faced once more the country of the tide-water.

"And when all the tribe made welcome to him in one mighty Potlatch (a gift feast), his happy wife had but these words to say: 'It was the children's hearts that led them to you.'"

The legend was ended; for a long time the chief and his wife and I sat beneath the singing pines beside the murmuring river; sat silent and motionless, with our thoughts wrapped in the long ago. Then the chief spoke:

"It was here, where we are sitting, that he built his fir-bark lodge, those many hundred years ago. Here on this spot, he dwelt those ten long years, alone." Then he arose. "It is growing late," he said regretfully. "The mountain airs at night are cool. The legend is ended."

I knew he meant it was time for us all to turn city-wards, so, like the older Squamish chief, I, too, arose, and with outstretched arms, said:

"Good-by, my mountains, my brothers, my crags, and my canyons."

THE LEGEND OF THE SEVEN SWANS[7]

"Did you ever know a mother who did not love her crippled baby more than all her other children?" asked the old Klootchman, glancing up from her basket-weaving, and for a moment allowing her slender hands to lie idly in her lap.

"One always loves the weak ones," I commented. "We admire the strong, we are proud of the deft, the agile, we applaud the skillful, the clever, but we *love* the weak."

"It is always so," she agreed. "Always so when the one who loves is a mother-woman, and when the weak one is a baby." As she spoke the old Klootchman looked away across the canyon, her eyes were very dreamy, and I knew her thoughts were winging their pathless way back to the olden years and the early history of her tribe.

I crouched down beside her, settling comfortably in a natural shelf of rock, and for a time watched in silence the mad tumble of the sleepless Capilano River,[8] as it crowded through the throat of the canyon[9] three hundred feet below us.

A swirl of melodies arose from its myriad waterfalls, its countless rapids—melodies soft and fresh as a robin's whistle, and their singing intensified the fragrance of damp mosses and pungent firs and cedars that frame this most exquisite beauty spot in British Columbia.

"There are not many song birds here," I remarked. "I sometimes think that Nature so richly favored this wonderful province that she kept the birds for some less beautiful country. Here the forests and the rivers sing to us. Their voices are more like a heavenly orchestra, like unseen hands playing on a thousand strings. The winds, the firs, the whispering rivers, are like a Chopin Prelude sobbed from the throat of a violin."

The Klootchman looked at me longingly, and I caught myself back—I had been voicing my thoughts unmindful of her dear, uncomprehending mind. I smiled.

"You no savvy[10] what I talk of, eh, Klootchman?" I said.

"Some savvy," she answered, using the native phrase with quaint delight.

"What I mean is that here we cannot hope to have *everything*," I hastened. "The less lovely country east of the Rockies must be given *some* things that are denied to us. We have so much beauty that Nature balanced things a little by giving the East its song birds."

"Yes," she agreed; "but we have many other birds. The Sagalie Tyee (God) gave us birds for food here, not for song. The winds sing, but cannot feed the Indian people. The waters laugh, but cannot keep us from starving by their pretty voices. So, the Sagalie Tyee gave us the fish and the birds for food—many gray geese, russet pheasants, wild ducks, whistling swans—"

"Oh, Klootchman!" I interrupted, "yesterday I saw a band of magnificent white swans fly directly over the city—seven of them. They were heading for the southeast."

She turned abruptly and looked at me with a half-curious, half-affectionate expression illuminating her rugged old face.

"You see *seven* swans?" she asked, with intense interest.

"Yes," I assured her. "Seven wonderful white swans. They were the most graceful things I ever saw. They sailed overhead like delicate white-winged yachts drifting on the blue sea—the far waterless sea of the skies."

"Very good sign," she said emphatically. "Very great luck for you—for *sure* you count *seven* of them?"

"Yes," I assured her. Then I told her how I happened to be at the door of "my wigwam" when I heard a faint whistle skyward, and looking aloft I saw them—seven white-feathered beauties sailing southward into the lands of sun and warmth. I could picture them idling away the winter in some far southern lagoon, while the lazy tropic weeks drifted by as they waited for the call of the North that would come with the early days of April—the sweet, clear call of the North that would mean mating time—that would mean days of nesting along the reeds and rocks of cooler climes, and a long, joyous summer in the far reaches of the upper Pacific Coast.

I watched them for many moments; their slender white throats were outstretched with the same keen eagerness to reach the southern suns as a finely bred horse displays near the finish of a race. Their shining pinions were like silken sails swelling to the breeze, and lofty as their flight was, I could distinguish a hint of orange from the web of their trailing feet. Their indifference to the city beneath them, their direct, though deliberate course, their unblemished whiteness were like a glimpse of some far perfect thing, that human hands may not defile. Farther and farther they winged their way, fainter and fainter drifted backward their clear whistling, until they were but a blur against the blue, like an echo of a whisper their voices still floated behind them, then a pearl-gray scarf of cloud enveloped them—they were gone.

The Klootchman listened like one absorbed. "*Very* good sign," she repeated, as I concluded my story.

"In what way?" I asked.

"What is it the palefaces call the one who loves you?" she questioned. Then answering her own query with, "Sweetheart—is that not it? Yes? Well, sign is your sweetheart very true to you. He not got two faces, one for you, another for when he is away from you. He's *very* true."

I laughed skeptically. "A woman's sweetheart is never true to her, but a man's always is," I remarked, with a cynicism born of much observation and some little experience.

"You know the big world too well for be happy," she began.

"Oh, I am the happiest-hearted woman alive," I hurried to explain. Then, teasingly, "And I'll be happier still if what you say of the seven swans is *really* true."

"It's true," she replied in a tone that compelled belief. "It is strange thing that you see and talk of seven swans, when an hour ago I speak to you of crippled baby and how the mother-women love them, care for them, protect them. You see—Tillicum (friend), there is a Squamish story—what you call it? Legend? Yes, legend about a crippled child and a band of seven swans."

I edged nearer to her. Then she told me the whimsical tale, while the restless Capilano murmured, and chanted, laughed and rollicked, sang and sobbed out its music far, far below us.

THE LEGEND OF THE SEVEN SWANS

"The little girl was born a cripple. There was no ugliness, nothing crooked in her form, just one little foot that was weak, and limp, and nerveless, and when she learned to walk, this foot trailed slightly behind the other. But, oh! the love of her Squamish mother that hovered over her, protected her, petted her, nursed her, waited on her; it was the all-powerful love of a mother-woman for a weak child, and the baby grew into girlhood, then to womanhood, wrapped around with this wonderful garment of love, as the clinging fragrant moss wraps the foot of a tree.

"Her mother called her 'Kah-lo-ka' (accent on lo), which in the Chinook means 'The Swan,' for the girl was very beautiful. Her face was as a flower, her form slender and filled with grace, only the trailing foot stood between her and the perfection of young womanhood. But her soul was yet more beautiful than her face. She was kind, joyous, laughter-loving. She never said a bitter word, never gave a sneering smile. Her heart was light, her hands skillful, her voice gentle. Her fingers were swift to weave baskets and blankets, her eyes keen and lustrous in selecting the dyes for the quills, and fibers, and furs, for her home-making and her garments, and she loved little children as her mother had done before her.

"And many a brave wanted her for his wife—many a young fisherman, many a warrior, many a trapper, but her heart loved none, until a young hunter came from the North, and said, 'I will be strong for both of us, I will be fleet of foot for both. My arrows are true and never fail, my lodge is filled with soft, warm furs, your frail little feet will rest upon them, and your heart will rest in my heart—will you come?'

"The shadows crossed her face as she looked at her trailing foot. 'But I can never run to meet you when you return from the forest with the deer across your shoulders or the beaver across your arm,' she regretted. 'My step is slow and halting, not swift like the other maidens of my tribe. I can never dance for you at the great potlatches for hours and hours, while the old people sing and the young people admire. I must sit with the old women—alone with the old ones and the ugly ones—alone.'

"'You will never be old, never be ugly,' he assured her. 'Your face and your soul are things of beauty. They, with your laughing heart, will always be young. Your mother named you Kah-lo-ka, The Swan, and you are always that—shall ever be that to me. Come, will you come with me—will you come from your mother's love—to mine?'

"And, womanlike, she went with him and her father's lodge knew her no more.

"But daily her mother would come to see her, to rejoice in the happiness of the young wife—the happiness that made her forget her trailing foot, that made her ever lovely face still more beautiful, and she would call the little bride-wife, 'Be-be, Be-be,' as though she were still her frail baby girl. It is the way with mothers and a crippled child.

"The years drifted on, and Kah-lo-ka bore her hunter husband six beautiful children, but none of them had the trailing foot, nor yet the lovely face of their laughter-loving mother. She had not yet grown old to look upon as the Squamish women are apt to do while even yet young, and her face was like a flower as she sat among the old and ugly at the great potlatches, while the maidens and the young men danced and chanted, and danced again. How often she longed to join them none ever knew, but no shadow ever blurred her eyes, no ache ever entered her always young heart until the day her husband's cousin came, a maiden strong, lithe, tall as the hunter himself, and who danced like the sunlight on the blue waters of the Pacific.

"For hours and hours this cousin would dance tirelessly, and through all the hours he watched her, watched her sway like the branches of the Douglas fir when storm-beaten, watched her agile feet, her swift, light steps, her glorious strength, and when she ceased, Kah-lo-ka's husband and the young braves and warriors gathered about her with gifts of shell necklaces and fair speeches.

"And Kah-lo-ka looked down at her own poor trailing foot—and the laughter died in her eyes. In the lodge with her six little children about her she waited for him many days, many weeks, but the hunter husband had left her for one who had no trailing foot to keep her sitting among the old and the ugly.

"So Kah-lo-ka waited, and waited, long, long years through, and the friends of her youth grew old and wrinkled, her tribes-people grew infirm and feeble with age, but the face of the woman with the trailing foot remained as beautiful, as young, as unlined as when she first met and loved the young hunter, who had gone out of her life many scores of moons ago.

"And far away in his distant lodge the hunter husband grew old and weakened in body and mind; his aim was no longer sure, his eye no longer keen, and at his side sat his cousin, she who was once so light of foot, so joyous in the dance, so strong, and straight, and agile, but the years had weighted her once swift feet, had aged her face, had stooped her shoulders, had stiffened her muscles, her ankles, her hands. Old and wrinkled she crouched in her blanket, for her blood ran slowly, her youth was gone—she danced no more.

"And one day he returned—returned to look upon her beauty, to hear her laughter, and to learn that a true woman's love will keep her young and flowerlike forever. With a great cry he bowed himself before her, and though he was old, and feeble, and ugly, although he was false and had failed her, and had forgotten her—womanlike she outstretched her arms towards him, for was he not the father of her children?

"But the Sagalie Tyee (the Almighty) spoke out of the sky, and His word is law to all races, to all people. 'You shall not have her again O! Hunter,' spoke the Voice. 'You have been untrue. She has been true—untruth cannot mate with truth, dishonor cannot mate with honor, falsity cannot mate with fidelity. I, the Sagalie Tyee, chief of the skies and of earth and of the seas, shall place her and her children where their youth and their beauty and their laughter shall forever taunt and reproach your crooked, misshapen heart. They shall never grow old or ugly, and she with her trailing foot shall become that most beautiful and graceful thing that I have ever created. Watch the morning skies oh! Hunter of the double face, the double heart, and in the first light of the rising sun you will see seven perfect things, Beauty, Grace, Laughter, Youth, Fidelity, Love and Truth—seven glorious things that you have forfeited, have cast aside.'

"In the morning the aged hunter sought Kah-lo-ka's lodge. It was empty, but against the gold of the rising sun there arose a group of seven pearl-white swans. They poised above him for a moment, then winged their way southwards. He watched in an agony of loneliness their graceful flight; he listened in an agony of heartache to their clear, wild piping laughter, that drifted backwards like the notes of a distant flute, his aged eyes watched and watched as those seven beautiful birds sailed away on wings like silken webs, and whose feet trailed a blur of orange against the blue of the morning sky. He bowed his head then—for he knew that those trailing, graceful feet were his Kah-lo-ka's one defect—glorified."

"Do they always travel in flocks of seven?" I asked.

"Not always, but often so," she replied. "So when you count seven white ones, it will be sure to be Kah-lo-ka and her children; that is why I say you have good luck, and a true Sweetheart. It is only an Indian story, but it means much."

"I supposed, Klootchman, it means that like begets like?" I half questioned. "That truth bears truth. That fidelity bears fidelity—is that it?"

"Yes, did not the Sagalie Tyee say that truth could not mate with untruth?" she said very reverently.

THE LEGEND OF LILLOOET FALLS[11]

No one could possibly mistake the quiet little tap at the door. It could be given by no other hand west of the Rockies save that of my old friend the Klootchman. I dropped a lapful of work and sprang to open the door, for the slanting rains were chill outside, albeit the December grass was green and the great masses of English ivy clung wet and fresh as in summer about the low stone wall that ran between my veranda and the street.

"Kla-how-ya, Tillicum!" I greeted, dragging her into the warmth and comfort of my "den," and relieving her of her inseparable basket, and removing her rain-soaked shawl. Before she spoke she gave that peculiar little gesture common to the Indian woman from the Atlantic to the Pacific. She lifted both hands, and with each forefinger smoothed gently along her forehead from the parting of her hair to her temples. It is the universal habit of the red woman, and simply means a desire for neatness in her front locks. I busied myself immediately with the teakettle, for, like all her kind, the Klootchman dearly loves her tea.

The old woman's eyes sparkled as she watched the welcome brewing, while she chatted away in half English, half Chinook, telling me of her doings in all these weeks that I had not seen her. But it was when I handed her a huge old-fashioned breakfast cup fairly brimming with tea as strong as lye that she really described her journeyings.

She had been north to the Skeena River, south to the great "Fair" at Seattle, but, best of all seemingly to her, was her trip into the interior. She had been up the trail to Lillooet in the great "Cariboo" country. It was my turn then to have sparkling eyes, for I traversed that inexpressively beautiful trail five years ago, and the delight of that journey will remain with me for all time.

"And, oh! Tillicum," I cried, "have your good brown ears actually listened to the call of the falls across the canyon[12] – the Falls of Lillooet?"

"My ears have heard them whisper, laugh, weep," she replied in the Chinook.

"Yes," I answered, "they do all those things. They have magic voices—those dear, far-off falls!"

At the word "magic" her keen eyes snapped, she set her empty cup aside and looked at me solemnly.

"Then you know the story—the strange tale?" she asked almost whisperingly.

I shook my head. This was always the crucial moment with my Klootchman, when her voice lowers and she asks if you know things. You must be diplomatic, and never question her in turn. If you do, her lips will close in unbreakable silence.

"I have heard no story, but I have heard the Falls 'whisper, laugh and weep,' that is enough for me," I said, with seeming indifference.

"What do you see when you look at them from across the canyon?" she asked. "Do they look to you like anything else but falling water?"

I thought for a moment before replying. Memory seemed to hold up an indistinct photograph of towering fir-crested heights, where through a broken ridge of rock a shower of silvery threads cascaded musically down, down, down, until they lost themselves in the mighty Fraser,[13] that hurled itself through the yawning canyon stretched at my feet. I have never seen such slender threads of glowing tissue save on early morning cobwebs at sun-up.

"The Falls look like cobwebs," I said, as the memory touched me. "Millions of fine, misty cobwebs woven together."

"Then the legend must be true," she uttered, half to herself. I slipped down on my treasured wolfskin rug near her chair, and with hands locked about my knees, sat in silence, knowing it was the one and only way to lure her to speech. She rose, helped herself to more tea, and with the toe of her beaded moccasin idly stroked one of the wolfskin paws. "Yes," she said, with some decision, "the Indian men of magic say that the falls are cobwebs twisted and braided together."

I nodded, but made no comment; then her voice droned into the broken English that, much as I love it, I must leave to the reader's imagination. "Indian mothers are strange," she began. I nodded again.

"Yes, they are strange, and there is a strange tie between them and their children. The men of magic say they can *see* that tie, though you and I cannot. It is thin, fine, silvery as a cobweb, but strong as the ropes of wild vine that swing down the great canyons. No storm ever breaks those vines; the tempests that drag the giant firs and cedars up by their roots, snap their branches and break their boles, never break the creeping vines. They may be torn from their strongholds, but in the young months of the summer the vine will climb up, and cling again. *Nothing* breaks it. So is the cobweb tie the men of magic see between the Indian mother and her child.

"There was a time when no falls leapt and sang down the heights at Lillooet, and in those days our men were very wild and warlike; but the women were gentle and very beautiful, and they loved and lived and bore children as women have done before, and since.

"But there was one more gentle, more beautiful than all others of the tribe. 'Be-be,' our people call her; it is the Chinook word for 'a kiss.' None of our people knew her real name, but it was a kiss of hers that made this legend, so as 'Be-be' we speak of her.

"She was a mother-woman; but save for one beautiful girl-child, her family of six were all boys—splendid, brave boys, too, but this one treasured girl-child they called 'Morning-mist.' She was little and frail and beautiful, like the clouds one sees at daybreak circling about the mountain peaks. Her father and her brothers loved her, but the heart of Be-be, her mother, seemed wrapped round and about that misty-eyed child.

"'I love you!' the mother would say many times in a day, as she caught the girl-child in her arms. 'And I love you!' the girl-child would answer, resting for a moment against the warm shoulder. 'Little Flower,' the woman would murmur, 'you are morning to me, you are golden midday, you are slumberous nightfall to my heart!'

"So these two loved and lived, mother and daughter, made for each other, shaped into each other's lives as the moccasin is shaped to the foot.

"Then came that long, shadowed, sunless day, when Be-be, returning home from many hours of ollallie picking, her basket filled to the brim with rich fruit, her heart reaching forth to her home even before her swift feet could traverse the trail—found her husband and her boys stunned with a dreadful fear, searching with wild eyes, hurrying feet, and grief-wrung hearts for her little 'Morning-child' who had wandered into the forest while her brothers played—the forest which was deep and dark and dangerous—and had not returned."

The Klootchman's voice ceased. For a long moment she gazed straight before her, then looking at me said:

"You have heard the Falls of Lillooet weep?" I nodded.

"It is the weeping of that Indian mother, sobbing through centuries, that you hear." She uttered the words with a cadence of grief in her voice.

"Hours, nights, days, they searched for the Morning-child," she continued. "And each moment of that unending agony to the mother-woman is repeated to-day in the call, the wail, the everlasting sobbing of the falls. At night the wolves howled up the canyon. 'God of my fathers, keep safe my Morning-child,' the mother would implore. In the glare of day eagles poised, and vultures wheeled above the forest, their hungry claws, their unblinking eyes, their beaks of greed shining in the sunlight. 'God of my fathers, keep safe my Morning-child' was again wrung from the mother's lips. For one long moon, that dawned and shone and darkened, that mother's heart lived out its torture. Then one pale daybreak a great fleet of canoes came down the Fraser River. Those that paddled were of a strange tribe, they spoke in a strange tongue, but their hearts were human, and their skins were of the rich copper-color of the Upper Lillooet country. As they steered downstream, running the rapids, braving the whirlpools, they chanted, in monotone:

"'We have a lost child,
A beautiful lost child.
We love this lost child,
But the heart of the child
Calls the mother of the child.
Come and claim this lost child.'

"The music of the chant was most beautiful, but no music in the world of the white man's Tyee could equal that which rang through the heart of Be-be, the Indian mother-woman.

"Heart upon heart, lips upon lips, the Morning-child and the mother caught each other in embrace. The strange tribe told of how they had found the girl-child wandering fearfully in the forest, crouching from the claws of eagles, shrinking from the horror of wolves, but the mother with her regained treasure in her arms begged them to cease their tales. 'I have gone through agonies enough, oh, my friends,' she cried aloud, 'let me rest from torture now!' Then her people came and made a great feast and potlatch for this strange Upper Lillooet tribe, and at the feast Be-be arose and, lifting the girl-child to her shoulder, she commanded silence and spoke:

"'O Sagalie Tyee (God of all the earth), you have given back to me my treasure; take my tears, my sobs, my happy laughter, my joy—take the cobweb chains that bind my Morning-child and me—make them sing to others, that they may know my gratitude! O Sagalie Tyee, make them sing!' As she spoke, she kissed her child. At that moment the Falls of Lillooet came like a million cobweb strands, dashing and gleaming down the canyon, sobbing, laughing, weeping, calling, singing. You have listened to them."

The Klootchman's voice was still. Outside, the rains still slanted gently, like a whispering echo of the far-away falls. "Thank you, Tillicum of mine; it is a beautiful legend," I said. She did not reply until, wrapped in her shawl, she had clasped my hand in good-bye. At the door she paused: "Yes," she said—"and it is true." I smiled to myself. I love my Klootchman. She is so *very* Indian.

THE LEGEND OF THE ICE BABIES[14]

As you journey across Canada from east to west, and have been absorbed in the beauty of the St. Lawrence, the Great Lakes, the prairies, the Rockies, the Selkirks, and finally the fiercely-rugged grandeur of the Fraser River,[15] as you are nearing the rim of the gentle Pacific, you will pass through one of the most fruitful valleys in all the Great Dominion. Orchards and vineyards, gardens and blossoming flowers stretch on every side, and in the misty distance there circles a band of bubbling mountains, and great armies of the giant Douglas firs and cedars that only the Western slope could ever give birth to. Through this valley stretches many a lazy arm of the sea, but there are also to be found several beautiful little fresh-water lakes. One in particular is remarkably lovely. It is small, and the shores so precipitous that winds seldom ruffle its clear, blue-green waters. The majestic old forest trees, the mosses, the trailing vines, the ferns and bracken crowd so closely down to the margin that they are mirrored in the lake in all their rich coloring and exquisite design. In looking on this secluded beauty one instinctively feels the almost sanctity of purity that can be found only in the undefiled forest lands. Nature has not been molested, and the desecrating hand of man has not yet profaned it. A happy chance had taken me along the shores of this perfect little gem, molded in its rocky setting, and one day when the Klootchman and I sat together on the sands watching the Pacific as it slept under an autumn sun, I spoke to her of the little fresh-water jewel up in the Chilliwack Valley.

"You have seen it?" she asked with great interest. I nodded.

"I am very glad. We Squamish women love it. The mothers love it most. We call it the Lake of the Ice Babies."

I remarked on the beauty of the name, and then on its oddity. "For," I said, "surely it does not freeze there!"

"Yes," she replied, "it always freezes over at least once in the winter, if only for a day. The lake is so still there is no wind now to keep it open from the frost."

I caught at the word "now." "Was there ever a wind there?" I ventured, for one must voice his thoughts delicately if one hopes to extract a tradition from my good, old reticent Klootchman.

"Yes, once it used to be very stormy; terrible gales would get imprisoned in that cup of the mountains, and they would sweep round and round, lashing up the waters of the lake like a chained wild animal," she answered. Then she added that ever-present pitiful remark: "But that was long ago—before the white man came." It has been the redskin's cry for more than a century, that melancholy "before the white man came."

Presently she picked up a handful of silver sand, and while she trailed it leisurely from palm to palm, threading it between her thin, dark fingers, her voice fell into the sonorous monotone, the half whisper, half chant, in which she loved to relate her quaint stories, while I sat beside her, sun-bathed and indolent, and listened to the

"LEGEND OF THE ICE BABIES."

"There were two of them—two laughing, toddling little children but just released from the bands of their cradle baskets. Girls, both of them, and cousins, of the same age, happy-hearted and playful, and the treasures of their mothers' lives. It was a warm, soft day of late autumn, a day like this, when not a leaf stirred, not a wave danced, that the wandering band of Squamish encamped in the bluffs about the little lake, and prepared to stay the night. The men cut branches and built a small lodge. The women gathered firewood and cooked venison and grouse, and the children and babies played about, watching their elders and sometimes replenishing the camp fires. The evening wore on, and with the twilight came a gentle rising wind, that whispered at first through the pines and cedars like a mother singing very softly to her sleeping child. Then the wind-voice grew louder, it began to speak harshly. The song in it died, and the mighty voices of the trees awoke like the war cry of many tribes in battle. The little lake began to heave and toss, then lash itself into a fury; whirlpools circled, waves rose and foamed and fought each other. The gale was shut within the cup of the shores and could not release itself.

"In the stir of fitting the camp for the night and protecting the frail lodge against destruction, the two girl babies were unnoticed, and hand in hand they wandered with halting, childish steps to the brink of the shore. Before them the waves rose and fell, frothed and whirled like some playful wild thing, and their little hands longed to grasp the curling eddies, the long lines of combers and breakers. Laughingly the babies slid down the fern-covered banks and stepped into the shallow waters at the margin, then wandered out over the surface of the lake, frolicking and playing in the tossing waves and whirlpools, but neither little body sank. The small feet skimmed the angry waters like feathers dropped from the wings of some passing bird, for under those dancing innocent feet the Sagalie Tyee had placed the palms of his hands, and the soft baby soles rested and romped in an anchorage greater than the most sheltered harbor in all the vast Pacific coast.

"From the shore their mothers watched them, first in an agony of fear, then with wonder, then with reverence.

"'The Great Tyee holds them in his hand,' spoke one with whispered awe.

"'Listen, he speaks.'

"'Will you give these babies to me, oh, mothers of the Squamish?' said a voice from above the clouds. 'To me to keep for you, always as babies, always as laughing, happy little ones, or will you take them back to yourselves and the shore, to have them grow away from their innocence, their childhood; to have them suffer in heart and body as women must ever suffer; to have them grow ill with age, old with pain and years, and then to die, to leave you lonely, and to go where you may not follow and care for them and love them? Which will you, oh, mothers of the Squamish? If you love yourselves best, you shall have your babies again. If you love your babies most, you will give them to me.'

"And the two mothers answered as one voice: 'Keep them always as babies, always innocent, always happy—take them, oh, Great Tyee, for we love them more than we love ourselves!'

"The winds began to sob lower. The waves ceased swirling, the roar of tempestuous waters calmed to whispers, then lulled into perfect tranquility, but the babies still played and laughed on its blue surface. The hands of the Sagalie Tyee still upheld them.

"That night the lake froze from shore to shore. When morning dawned the two mothers were 'wakened by a voice that spoke very gently, but it came from invisible lips, and they knew it to be a message from the Tyee of the Happy Hunting Grounds. 'The babies are yours forever,' he said, 'although I, the Sagalie Tyee of all men, shall keep them in the hollow of my hands. I have bridged the waters with eternal stillness, for their little bodies are young and tender, their little feet too soft for rough waves, their little hands too frail to battle rough winds. No storm shall ever again fret this lake, no gale churn its surface to fury. I have tempered their little world to their baby needs, and they shall live in shelter for all time. Rise, oh, mothers of the Squamish, and look upon your gifts to me, which I shall keep in trust for you forever.'

"The women arose, and creeping to the door of the lodge beheld their babies dancing on the frail, clear ice far out across the lake. They could see the baby smiles, hear the baby laughter, and they knew their mother-hearts would never mourn for their children's lost innocence or lost babyhood. And each year since that time, when the first frosts of late autumn touch the little lake with a film of ice, the babies come to play and laugh, like elves of the air, upon its shining surface. They have never grown older, never grown less innocent. They are pure as the ice their soft, small feet touch with dancing step, and so they will remain for all time."

The silver sands were still filtering between her brown fingers as the Klootchman ended the tale, and I still lay watching the sunlight glint on the lazy Pacific, and wondering if it, too, were not the dancing feet of some long-ago children.

"Do people ever see these ice babies now?" I asked dreamily.

"Only those who are nearing the country of the Great Tyee," she replied. "As one nears that land one becomes again as a little child, one's eyes grow innocent, one's heart trusting, one's life blameless, as they go down the steep shores of age to the quiet, windless, waveless lake where they must rest forever in the hollows of the Great Tyee's hands, for he has kept these pure Ice Babies there for many hundreds of years because he wishes his Indian children to become like them before they cross the lake to the Happy Hunting Grounds on the far shore."

She was silent for a moment, then added: "I am growing old, Tillicum (friend); perhaps I shall see them—soon."

INTERVIEWS

INTERVIEW WITH RICK MONTURE

Dr. Rick Monture is Mohawk, Turtle clan, from Six Nations of the Grand River Territory, and an Associate Professor in the Department of English and Cultural Studies and Indigenous Studies at McMaster University. He is the author of *We Share Our Matters: Two Centuries of Writing and Resistance at Six Nations of the Grand River* (2014).

This excerpt is taken from two recorded interviews with Alix Shield, the first taking place at SFU Burnaby by phone on 25 August 2017, and the second in person at McMaster University's Indigenous Student Services space on 25 October 2017.

AS: Do you have a sense of the community's attitudes towards E. Pauline Johnson as a writer? And towards the relationship between Johnson and the Capilanos?

RM: I'd say at Six Nations people are quite proud of Pauline as a personality, but they're not so familiar with her work anymore. A lot of people are puzzled by her, I think even while she was alive. Her legacy now is her family's house called Chiefswood—the house is still very much a presence on the reserve. People know about it. We've put a lot of money into restoring it and keeping up the grounds. It's quite a showpiece, and we take a lot of pride in keeping it up. So her legacy and her presence is very much around and part of the community; her written legacy not so much. But how much do people know anybody's literary work from the 1800s anywhere, right? It's not that celebrated or talked about. However, there's a small but vocal group of us who have championed her writing for a long time and continue to do so. I think people are sympathetic towards her now. I know growing up they saw her—I wouldn't say as a sellout, or anything like that. But because her connection to the reserve was so minimal, especially in the last few years of her life, there wasn't much really to talk about. We're pretty sure that she never did a reading that we know of on the Reserve. We haven't found any record. I've talked to Tom Hill, Paula Whitlow, and others who have dealt many years with her archive, but they've never come across any kind of evidence that she gave a reading "at home." Which is interesting. She probably did a reading in Brantford or in Hamilton. I'm sure a handful of people might have found their way out for that, but travel was difficult then.

AS: What do people from the Six Nations community know about the Capilanos?

RM: People here haven't really paid a whole lot of attention to *Legends of Vancouver* because it deals with another nation in a faraway place. But people have focused on the Iroquoian content of her work, which is considerable for sure—especially the early stuff, like her poems about Joseph Brant or Red Jacket.[1] I focused on some of this material a little bit in my book to give it some cultural relevance,[2] and I find a lot of her language kind of puzzling at times. Bending towards stereotypes if you will. In doing work with her stuff, I sometimes wonder: is she just pandering to audiences, or does she really believe this, has she bought into this? Or is she just fulfilling audience expectations of what Native people were about?

One of the stories that I take up in my book, which I still like a lot and teach when I can is "Wehro's Sacrifice."[3] I find it an intriguing story because she does accurately describe the really important ceremony that takes place in our community every year. The particular part of it that she talks about, the burning of the white dog, was a big part of that ceremony for many, many years but had been outlawed—well not outlawed—but was dropped from the program in the 1930s. So what she's talking about is an accurate thing, it's not made up by any means. She's taken some poetic licence to embellish the story of the little boy and his dog, but I think she gets some things right in terms of the openness with which our people invited other religious men into our ceremonies. We were always an inclusive people—we still are—but our ceremonies have, for about fifty years now (since the 1960s), been closed off to non-Native people. But for years non-Native people were welcomed into our ceremonies. And she documents that time. It's not without its problems, especially the stereotypical language she includes—you know, she talks about weird, mournful chanting of the singers, and this and that. If I didn't know any better it would paint this weird, exotic image of what it is that we do and did back then. But I think the story itself about self-sacrifice and being proud of your spiritual traditions is neat, considering that time. But in typical Pauline style she's presenting both sides, and that's what makes her so compelling for us today. What did she really think? I don't know what she really thought.

AS: Can you tell me a bit about your relationship with Johnson's life and work?

RM: I grew up on the Reserve, and we'd visit her home and everyone was afraid of it because it wasn't very well-kept at a particular time when we were school kids. It was always considered haunted and it probably still is. But I've been around there a lot, and it doesn't seem nearly as dark and dreary as it once did—it's been nicely restored.

I continue to teach her stuff, though I pick and choose the poems. Some of it isn't that teachable because to do the cultural-historical explanation of the context of what she's getting at is difficult, and kind of bogs down the story. I've taught mostly the Iroquoian poems and I've written about them in my book a little bit. I sort of scratch my head as to whether she really believed that assimilation was best for our people, or if she was very proud of our traditions and history.

There's always been two segments on the Reserve—the Traditional and the Christian community in our territory. And it's still that way. From everything I've ever heard, we were always very tolerant of each other, the Christian and Traditional people, and still are to this day. But if you were to read other anthropologists and historians in the last century or so, you'd hear otherwise. They represent us as a divided community around religious differences, and that's not really true.

My own family is of Traditional and Christian backgrounds throughout, as are many, many people. To me it was always about how well you get along; it doesn't really matter what you do or don't do on Sunday. It's about tolerance for each other and respect for people's religious beliefs. Which I think is very much a part of our community, even though it may not appear like that to outsiders sometimes. A lot of the conflicts are mostly in a joking way, you know—at the end of the day we all get along pretty well. Pauline did a pretty good job of documenting some of that stuff. I was just telling you about "Wehro's Sacrifice," about the pride in our traditions that our traditional people carry with them. They're unashamed of stuff even though we were made to feel ashamed. They were not.

As surrounded as we are by the most populated region in Canada, here in Southern Ontario, we do maintain these ceremonies. Probably all the ceremonies that were around in Pauline's time are still conducted throughout the year in our community and in our languages. And that's something to be proud of, because again it's a responsibility that our people have felt for a long time. Her grandfather, John "Smoke" Johnson, was an advocate for tradition, so she would have grown up around it. It would have been during her time, in the late 1800s, when the people in the community would have been asking: how do you navigate tradition, history, progress, assimilation, and survival—all that kind of stuff. In many ways she probably didn't see a real threat to language and culture and tradition the way we face it now in 2017 and have for the last half century. Back then all of our things were pretty strong. So she was documenting both sides of that, reflecting a community that was partly Christian and assimilated, and partly Traditional and—I don't want to use the word conservative because that paints a different kind of picture—but adaptable, and proud of our culture and traditions. And this was through one of the worst eras of the Indian Act and residential schools. Our people have survived and shown remarkable resilience to keep these traditions alive despite a lot of these measures taken against us and our traditional government. All of this was in place when Pauline was alive.

After twenty years of working with her stuff, I'm still trying to figure her out. Which I think is great—it shows real substance and depth to her work that I find quite fulfilling and fun to dig into. If it was one-dimensional, then that would be easy—we'd have her all figured out. But 100 years after she's gone, we're still talking about her, and we're seeing a lot of what she was concerned with in her lifetime being talked about today. The roles and importance of Indigenous women, identity issues, non-recognition of history and treaties—all that stuff. She addressed all those things 100 and more years ago. We're still talking about them, still trying to figure them out.

People say she was too soft in her politics, and I've said this a bit too. But I also know that it would have been difficult to really stand up and voice real criticism at that time because she wanted to be published—she was trying to survive. As I was saying earlier, I'm not really sure what she actually thought. I'm sure what she said or thought was very tempered by her need to sell tickets, publish her books, and keep everybody happy. She couldn't be too critical. She chose her moments, and I think she chose them pretty well. That's why I hold her up as someone who fought the good fight, in her time, when very few Native people had that stage—literally had that stage, let alone a woman. And so that really excites students, Native and non-Native, about an early feminist. All the travelling she did by herself, didn't feel the need to marry—or maybe she did, we don't know, her love life is a whole other mystery to us all. But yeah, she's a really compelling, intriguing figure that we're still trying to figure out all these years later.

AS: Definitely. In your article, "Beneath the British Flag: Iroquois and Canadian Nationalism in the Work of Pauline Johnson and Duncan Campbell Scott" (2001), you talk about Johnson's story, "A Royal Mohawk Chief." This story concludes *Legends of Vancouver* with an idealistic, reconciliatory gesture between the English and the Iroquois, and your article discusses how this comes across as disingenuous. Could you speak to that?

RM: Sure. It's quite accurate the way she brings her father into the story; that much is true. But he wasn't a big deal Chief. At the time, he was more of an interpreter; there are stories about how his mother forced his way into a leadership position. That's 150 years ago so we can't really know, but she takes a lot of licence with his portrayal. It is true that her grandfather and father played a role during that time in 1869;[4] but that was essentially a Six Nations response to the recent Confederation of Canada, and they were building relationships, reminding the Crown of our ally-to-ally relationship way back before Confederation.

Johnson had an imperfect understanding of our culture and ceremony; she wasn't raised traditionally, and she wasn't that interested in understanding or portraying traditional culture accurately. You see it in some of the language in "A Royal Mohawk Chief" where she mentions the "weird monotones" and the adjectives she uses to describe Iroquois ceremony. It's a complete misrepresentation of what took place that day. She makes it sound like Prince Arthur was raised above all else. And that's wrong.

And so this story would have been a reminder—we call it polishing the chain—that we were once again reaffirming those ties in the wake of Confederation. We're not Canadian, we are a sovereign nation—remember, England? That's what that whole moment was about, and that's not how she portrays it. I don't know if she's trying to make that connection between Six Nations and England again—isn't that where she met Joe Capilano?

AS: In London, yes.

RM: So I don't know if she's trying to harken back to all of our ties to the Crown, but that's imperfect too given B.C.'s history. Maybe she just needed a place for that story to appear, so it got tacked on at the end. It really has no connection to *Legends of Vancouver*.

I can see why she sort of sprinkles, "well my people do this or that" in a couple of the other stories; it makes some sense, even though when she does this it's often wrong. There's one point where she talks about twins as being unwelcome, and known as "rabbits" ("The Recluse" 88). Well, I've never heard that. My dad's an identical twin. We've never heard that. No one's ever said that to me, and they've never heard it said. So I don't know where she is getting that from. It's moments like that where you just raise your eyebrows.

AS: The book has been in publication now for over 100 years, and yet no edition thus far has attempted to involve members of the Sḵwx̱wú7mesh or Mohawk communities. What are your thoughts and/or experiences in regards to community-based projects today, and the difficulty in negotiating the demands of the institution/academia while respecting the cultural protocols of Indigenous communities?

RM: I can't speak for the accuracy of her portrayal of the Sḵwx̱wú7mesh traditions, that's for Rudy to take up, but if it's anything like the way in which she portrays traditional Iroquoian culture, there are problems. It seems that she gets the general philosophies right about our ceremonies—thankfulness, inclusivity, men's roles and women's roles—but she doesn't go into depth about these things either. Yet I think it's important that they be documented.

It's always difficult to talk about cultural representation when there's a language barrier. Even if she's transcribing or relaying Sḵwx̱wú7mesh stories in English, there's always a kind of translation barrier, right? That's huge. Even the way stories work: they're not always accurate portrayals of authentic narratives, because it's always depending on the teller. At home there were always moments in which traditional folks—let's call them informants—would talk to ethnologists and anthropologists, but they didn't always give them the most accurate information. They weren't going to give away too much of our knowledge. Who knows if Pauline might have heard some of that. That's how the misinformation gets generated and perpetuated, because it was never told to be completely accurate to begin with, and they had their reasons, right? They didn't want to share too much. Some of it was sacred knowledge, and not for a general public. So they would self-censor. And maybe that's what's happening here.

AS: I'm wondering if you could speak about doing this type of work, about republishing and re-framing a book that's been in publication for such a long time. What are your thoughts on this as a scholarly practice, as something that we can do to re-centre the stories and roles of Indigenous storytellers?

RM: That's a good question, and a big question. That's part of the larger project of The People and the Text.[5] I think it's vital that we keep these texts in circulation, and keep talking about the old ones.

I see the use and value of having annotated critical editions; I can see *Legends of Vancouver* appearing alongside some essays by Indigenous folks that talk about Pauline's legacy, and maybe the cultural inaccuracies or accuracies, that kind of thing, or modern-day retellings of those same stories, or any number of things. I know that I would certainly welcome the opportunity to do that in an Iroquoian setting where you separate her Iroquoian poems and stories into one text that then is followed by essays that take those things up critically and challenge some of the more inaccurate language that I've described. There's a way of being critical but also holding her up as someone who was telling these stories and finding beauty and truth in the ceremonial aspects.

INTERVIEW WITH RUDY REIMER

Dr. Rudy Reimer (Yumks) is an Indigenous Archaeologist from Sḵwx̱wú7mesh Úxwumixw who implements Indigenous perspectives into his research. He is an Associate Professor in the Department of Archaeology at Simon Fraser University, where he is currently holding a Canada Research Chair position in Community Engagement. Dr. Reimer is also the host of *Wild Archaeology* on the Aboriginal Peoples Television Network.

This excerpt is taken from a longer interview with Alix Shield, recorded in-person at SFU's Burnaby campus on 5 December 2017.

AS: Do you have a sense of how the Sḵwx̱wú7mesh community feels about this collection of stories, the *Legends of Vancouver* stories, in general?

RR: I think overall in the Sḵwx̱wú7mesh Nation community the work by Pauline Johnson and the *Legends of Vancouver* book are fairly well-respected. There's a certain amount of pride there, that going that far back, there was someone, you know another First Nations person, who had an interest in Sḵwx̱wú7mesh/Coast Salish culture and was accepted into the community. The book, I know, is on many shelves within the Sḵwx̱wú7mesh nation community; having gone and done interviews myself, people go to their bookshelf and go "oh, is this what you're talking about?," and I say yes, but no, at the same time. And that's just the result of various historical contingencies of colonization. I've heard in other communities where I've been, people will bring down another James Teit book, on ethnography in the Interior, and go "here, this is the source," and it's an interesting process where those people know what's in that book, but they don't feel authoritative enough to speak about it. Very often people will grab a book like *Legends of Vancouver* and go "okay, it's in here, some of our history." Yes, there's a certain amount of pride that there's something to access. But I think with younger generations people in the Sḵwx̱wú7mesh nation are questioning what might be in there and in other texts, like *The Salish People* by Charles Hill-Tout, or what other anthropologists like Wayne Suttles and others have written about Sḵwx̱wú7mesh and other Coast Salish communities. I think maybe the appreciation for *Legends of Vancouver* with younger generations might be substantially less, or they might just not know about the book, because it's over a hundred years old.

AS: The next question is about the Chinook jargon. I'm wondering what your sense is of the use of Chinook jargon within the Sḵwx̱wú7mesh community. Is it still a language known or used? Do you think that Chief Joe Capilano's or Mary Capilano's use of Chinook to communicate with Johnson was reflective of a wider phenomenon or practice during the early twentieth century?

RR: I think definitely it was. And if we go further back—I'm thinking as an archaeologist here—talking with people in various communities, prior to contact with Europeans, people in Sḵwx̱wú7mesh or Sechelt or Musqueam or up in Stó:lō or even Lil'wat and other places, people in our communities didn't speak just one language. People were involved, either through exchange of goods or even through conflict, or more often likely through family connections to these different places. If your son or daughter would marry off into another group, you would come to know that family, and you'd come to know their language. Our languages were similar, but they were distinct. So prior to contact I think people in our communities spoke multiple languages, similar to modern-day Europe where someone living in Germany probably knows Italian, Swiss, French, and English, as an example. But when Europeans showed up, it was an entirely different ball game, because there was the advent of the Maritime fur trade in the early 1800s. There were Americans, Russians, British, and Spanish, a multitude of people from totally foreign places speaking different languages. And so that's where Chinook comes in. I believe its origins are down around the Columbia River. It was a language mixed of Salishan, French, English—it's a really interesting mish-mash. It became heavily relied upon and quickly learned by many people who were involved in these endeavours.

Also at that time there was a lot of social, political, and population change. There was the smallpox and other epidemics that came in and decimated our populations. There were changes in settlement patterns, where villages were abandoned and others sprung up, or congregated together. And so there was a need for a language to converse amongst multiple communities. I think it grew organically and served a purpose probably for a number of generations. But in my lifetime, no one really speaks Chinook. I remember growing up in Sḵwx̱wú7mesh, we would use certain words—we thought they were cool, but we never really knew what they meant. But there are no "fluent" speakers, and today people in the community are more interested in reviving our language, and that's very active with some of my relatives. That's also happening in other communities as well.

As an anthropologist/archaeologist, or even as an historian, we have to be wary about the telling of a story or history by someone speaking in a given language—whether it be Sḵwx̱wú7mesh, or Chinook, or English. The way they tell it and the choice of words are very important. If that's going through the ear of a translator, and then to a third person—so from Chief Joe Capilano, or Mary, to Pauline—there may be changes. And what words are stressed, because I've heard language speakers say, "In Sḵwx̱wú7mesh we don't have a word for that," and so something is substituted or changed. By the time it gets to someone like Pauline, she is writing notes or drawing from memory, which is probably a reflection of how she was brought up at Six Nations. That's oral history. She may have had a slightly different process as well, of taking in those stories, remembering them, and then writing them down. There may have been changes, there may have been embellishments, or stressing the importance of one thing more than something else. That's something from my archaeological training that I've been trained to be wary of.

It's interesting to look at the version of a story in *Legends of Vancouver*, and if there are the same stories, published or unpublished, elsewhere. You can put them side-by-side and go, "this is the same story but it's being told in different ways." And to some people that might be a very troublesome thing to deal with, but in essence when you boil down those histories, those narratives, what is the essence of the story? What's being stressed? It gets down to who is telling the history, and what they are trying to convey to the person who is learning or interested in it. And that's the process we need to be wary about. If you have three or four different versions of a story, that's not necessarily a bad thing; every oral history, our history, has multiple layers. This is why we need to consider place names, and the names of people, and where they're from, to give us insight about how those stories are told.

AS: The book has been in publication now for over one hundred years—it was published first in 1911—and yet no edition thus far has attempted to involve members of the Sḵwx̱wú7mesh or Mohawk communities. What are your thoughts/experiences in regard to community-based projects today, and the difficulties of negotiating the demands of the institution while also respecting the cultural protocols of these Indigenous communities?

RR: I think what you're doing is great. It's a big endeavour. I'm glad to know you're working with the Mathias family in the community, that's a great starting point. And there are other people too, I'm sure they have some relation and would like to be involved. But I don't think it would be negative. I think people would welcome that. I've seen that change throughout my career, over the last twenty years in the Sḵwx̱wú7mesh community, where I'm going back to my community and saying "I'm an archaeologist, I would like to talk to you about this" and they go "oh, what are you going to do, dig up my ancestors?" There's been a change historically, and people in the community have a better sense of who historians are, anthropologists, archaeologists, or other academics in different disciplines. There's a better sense of trust, maybe? Maybe that's a strong word. But acceptance, because I think they've seen, not just through myself but other researchers making the attempts—successful attempts—of learning the protocols, of going about things the right way. And I understand that you're doing that, and so coming at it from that direction, not just sort of bombing into the community saying "I'm going to do this, and I just need to check off my boxes, see you later" or "I'm going to republish the book, maybe make some money out of it, and you're not going to get anything," right? So we do things differently. Which is good. The book being republished, I think you mentioned under a different name—*Legends of the Capilano*—would go a long way; not just within the Sḵwx̱wú7mesh community, but other neighbouring communities, because Joe Capilano had relations to other places. But I can say with some degree of confidence that within the Sḵwx̱wú7mesh community it would be very interesting, particularly for older people in the community, who are probably more aware of the book. And maybe having a Foreword or a section where the family can come together and become part of the book. I've seen that open doors to older texts. I'm looking at my bookshelf here at the *Conversations with Khahtsahlano*—I would love for someone to tackle that book, to literally tear it apart and glue it back together. Because a book like that was created haphazardly, where there's two indexes. It's confusing to go through, but when you learn the system of how to get through it, there's some really good information in there. Pauline's work, though, is a lot easier—as a version of our history, it's got a historical legacy that people can look at and create a sense of curiosity for themselves and say, "I've heard that story but it was told differently. Why is this version here?" At first people might be confused, but as people think about it more, they'll realize, "oh okay, I can go and talk to so-and-so about this," and I think that just engages people more into learning our history.

AS: And as a follow-up to that, thinking about how the book has been in publication for so long, and has always been in the hands of non-Indigenous editors and publishers?

RR: That's the historical legacy of a lot of academia. You know, archaeology was the bad poster-child for decades, right? We archaeologists went and dug up burials and other things without consent. It was that criticism from Indigenous communities that forced the discipline to change, and thankfully the discipline has changed. So what we have now in archaeology, working with Indigenous communities is called "Indigenous Archaeology." There are guidelines and ethics, and standards of practice. I see this happening in other disciplines. Scholars are realizing, "okay, if we want to move forward, this is the way we have to do things." And if it's publishing or re-publishing a book, having knowledge about the community protocols and processes, I think that's very important. As long as that's followed, I don't think there will be any issues.

AS: I know you've done some work on the "Sea Serpent" story. In Johnson's story, "The Sea-Serpent" (107), she writes about the vice of "avarice," or greed, and in the story she likens this idea of greed to a slimy, two-headed sea-serpent that can only be destroyed by a warrior who embodies upstanding morals and virtues. Are there are any other versions of this story that you are familiar with? And does her interpretation of the story resonate with the version(s) that you know?

RR: Yes, well partially it does, and again there are multiple versions of that narrative. The one that I tell is to the place names, to the archaeological sites, that are along the eastern flank, the shores of Eastern Howe Sound. These places, you can't understand their meaning, their literal translations don't make any sense, until you knit them together with the narrative of Sinulhkai and Xwechtaal. Pauline's version is correct, where Xwechtaal is the warrior brandishing the weapons of purity and strength and vitality, and in the version that I tell I agree with that. That's something he had to achieve through a lot of training, physically, mentally, spiritually, and emotionally. He had to go into the mountains, into the lakes, into the saltwater, and get the powers from all of those different places to be able to take on something so large and powerful. Pauline probably used the term "avarice" or greed because that is a very potent thing that is associated with bad things. But in the versions I've always heard, and what I've been told, is that the serpent has two heads for a reason. It's sort of an analog, or for lack of better words, there's your good side and your bad side, and there's a centre where they come together. And so whenever you look at how Sinulhkai and Xwechtaal are portrayed in art, there's always the two heads, and it comes together in the middle and there's usually a face—and that's typically Xwechtaal. That's the coming together, where you always have some good, you always have some bad, and it's about finding that balance within your life, through doing similar training—through bathing or fasting, going into the saltwater, encountering animals, knowing about plants and about our landscape. That's how you figure out how to find balance in your own life.

In Pauline's version, greed was probably the most powerful word at the time, because there were changes in our economy, there were changes in flux with Christianity, the missionaries, and the residential schools, right? I remember going to Catholic school as a child, and the first thing you learn is that greed is bad. These things are hammered into you. Whereas I think traditionally it would have been different things. It goes back again to that process of when someone comes to you and asks, "can you tell me that story?" And you say, "well, why do you want to hear it?" and you get a sense from that person of what they're about, or what they are seeking. And then you can tell the story in a certain way, so that they can get something out of it. That's why we have multiple versions of that story. It's about who is telling the story, and who they are telling it to. And who is the bigger audience.

In the version I tell, Xwechtaal cuts off the Sinulhkai's heads, and those are islands just off Whytecliff Park in West Vancouver. When the tide is low, there's a little bridge that goes out and connects the islands to the land. But when the tide comes up, that's the history of the serpent getting its head cut off. There's another version of the story of Sinulhkai and Xwechtaal over at Bunsen Lake and in Indian Arm. It's a very similar story, but it's different, because their version reflects their history and where they are located. It's a big story all up and down the coast. When I was up at Tla'amin territory up on the Sunshine Coast many years ago, I went on a little tour and one of the community members pointed out a rock ardament or pictograph. He goes, "that's the Sinulhkai and this is where it met its end." And I was like, "we have pretty much the exact same story in Sk̲wx̲wú7mesh." But they have a slightly different version.

AS: The stories collected in *Legends of Vancouver* are essentially Sk̲wx̲wú7mesh stories reinterpreted through Johnson's own Mohawk/English imagination and memory. Do you recognize these stories as Sk̲wx̲wú7mesh stories?

RR: Yes and no, I guess. I guess no because I've heard different versions, and that probably gets back to my own family history and experiences. But I'm sure that other people in the Sḵwx̱wú7mesh Nation community would say yes, and I don't think there's any definitive yes or no to that. Again, it gets back to why she was accepted by the people in the community—she was essentially adopted in, and she's still known and respected today, and I have no problem with that. I think she just went through a different process than what we do in modern day, and that's a challenge for us as scholars, looking at these historical texts and thinking, "how did this come together, and under what circumstances?"

AS: Is there anything that we haven't touched on that you would like to say in conclusion?

RR: I think this could be the interesting start to a whole career—if one chose to go about doing this. There are multiple texts like this that could be examined or re-evaluated; and I'm glad you're doing it. It's timely. It will be interesting, and a good contribution. And it resonates with the philosophy of how I do archaeology now. You know, earlier in my career, I would go and dig up sites, and collect things and bring them back. I, and many others throughout Sḵwx̱wú7mesh territory have done that, and there's this huge collection of stuff up in my lab, and I said to the community, "I'm not going to dig anything up anymore." And they said, "why not?" And I said, "there's just too much here to look at." And so my form of "texts" are different than yours—you're looking at books, and I'm looking at stone tools. For you there are multiple texts out there, and for me there are multiple boxes of tools. It's good that we are at a point in academia that we can realize the importance of re-evaluating and revisiting some of this older stuff. It keeps that stuff alive. For me, that stuff is not just collecting dust in a box. It's stuff I can talk about in a publication, or through presentations to the community, or involve youth, or even grad students so that somebody gets something out of it. Keep it relevant.

GLOSSARY

"Yet I knew that my Chinook salutation would be a drawbridge by which I might hope to cross the moat into his castle of silence."

—Johnson, "The Grey Archway"

Chinook is a hybridized trade language that came into common use in the Pacific Northwest during the nineteenth to early-twentieth centuries as a means of communication across cultures. It comes from an amalgamation of language patterns among the Nootka and Coast Salish nations, as well as French and English. As Edward Harper Thomas argues in *Chinook: A History and Dictionary* (1935), "the Jargon was so widely used because—though short on beauty and refinement of detail—it was able to communicate successfully between persons of different tribes, nationalities, and races" (ix). Thus, the language developed from practical uses and often served as a kind of "drawbridge" between cultures. Those words marked with an asterisk (*) come from the additional legends narrated by Mary Capilano.

***Be-be:** a kiss

chickimin: money

hyiu:[1] much, plenty, abundance

[1] In Thomas's dictionary, this word is spelled "hiyu"; this spelling is also replicated in the 1990 Quarry Press edition of *Legends* in the book's Glossary (although spelled "hyiu" where it appears in the text).

hyiu chickimin: plenty of money

hyiu muck-a-muck: plenty of food

hykwa: large shell-money

***Kah-lo-ka:** a swan

kla-how-ya: good day/how do you do, friends?; (used in phrase, "kla-how-ya, tillicums?")

klootchman: a woman

Leloo: the timber-wolf or the big grey wolf

muck-a-muck: food

ollallie (or o-lil-lie): berries, fruit

potlatch: a gift, and to give

Sagalie Tyee: God, the Chief above, the Great Creator

Salt chuck: saltwater, the sea

Salt-chuck Oluk: sea-serpent (definition provided in-text in "The Sea-Serpent")

Shak-shak: the Hawk (definition provided in-text in "The Sea-Serpent")

skookum chuck: rapids

skookum tumtum: a brave spirit

Tenas Tyee: Little Chief (definition provided in-text in "The Sea-Serpent")

Tillicum (or tillikum): friend

Tyee: a chief or superior

Sources: Gill, John Kaye. *Gill's dictionary of the Chinook Jargon: with Examples of Use in Conversation and Notes Upon Tribes and Tongues*. Portland: J.K. Gill & Co., 1902.

Thomas, Edward Harper. *Chinook: A History and Dictionary of the Northwest Coast Trade Jargon*. Oregon: Metropolitan Press, 1935.

ACKNOWLEDGEMENTS

I am thankful for the guidance and support I've received along the way, and wish to give special thanks to Carole Gerson, Deanna Reder, Sophie McCall, Margery Fee, Kate Hennessy, Linda Quirk, Jolene Cumming, Rick Monture, Rudy Reimer, Warren Cariou, Jill McConkey, and everyone at UMP. I am particularly grateful to the late Gregory Younging for supporting this work, and for inviting me to speak about *Legends* at the Indigenous Editors Circle in August 2017. I also owe thanks to Myron Groover and the staff at the McMaster University Archives for graciously hosting me during a month-long research trip in 2017, and to the staff at SFU's Special Collections library for digitizing the book covers included in this edition. Thanks also to MONOVA Archives of North Vancouver, the Vancouver Public Library, the City of Vancouver Archives, and the University of British Columbia Library Rare Books and Special Collections for providing access to their collections.

I would like to thank the Mathias family, descendants of Chief Joe Capilano and Mary Agnes Capilano, for their support and kindness over the past five years. As per the family's wishes, all royalties from the sale of this book will go to The Chief Joe Mathias BC Aboriginal Scholarship Fund.

To Agi, Rocky, Gerda, Rose, Katie, Mandy, Florence, Cody, Dulcie, Ellan, and others: This book is dedicated to you and your great-great grandparents. I raise my hands to you all. Huy chexw.

NOTES

Introduction

1 Throughout this introduction, I employ a range of terms when referring to members of Indigenous Nations, reflecting specific contexts of use. For example, I use the terms "Mohawk" and "Iroquois" when referring to E. Pauline Johnson and her writing, using the terms that she would have used to describe herself. Today, the term "Kanien'kehá:ka" is being used instead of "Mohawk" to describe the Mohawk people, or People of the Flint. See Taiaiake Alfred, *Peace, Power, Righteousness: An Indigenous Manifesto* (Don Mills: Oxford University Press, 1999), xxv. And the term "Haudenosaunee" is used to refer to the Iroquois or Six Nations. See Rick Monture, *We Share Our Matters: Two Centuries of Writing and Resistance at Six Nations of the Grand River* (Winnipeg: University of Manitoba Press, 2014), xi. I use these terms when referring to these communities at present time.

2 Maria Campbell, Keynote, Indigenous Literary Studies Association (ILSA) Conference, UBC First Nations House of Learning, Vancouver, BC, 8 June 2019.

3 The interview with Rick Monture took place over two recorded sessions—the first was by phone on 25 August 2017, and the second was in-person at McMaster University's Indigenous Student Services space on 25 October 2017. The interview with Rudy Reimer took place in person on 5 December 2017 at SFU's Burnaby campus. Edited transcripts from these interviews are included in this edition.

4 Betty Keller, *Pauline: A Biography of Pauline Johnson* (Vancouver: Douglas and McIntyre, 1981), 7, 47.

5 Veronica Strong-Boag and Carole Gerson, *Paddling Her Own Canoe: The Times and Texts of E. Pauline Johnson (Tekahionwake)* (Toronto: University of Toronto Press, 2000), 116–17.

6 Johnson's "A Strong Race Opinion" was first reprinted in 2000 in Misao Dean's *Early Canadian Short Stories: Short Stories in English Before World War I* (Ottawa: Tecumseh Press) and in 2002 in Carole Gerson and Veronica Jane Strong-Boag's *E. Pauline Johnson, Tekahionwake: Collected Poems and Selected Prose* (Toronto: UTP); it has since been reissued in whole or in part in a number of anthologies, including Margery Fee and Dory Nason's

Tekahionwake: E. Pauline Johnson's Writings on Native North America (Peterborough, ON: Broadview Press, 2016) and Deanna Reder and Linda M. Morra's *Learn, Teach, Challenge: Approaching Indigenous Literatures* (Waterloo, ON: Wilfrid Laurier University Press, 2016).

7 James Clifford, "The Others: Beyond the Salvage Paradigm," in *The Third Text Reader on Art, Culture, and Theory*, ed. Rasheed Araeen et al. (London/New York: Continuum, 2002), 160–65.

8 Letter from Elizabeth Ansley to E. Pauline Johnson, 13 August 1907, The William Ready Division of Archives and Research Collections, McMaster University Library, E. Pauline Johnson fonds, Box 1.

9 Rick Monture, personal interviews, 25 August 2017 and 25 October 2017.

10 Gerson and Strong-Boag, eds., *E. Pauline Johnson, Tekahionwake*, xxi.

11 Charlotte Gray, *Flint & Feather: The Life and Times of E. Pauline Johnson, Tekahionwake* (Toronto: HarperCollins, 2002), 390–91.

12 For further biographical reading on Johnson, see: Mrs. W. Garland Foster, *The Mohawk Princess: Being Some Account of the Life of Tekahion-Wake (E. Pauline Johnson)* (Vancouver: Lions' Gate Publishing Company, 1931); Johnson, *Collected Poems and Selected Prose* (eds. Gerson and Strong-Boag); Gray, *Flint & Feather*; Sheila M.F. Johnston, *Buckskin and Broadcloth: A Celebration of E. Pauline Johnson—Tekahionwake, 1861–1913* (Toronto: Dundurn Press, 2008); Keller, *Pauline: A Biography*; and Strong-Boag and Gerson, *Paddling Her Own Canoe*.

13 Though Sahp-luk is the modern spelling (see Fee and Nason, *Tekahionwake*, 2016), this name has also previously been written as Su-á-pu-luck (see Strong-Boag and Gerson, *Paddling Her Own Canoe*).

14 Robin Fisher, "SU-Á-PU-LUCK," in *Dictionary of Canadian Biography*, vol. 13, University of Toronto/Université Laval, 2003–, accessed 9 November 2021, http://www.biographi.ca/en/bio/su_a_pu_luck_13E.html.

15 Mathias Family, "Squamish Family Histories" document, 2390. According to one of Letekwamcheten's other sons, Charley Squamish Sxeliltn (of False Creek or Seymour Creek circa 1853), Letekwamcheten also went by the name Peter (see endnote 294 in "Squamish Family Histories"). Letekwamcheten was born around 1835.

16 James Morton, *Capilano: The Story of a River* (Toronto: McClelland and Stewart, 1970), 25; Simon Baker, *Khot-La-Cha: The Autobiography of Chief Simon Baker* (Vancouver: Douglas & McIntyre, 1994), 7. Robin Fisher (in "SU-Á-PU-LUCK") alternatively suggests that Joe and Mary were "probably" married at Mission Indian Reserve No.1.

17 Robin Fisher, "SU-Á-PU-LUCK," in *Dictionary of Canadian Biography*, vol. 13, University of Toronto/Université Laval, 2003–, accessed 9 November 2021, http://www.biographi.ca/en/bio/su_a_pu_luck_13E.html.).

18 Morton, *Capilano*, 25.

19 Ibid., 25–26; Louis Miranda, interview by Ruben Ware, Item AAAB8169, Tape 0001, BC Archives, 16 February 1979.

20 Ibid., 25.

21 Baker, *Khot-La-Cha,* 99.

22 Ibid., 10–11.

23 Morton, *Capilano*, 28.

24 "Chief Capilano is interviewed," *The Vancouver Daily Province* (Vancouver, BC), 14 August 1906, 8. James Morton suggests that newspaper accounts of Joe Capilano's speeches reflected more than just his own words: "the London scribes no doubt polished, Simon Pierre no doubt translated freely, and Joe no doubt embellished" (1970, 29).

25 Martha L. Viehmann, "Speaking Chinook: Adaptation, Indigeneity, and Pauline Johnson's British Columbia Stories," *Western American Literature* 47, no. 3 (2012): 278; Keller, *Pauline*, 220–21; Gray, *Flint & Feather,* 324–25.

26 "Blames Capilano Joe," *The Hedley Gazette* (Hedley, BC), 11 June 1908; "Joe Capilano Sees Laurier," *The Hedley Gazette* (Hedley, BC), 18 June 1908 in UBC's "BC Historical Newspapers" Open Collections.

27 Morton, *Capilano*, 30–31.

28 "Capilano Will Deliver the King's Message," *Ladysmith Daily Ledger* (Ladysmith, BC), 17 September 1906 in UBC's "BC Historical Newspapers" Open Collections.

29 Louis Miranda, interview by Ruben Ware, Item AAAB8169, Tape 0001, BC Archives, 16 February 1979; "Old Quarrel Has Now Been Adjusted," *The Province* (Vancouver, BC), 31 August 1921.

30 Garland Foster, *The Mohawk Princess*, 135.

31 For records of this alternative spelling, see: Morton, *Capilano*; Reg Ashwell, *Coast Salish, Their Art, Culture and Legends* (Surrey: Hancock House, 1978); Mildred Valley Thornton, *Potlatch People: Indian Lives & Legends of British Columbia* (Surrey: Hancock House, 2003); and records at the City of Vancouver Archives.

32 "Princess Mary Capilano: Birth a Century Ago Sealed Peace Between Warring Tribes," *The New York Times*, 17 December 1940, 25.

33 "Chief Mathias Loyal," by Andy Paull for *The Province* (Vancouver, BC), 1 June 1953, 7. See also Figure 7, "Indians—Capilano genealogy" on p. 13, this volume.

34 Bob Baker, email correspondence, 2 October 2017.

35 Mary Paul (daughter of Agi Mathias Paul), personal interview, 12 May 2022.

36 Mathias Family, "Squamish Family Histories" document, 2384. Charlie was also identified as Chief Charlie in "The Old Lady of the Siwashes," *Vancouver Daily World* (Vancouver, BC), 12 March 1910, 45.

37 Mathias Family, "Squamish Family Histories" document, 2384.

38 Agi Mathias Paul, personal interview, 12 May 2022. Agi explained that Mary's refusal to build a church at Capilano caused some tension in the community. Sḵwx̱wú7mesh Elder Louis Miranda also reflects on religion as a point of division, stating: "So the priest, after they blessed this place as a Catholic Mission, there was no one else allowed on here except a devoted Catholic person. So after Kiapalano died, Lahwa died, they had no one here to represent Capilano. And the bishop—Bishop Durieu, who was then the ruler of this place, he picked the man because the people down at Capilano wouldn't join the Catholics—they stayed Pagan or non-Catholic" ("interview with Ruben Ware"). Today, the church is known as St. Paul's Parish, and is located on Esplanade Street W. in North Vancouver.

39 The exact number of children Mary and Joe had is not certain, but most sources suggest at least ten. In Robin Fisher's entry for "SU-Á-PU-LUCK (Joseph Capilano)" in the *Dictionary of Canadian Biography*, Fisher states that Joe and Mary together had twelve children; it is likely that most of these children died at a young age, as they are not mentioned in other biographical resources. The 1910 *Vancouver Daily World* newspaper article, "The Old Lady of the Siwashes," claims that Mary "has mothered a brood of fifteen little ones, but of that number, only three are living today" (45). Similarly, in Mildred Valley Thornton's article on Mary in *The Vancouver Sun*, she writes: "She must have been the mother of many children, for the little cemetery records their interment two by two" ("Mary Capilano, Daring, Venturous"). These numbers reflect the staggering rates of infant mortality amongst Indigenous Peoples during the early twentieth century: see Tina Moffat, "Infant Mortality in an Aboriginal Community: A Historical and Biocultural Analysis," (McMaster University, Master's thesis, 1992); see also, Magda Fahrni and Esyllt W. Jones (eds), *Epidemic Encounters Influenza, Society, and Culture in Canada, 1918–20* (Vancouver: UBC Press, 2012). Such numbers are similarly described in Emily Carr's 1941 story, "Sophie" (published in *Klee Wyck*), where Carr writes of her Sḵwx̱wú7mesh friend Sophie Frank: "Every year Sophie had a new baby. Almost every year she buried one. Her little graves were dotted all over the cemetery. I never knew more than three of her twenty-one children to be alive at one time" (56).

40 Baker, *Khot-La-Cha*, 3.

41 Noel Robinson, "Letters to the Editor: Inability to Present Indians to their Majesties Regretted," *The Province* (Vancouver, BC), 3 June 1939.

42 Noel Robinson, "Mrs. Capilano's Deception," *The Province* (Vancouver, BC), 4 September 1937.

43 Agi Mathias Paul, personal interview, 20 September 2017.

44 Baker, *Khot-La-Cha*, 2.

45 Noel Robinson, "Mary Capilano," speech typescript, City of Vancouver Archives, Box 506-A-02, folder 4.

46 Mamie Moloney, "In One Ear" column, *The Vancouver Sun* (Vancouver, BC), 22 May 1953.

47 Jean Barman, *Stanley Park's Secret: The Forgotten Families of Whoi Whoi, Kanaka Ranch and Brockton Point* (Madeira Park: Harbour Publishing, 2005), 89.

48 Ibid., 80–82.

49 Ibid., 186.

50 For detailed accounts of the Stanley Park Dispossession Cases and trial proceedings, see Barman, *Stanley Park's Secret*, 186–96. Barman's text erroneously lists Mary Capilano's interpreter as Chief Joe Mathias (193), where it should have been Chief Mathias Joe. See also "Att'y-Gen'l of Canada et al. v. Cummings, et al., 1925 CanLII 468 (SCC)," https://www.canlii.org/en/ca/scc/doc/1925/1925canlii468/1925canlii468.html?searchUrlHash=AAAAAQA-TY2FuYWRhIHYuIGdvbnphbHZlcwAAAAAB&resultIndex=6.

51 Though Mary's exact age was unknown, Vancouver writer Noel Robinson estimated Mary to be over 100 years old. This caused a point of contention between Robinson and The City of Vancouver archivist Major Matthews, who claimed Mary to be only 83 at her time of death. See letters in the City of Vancouver Archives, "Capilano Genealogy" file, for their correspondence back and forth (including a response from Matthews where he states, 'THIS IS NONSENSE').

52 For more on this initial meeting in London, and how Johnson "took credit for only easing the men's homesickness," see Viehmann, "Speaking Chinook," 278.

53 Agi Mathias, personal interview, 25 November 2017.

54 Baker, *Khot-La-Cha*, 10–11.

55 Louis Miranda, interview by Ruben Ware, Item AAAB8169, Tape 0001, BC Archives, 16 February 1979. See also Baker, *Khot-La-Cha*; Morton, *Capilano*.

56 Baker, *Khot-La-Cha*, 11.

57 Ibid., 13.

58 Walter McRaye was Johnson's stage partner and manager between 1901 and 1909; they remained close friends until her passing. See: Johnson, *E. Pauline Johnson, Tekahionwake*, eds. Gerson and Strong-Boag, xviii.

59 Viehmann, "Speaking Chinook," 265.

60 Richard M. Steele, *The Stanley Park Explorer* (Vancouver: Whitecap Books, 1985), 76.

61 Linda Quirk, "Labour of Love: *Legends of Vancouver* and the Unique Publishing Enterprise that Wrote E. Pauline Johnson into Canadian Literary History," *Papers of the Bibliographical Society of Canada/Cahiers de la Société Bibliographique du Canada* 47, no. 2 (2009): 209.

62 Gray, *Flint & Feather*, 363. In the "Sources" section in Gray's *Flint & Feather*, she lists her source for this quote as Bertha Jean Thompson Stevinson's book of collected columns, titled *Up and Down the Pacific Coast* (1989, privately published). These columns first appeared around 1906 in Thorold, Ontario's *Thorold Post* newspaper (https://digital.lib.sfu.ca/ceww-703/thompson-bertha-jane).

63 This was suggested by Bob Baker (who today carries the ancestral name Sahplek) in an email communication (2 October 2017) and in conversations with Agi Mathias Paul and the Mathias family.

64 I credit Carole Gerson's article, "Periodicals First: The Beginnings of Susanna Moodie's *Roughing It in the Bush* and Pauline Johnson's *Legends of Vancouver*," in *Home Ground and Foreign Territory: Essays on Early Canadian Literature*, edited by Janice Fiamengo, 45–66 (Ottawa: University of Ottawa Press, 2014), for the first part of this title.

65 Strong-Boag and Gerson draw on surviving financial documents in *Paddling Her Own Canoe* to suggest that Johnson was paid six dollars per thousand words at *Mother's Magazine* in 1907 (166).

66 Viehmann, "Speaking Chinook," 269.

67 Letter from Elizabeth Ansley to E. Pauline Johnson, 13 August 1907, The William Ready Division of Archives and Research Collections, McMaster University Library, E. Pauline Johnson fonds, Box 1.

68 For a thoughtful analysis of Johnson's use of sentimentalism, particularly how Johnson's phrases like "she is so very Indian" often function to essentialize Indigenous women, see Viehmann, "Speaking Chinook," 163.

69 Strong-Boag and Gerson, *Paddling Her Own Canoe*, 137.

70 Garland Foster, *The Mohawk Princess*, 135.

71 Alfred Buckley, "The Spectator," *The Vancouver News-Advertiser* (Vancouver, BC), 23 March 1913, 23.

72 Ibid.

73 Keller, *Pauline*, 250. See also: J.N.J. Brown, "Legends of Vancouver," *The Province* (Vancouver, BC), 18 June 1929.

74 Strong-Boag and Gerson, *Paddling Her Own Canoe*, 177.

75 Jenny L. Davis, "Famous 'Last' Speakers: Celebrity and Erasure in Media Coverage of Indigenous Language Endangerment," in *Indigenous Celebrity: Entanglements with Fame*, eds. Jennifer Adese and Robert Alexander Innes (Winnipeg: University of Manitoba Press, 2021), 165.

76 Ibid.

77 Christine Marshall qtd. in Strong-Boag and Gerson, *Paddling Her Own Canoe*, 177.

78 For a detailed analysis of Johnson's framing techniques in *Legends*, see Deena Rymhs, "But the Shadow of Her Story: Narrative Unsettlement, Self-Inscription, and Translation in Pauline Johnson's *Legends of Vancouver,*" *Studies in American Indian Literatures: The Journal of the Association for the Study of American Indian Literatures* 13, no. 4 (2001): 51–78. See also Strong-Boag and Gerson, *Paddling Her Own Canoe*, 175; and A. LaVonne Brown Ruoff, Introduction to E. Pauline Johnson's *The Moccasin Maker* (Norman: University of Oklahoma Press, 1998), 24.

79 Rymhs, "But the Shadow of Her Story," 58.

80 Monture, *We Share Our Matters*, 67.

81 Ibid.

82 Rick Monture, personal interviews, 25 August 2017 and 25 October 2017.

83 Johnson, "A Royal Mohawk Chief," this volume, 160.

84 Ibid., 233–34 n.18.

85 Rick Monture, personal interviews, 25 August 2017 and 25 October 2017; Monture, *We Share Our Matters*, 100.

86 Ibid.

87 Lionel Makovski, quoted in Johnston, *Buckskin and Broadcloth*, 210.

88 Garland Foster, *The Mohawk Princess*, 135.

89 The E. Pauline Johnson fonds at McMaster University includes letters from I.O.D.E. chapters in Canadian cities including Brandon, MB; Calgary, AB; Hamilton, ON; Collingwood, ON; and Brantford, ON among others. These letters, addressed to Johnson at the Bute St. Hospital, would request additional books to sell in their respective cities, and would often include kind, sympathetic messages with hopes for her speedy recovery.

90 Strong-Boag and Gerson, *Paddling Her Own Canoe*, 173.

91 E. Pauline Johnson, "The Legend of the Two Sisters," *Mother's Magazine* (Elgin, IL), January 1909, 12.

92 G.P.V. and Helen B. Akrigg, *British Columbia Place Names*, 3rd ed. (Vancouver: UBC Press, 1997), 154.

93 Steven Threndyle, *The Greater Vancouver Book: An Urban Encyclopedia* (Vancouver: Linkman Press, 1997), 155.

94 Johnson, "The Legend of the Two Sisters." Similarly, Chief Capilano is generally not named explicitly (aside from the Author's Foreword to *Legends of Vancouver,* and the opening to "A Squamish Legend of Napoleon"), and he is referred to throughout the stories as "Chief" or "my old tillicum."

95 Ibid.

96 Lionel Makovski, "For Now We See Through a Glass Darkly," *The Vancouver Daily Province* (Vancouver, BC), 26 March 1910.

97 Johnson, "The Legend of the Two Sisters," 13.

98 Rudy Reimer, personal interview, 5 December 2017.

99 Johnson, this volume, "The Two Sisters," 81; and "The Legend of the Two Sisters," 167.

100 Johnson, "The Legend of the Two Sisters," 12.

101 "The Legend of the Squamish Twins" has only minimal changes to the story across versions. With both the *Mother's* and *Province* versions appearing in July 1910, this story illustrates Johnson's ability to navigate between publishing venues—adapting her material according to the demands of each publication. Where the *Mother's* version of this story is narrated by Mary Capilano and Joe Capilano together, the *Province* version eliminates Mary as narrator, and instead presents the story as told only by Joe Capilano. Though the two versions follow each other closely, the *Mother's* version uniquely assigns storytelling credit to Mary Capilano alongside her husband.

102 Quirk, "Labour of Love," 213.

103 In Strong-Boag and Gerson's *Paddling*, it is erroneously stated in the "Chronological List of Pauline Johnson's Writings" that "The Legend of the Seven Swans" (appearing in *Mother's Magazine*, September 1911) was reprinted from the *Province*'s 1910 version. This is incorrect—the *Province*'s version is narrated by Chief Capilano, whereas the *Mother's* version is told in the voice of Mary Capilano.

104 The existence of Johnson's preferred title has also been observed in Ruoff, Introduction, 15; Quirk, "Labour of Love," 205; Gerson and Strong-Boag (eds.), *E. Pauline Johnson, Tekahionwake*, xxxii; Keller, *Pauline*, 257; Garland

Foster, *The Mohawk Princess*, 125; etc. This volume marks the first time this preferred title has been used.

105 Quirk, "Labour of Love," 205.

106 James Goulet (1866–1952) of Raleigh, Kent County, Ontario, was the son of John Goulet and Sophie Clark (originally hailing from Quebec). His brother, Louis, was a local historian/writer who documented some of the Goulet family's genealogy. See Louis Goulet, *Kent Historical Society: Papers and Addresses* Vol. 5 (1921) and the *Commemorative Biographical Record of the County of Kent, Ontario* (1904).

107 Gray refers to one of these letters, dated 27 August 1913, in *Flint & Feather* (2002), in which Evelyn responds to a recently published article by Charles Mair in *Canadian Magazine* (256–57). In the corresponding notes to this chapter, Gray writes that "Evelyn Johnson's 1913 letter to James Goulet came into the possession of Juanita Staples Brumpton in about 1942; a copy was kindly sent to me by Harry Brumpton of Windsor, Ontario" (412–13). These letters were eventually donated to McMaster University Archives, as noted in the "Recent Notable Gifts" section of the fall/winter 2002 *McMaster Library News* Bulletin: "Harry O. Brumpton, letters and news clippings from Evelyn H.C. Johnson to James Goulet regarding her sister, poet E. Pauline Johnson." In the Pauline Johnson fonds (Box 1, Folder 1) at Trent University Archives, a scrap of paper documents Evelyn Johnson's correspondences for the 1913 (including those with Goulet). This paper is divided into columns for each month, with the date, name, and general subject matter of letters received—presumably as a way for Evelyn to keep track of her increased mail, incoming and outgoing, following her sister's death.

108 City of Vancouver Archives, Box 504-E-02, fld. 44. This letter is typewritten, dated "March 18, 1906" but seems to be erroneously so; in her book *Pauline: A Biography* (1981), Keller estimates this letter to be dated c. 1935 (see Keller 297); Evelyn could not be referring to *Legends* in 1906 as the book had not been published and the stories not yet written. Also, Keller notes Evelyn's blindness near the end of her life in *Pauline: A Biography*, stating that in 1936 Eva was "almost totally blind" (279). Keller refers to this letter in her chapter on "Vancouver" in *Pauline: A Biography* (1981), where she argues that Pauline and Evelyn's reunion during her sickness was "ill-conceived" (261), as they had been estranged for several years beforehand. Keller depicts Evelyn (Eva) as being very bitter about Pauline's decisions, particularly those articulated in Pauline's Last Will and Testament.

109 See Cranbrook's *The Prospector* (23 July 1910) or North Vancouver's *The Express* (30 July 1909), both available through UBC's "BC Historical Newspapers" Open Collections.

110 Keller, *Pauline*, 257.

111 The William Ready Division of Archives and Research Collections, McMaster University Library, E. Pauline Johnson fonds, Box 1.

112 Walter McRaye, *Pauline Johnson and Her Friends* (Toronto: Ryerson Press, 1947), 130–31.

113 Mathias Family, personal interview, 2 September 2017.

114 Letter from Evelyn H.C. Johnson to Mr. James Goulet, 1 July 1913, The William Ready Division of Archives and Research Collections, McMaster University Library, E. Pauline Johnson fonds, Box 11.

115 Bernard McEvoy, "Preface" to E. Pauline Johnson's *Legends of Vancouver* (Vancouver: Privately Printed, 1911), vii.

116 For more on this concept, see Philip J. Deloria, *Playing Indian* (New Haven: Yale University Press, 1998).

117 The story of "Lillooet Falls" also appears in Johnson's *The Moccasin Maker*, which was first published in 1913 by William Briggs (Toronto).

118 The William Ready Division of Archives and Research Collections, McMaster University Library, E. Pauline Johnson fonds, Box 1, File 41.

119 *The British Columbia Federationist*, 9 January 1914. See UBC's "BC Historical Newspapers" Open Collections.

120 Quirk, "Labour of Love," 214.

121 These drawings appeared in the 1912 and 1913 printings of *Legends*, up until the seventh edition which was published in 1913 by Saturday Sunset Presses (Vancouver, BC).

122 Carole Gerson and Alix Shield, "Picturing E. Pauline Johnson/Tekahionwake: Illustration and the Construction of Indigenous Authorship," *The Cultural Performance of Authorship in Canada* 10, no. 1 (2021): https://doi.org/10.21825/aj.v10i1.20629.

123 O.B. Anderson, "In the Indian Past: Rapidly Vanishing Indian Lore," *British Columbia Magazine* (August 1912): 619.

124 Johnson, "The Two Sisters," this volume, 81.

125 Johnson, "The Recluse," this volume, 87.

126 The "George Parker Notes" on the early McClelland and Stewart records indicate the following agreement between M&S and Makovski: "1st record in Sales Book: Jan 16, 1914. Contract with Lionel W Makovski." The William Ready Division of Archives and Research Collections, McMaster University Library, McClelland and Stewart Ltd. Fonds, Box 122, George Parker Notes. See also Quirk, "Labour of Love," 216.

127 The Toronto-based publishing company, McClelland and Stewart, was started by John McClelland and Frederick Goodchild in 1906 (known then as McClelland and Goodchild); it then became McClelland, Goodchild and Stewart and eventually just McClelland and Stewart in 1919. The company was eventually taken over by John McClelland's son, Jack McClelland, who worked for the publishing house between 1946 and 1987. See pp. xx, 2–3 in James King, *Jack, a Life with Writers: The Story of Jack McClelland* (Toronto: Alfred A. Knopf Canada, 1999).

128 Marcus Van Steen, Introduction to *Legends of Vancouver* (Toronto: McClelland and Stewart, 1961), vii.

129 Indigenous literary legends are classified under the subheading "YG–Legends." Y = Indigenous Literature; YG = the subsection for Legends and Storytelling. See UBC's resources on Indigenous Librarianship: https://guides.library.ubc.ca/Indiglibrarianship/briandeer.

130 Hartmut Lutz, "Canadian Native Literature and the Sixties," *Canadian Literature*, vol. 152/153 (1997): 175.

131 Van Steen, Introduction, xv.

132 Parker observes that between July 1920 and May 1928, there were approximately 19,125 copies of *Legends of Vancouver* printed, and approx. 18,400 bound. "The last record of bindings of the 1928 printing is April 1934. These were prepared in cloth, paper, velvet calf, lambskin, Persian yapp." See McClelland and Stewart Ltd. fonds, The William Ready Division of Archives and Research Collections, McMaster University Library, Box 122, George Parker Notes. I would like to thank Dr. Leslie Howsam for deciphering the word "yapp," a form of soft binding, and linking me to this definition: https://www.biblio.com/book_collecting_terminology/yapp-binding-334.html.

133 McClelland and Stewart Ltd. fonds, The William Ready Division of Archives and Research Collections, McMaster University Library, Box 2Ca88.

134 Diana Shklanka, "Two Collections of Native Stories," *Canadian Children's Literature (CCL)* 75 (1994): 61–62.

135 Butt acknowledges Chief Joe Capilano's role in the original story briefly on the inner dustjacket: "The tale of The Two Sisters comes from the twentieth-century Canadian classic *Legends of Vancouver* and is her retelling of the legend first told to her by Joe Capilano, chief of the Squamish Nation."

136 See back cover of *The Lost Island* (Vancouver, BC: Simply Read Books, 2016) where Capilano is referred to as a "Salish chief;" see also page with text that reads: "guarding the peace of the . . . Coast and the quiet of the . . . Canyon . . ." in *The Two Sisters*.

137 Armand Garnet Ruffo and Heather Macfarlane, eds, "Preface: Opening a Window," *Introduction to Indigenous Literary Criticism* (Peterborough: Broadview Press, 2015), xv.

138 E. Pauline Johnson, "Glossary," *Legends of Vancouver* (Kingston: Quarry Press, 1991), 135.

139 See p. 134 of the Quarry Press edition: "The royalty on sales of this edition is being donated to the trust fund preserving Chiefswood, Pauline's beloved ancestral home."

140 Robin Laurence, Introduction, in E. Pauline Johnson, *Legends of Vancouver* (Vancouver, BC: Douglas and McIntyre, 1997), xvii.

141 Gerson, "Periodicals First," 62.

142 Midtown Press, personal communication, 28 April 2022. In this same correspondence with the Press, I learned that they were also the first to correct a typo of over 100 years old in their 2013 edition. "In the original publication in the Siwash legend, the sentence reads, 'For a time we paddled slowly; the rack detached itself from its background of forest and shore.' We replaced rack with rock." I am thankful to the Press for making this correction and have made this adjustment to the line in "The Siwash Rock" here.

143 See pp. 52–56 in Daniel Francis's *The Imaginary Indian: The Image of the Indian in Canadian Culture* (Vancouver: Arsenal Pulp Press, 2011). I am also thankful to a reviewer for urging me to also acknowledge that, despite the many criticisms we can make of Curtis, there are many Indigenous Peoples today who appreciate Curtis's work for his documentation of both individual Indigenous persons and aspects of Indigenous material culture.

144 This image appears as plate no. 373 in Volume 11 of Edward S. Curtis's *The North American Indian* (1916).

145 Midtown Press, personal communication, April 2017.

146 For examples of Indigenous editorial protocols, see Gregory Younging, *Elements of Indigenous Style* (Edmonton, AB: Brush Education, 2018) and other books in UMP's "First Voices, First Texts" series.

147 Midtown Press, personal communication, 28 April 2022.

148 "Last Will and Testament of Emily Pauline Johnson," British Columbia Archives, 26 February 1913, 5. See also p. 130 of McRaye's *Pauline Johnson and Her Friends* (1947), where McRaye explains how he personally purchased all remaining first edition copies of *Legends* to sell, signed, for twice the price; this enabled the Pauline Johnson Trust to issue a second print order of *Legends*, as they could not reissue the book until all copies had been purchased.

149 "Last Will and Testament of Emily Pauline Johnson," British Columbia Archives, 26 February 1913. Johnson appointed Lionel Makovski and Isabel Mackay as her executors.

150 Quirk, "Labour of Love," 216.

151 See pp. 38–41, Younging's *Elements of Indigenous Style* for more on copyright as it applies to Traditional Knowledge and Oral Traditions. Also, note that the current Canadian Copyright Act and concept of "public domain" do not account for or protect the unique, communal nature of Indigenous Knowledge. Just because something is in the "public domain" does not mean it should be circulating freely, out of context and without guiding protocols of use. See Canadian Federation of Libraries, "Position Statement: Indigenous Knowledge in Canada's Copyright Act" (2018).

152 Letter from Lionel Makovski to Messrs. McClelland and Stewart, Ltd. 15 August 1922. The William Ready Division of Archives and Research Collections, McMaster University Library, Jack McClelland Fonds, Box 32, File 1.

153 For examples of Rackham's line art, which appears visually similar to that of MacDonald, see Jeff A. Menges, *The Fantastic Line Art of Arthur Rackham* (Mineola: Courier Dover Publications, 2017).

154 A unique copy of this pamphlet can be found in The William Ready Division of Archives and Research Collections E. Pauline Johnson fonds at McMaster University Library, which appears to include hand-painted watercolour colouring throughout. McMaster Archives Librarian Myron Groover suggests that "the colours appear too unnatural to have been done by a printer" (24 October 2017).

155 Indigenous women writers like Mourning Dove, Anahareo, Mini Aodla Freeman, and Maria Campbell also worked within colonial publishing contexts. See Mourning Dove's *Cogewea, the Half-Blood: A Depiction of the Great Montana Cattle Ranch* (Lincoln: University of Nebraska Press, 1981), Anahareo's *Devil in Deerskins: My Life with Grey Owl* (Winnipeg: University of Manitoba Press, 2014), Mini Aodla Freeman's *Life Among the Qallunaat* (Winnipeg: University of Manitoba Press, 2015), and Maria Campbell, *Halfbreed* (Toronto: McClelland and Stewart, 2019).

156 Lionel Haweis, "The Legend of Siwash Rock," *British Columbia Magazine* 10 (1914): 136–41 at the University of British Columbia Library Rare Books and Special Collections.

157 Makovski and Haweis were invited guests to a Marlborough College (Wiltshire, England) reunion held in Vancouver in 1930, suggesting they may have been classmates or at least may have known each other. See "Headmasters Tour," letter, 7 April 1930. Lionel Haweis sous-fonds, Haweis Family fonds,

University of British Columbia Library Rare Books and Special Collections (Vancouver, BC).

158 Rick Monture, personal interviews, 25 August 2017 and 25 October 2017, this volume, 197.

159 Ibid., 201.

160 Rudy Reimer, personal interview, 5 December 2017, this volume, 206.

161 Ibid., 211–12.

162 Ibid., 211–12.

Legends of the Capilano

1 See Johnson's poem titled "The Happy Hunting Grounds" (1889).

2 Famous statues of four lions located in Trafalgar Square (a plaza in London, England) and named after the artist who created them, Edwin Landseer. Chief Capilano would have seen these lions during his 1906 delegation visit to meet with King Edward VII.

3 Likely referring to the "Southern Cross" constellation of stars located in the Southern Hemisphere, and visible year-round from most places in Australia.

4 Likely referring to Emma, the same daughter who prepared cedar baskets for King Edward VII and Queen Alexandra for the Chief's trip to London in 1906. See the 26 March 1910 tribute to Chief Joe Capilano (written by Lionel Makovski) in *The Vancouver Daily Province* magazine.

5 In Pacific Northwest Coast mythology, the Thunderbird is a giant supernatural bird who lives in the mountains; he is known to cause thunder and lightning when hungry. See Thomas George's "Thunder and Lightning," in *Raven and the First People: Legends of the Northwest Coast* (Edmonton: Eschia Books, 2009).

6 An island located in the estuary of the Fraser River (south of Vancouver, BC), known today as the city of Richmond and part of the city of New Westminster.

7 A snow-capped dormant volcano in eastern Turkey; also known as the resting place of Noah's Ark in the Bible's flood narrative (see Genesis 8:4).

8 An American stage actor (1866–1951) best known for his role as Anton von Barwig in *The Music Master*, which he played from 1904 to 1907 (and again during an eight-week revival in 1917). See his obituary in *The New York Times*, 28 June 1951, 22.

9 A pamphlet of this same name, *The Legend of the Salt-Chuck Oluk*, was published in the 1920s by Lionel Haweis and was based on Johnson's story "The Sea-Serpent." See pp. 66–67, 69 of Introduction, this volume.

10 The dry, interior region of British Columbia, known during Johnson's time for its mineral resources and mining opportunities. See Frank Bailey's *Nicola, Similkameen and Tulameen Valleys: The Richest Section of British Columbia* (Vancouver: Ward, Elwood and Pound, 1914), available online through UBC's Open Collections.

11 "A Many Sided Battle," *The Boundary Creek Times* (Greenwood, BC), 20 May 1899.

12 [Original footnote by Johnson] * Note—It would almost seem that the chief knew that wonderful poem of "The Khan's," "The Men of the Northern Zone," wherein he says:
If ever a Northman lost a throne
Did the conqueror come from the South?
Nay, the North shall ever be free . . . etc.

13 The Battle of Waterloo (18 June 1815) marked the defeat of Napoleon Bonaparte and the French Empire by two armies of the Seventh Coalition (British and Prussian).

14 Approximately ten years after the publication of *Legends of Vancouver*, Lionel Makovski would do just that in his book proposal to McClelland and Stewart for a "Pauline Johnson['s] book for boys and girls"(see Introduction, this volume, 66).

15 Old Chief Ki-ap-a-la-no (1792–1875) was a warrior and patriarch of Musqueam and Sḵwx̱wú7mesh descent, who was half-brother to Mary Agnes Capilano's grandfather, Paytsmauq. See Figure 7, "Indians—Capilano genealogy," on p. 13, and Morton's *Capilano*, 23–24.

16 Prince Arthur William Patrick Albert (1850–1942), Duke of Connaught and Strathearn, was the son of Queen Victoria and Prince Albert and member of the British royal family. He served as Canada's tenth Governor General, and was the first (and only) British prince to do so.

17 George H.M. Johnson (1816–1884), or Onwanonsyshon, was E. Pauline Johnson's father and elected hereditary chief of the Iroquois confederacy (Mohawk Wolf Clan). He was known for his work as an interpreter, first translating the sermons of Church of England missionaries for the Six Nations of the Grand River, and later working as a representative for the superintendent of Indian Affairs. See Strong-Boag and Gerson, *Paddling*, 46–47; and Monture, *We Share Our Matters*, 67.

18 John "Smoke" Johnson (1792–1886), or Chief Sakayengwaraton, was E. Pauline Johnson's grandfather. He was named by the Six Nations Council as an elected Pine Tree Chief for his service during the War of 1812, and was known on the reserve for his abilities as an orator—hence his nickname, "The Mohawk Warbler." In *We Share Our Matters*, Monture describes John "Smoke" Johnson as Pauline's "most significant connection to Mohawk identity and cultural life

on the reserve. . . . As a young girl, Pauline would listen as he told stories of Iroquois history and their prowess on the battlefield, as well as their great skills at diplomacy" (67).

19 Referring to Joseph Brant (1743–1807), Mohawk leader and Loyalist, who was responsible for relocating the Mohawk Loyalists to the Grand River following the American Revolution. See Johnson's poem "Brant, a Memorial Ode" (1886).

20 The Great Law of Peace, or Kaienerekowa, is the oral constitution of the Iroquois Confederacy. It was translated from the oral tradition to a written version in 1900, by the Hereditary Council of Chiefs at Six Nations. See Monture's *We Share Our Matters* and Horatio Hale's *The Iroquois Book of Rites* (Philadelphia: D.G. Brinton, 1883).

21 i.e. Prince Albert (1840–1861), husband to Queen Victoria.

22 Johnson incorporated the scarlet broadcloth blanket into her performance costume, often wearing it draped over the shoulder of her buckskin dress. When the Duke of Connaught visited Pauline in the hospital during September 1912, she produced the ceremonial blanket "and draped it over the chair he was to sit on" (Keller, *Pauline*, 263).

Stories of Mary Capilano

1 Copy-text taken from *The Mother's Magazine*, January 1909, 12–13.

2 The word "Canyon" was printed in the *Mother's* version as "Cañon"; Gerson notes that this is "the original Spanish spelling (the word comes from American/Mexican south)—which was quite common in the US" (personal correspondence, 24 January 2019).

3 Also known as Nelson's Column, this monument commemorates the war efforts of Admiral Horatio Nelson, who died at the Battle of Trafalgar in 1805.

4 [Original footnote: *In the Chinook tongue, in general usage as a trade language on the Pacific coast, "Klootchman" means woman, and is a word used with great respect among the Indian tribes.]

5 Printed in *Mother's* version as "Cañon" or "cañon."

6 This story was revised for publication in *The Province*, with the narrator changed to Chief Capilano and retitled "The Recluse." Some of the words from the original *Mother's Magazine* copy-text were indecipherable, and those words appear in square brackets in this volume.

7 Copy-text taken from *The Mother's Magazine*, September 1911, 17–18, 32. Note that in the *Province* version (October 1910) of this story, the girl character is named "Be-be," whereas in the *Mother's* version (September 1911), narrated by Mary Capilano, she is referred to as "Kah-lo-ka." This inconsistency

is somewhat puzzling, as the name "Be-be" appears again in Johnson's "The Legend of Lillooet Falls" story (published in January 1912).

8 Misprinted in *Mother's* version as "Capilain River."

9 Printed in *Mother's* version as "cañon."

10 Misprinted in *Mother's* version as "savay."

11 Copy-text taken from *The Mother's Magazine*, January 1912, 19, 45.

12 Printed in *Mother's* version as "cañon."

13 Misprinted in *Mother's* version as "Frazer" and "Fayer."

14 Copy-text taken from *The Mother's Magazine*, November 1911, 23–24.

15 Misprinted in *Mother's* version as "Frazer."

Interviews

1 Red Jacket (1750–1830) was a famous Seneca orator and elected chief of the Wolf clan; based in New York, he was a contemporary of Mohawk leader Joseph Brant. See Monture, *We Share Our Matters* (78–80), and also Johnson's poems, "The Re-interment of Red Jacket" (1884) and "'Brant,' A Memorial Ode" (1886).

2 For Monture's published discussion of this material, see *We Share Our Matters* (61–100).

3 This story was first published in *The Boy's World* magazine as "We-eho's Sacrifice" (19 January 1907), and was later reprinted and retitled in *The Shagganappi* (Toronto: Briggs, 1913).

4 Monture is referring to the plot of Johnson's "A Royal Mohawk Chief," which describes how Prince Arthur, Duke of Connaught, was given the honorary title of "Chief of the Six Nations Indians."

5 This is a five-year SSHRC-funded research project, led by SFU Associate Professor Deanna Reder (Cree-Métis), which investigates the neglected canon of Indigenous writing in northern North America up until 1992. Rick Monture and Rudy Reimer are both collaborators on this project.

SELECTED BIBLIOGRAPHY

Selected Bibliography for E. Pauline Johnson

The White Wampum. London: John Lane; Toronto: Copp Clark; Boston: Lamson, Wolffe, 1895.

Canadian Born. Toronto: Morang, 1903.

"When George Was King" and Other Poems. Brockville, ON: Brockville Times, 1908.

Legends of Vancouver. Vancouver: Privately Printed, 1911. Many subsequent editions.

Flint and Feather. Toronto: Musson, 1912. Many subsequent editions.

The Moccasin Maker. Toronto: Briggs, 1913; reprinted 1927. Several subsequent editions.

The Shagganappi. Toronto: Briggs, 1913; reprinted 1927.

E. Pauline Johnson, Tekahionwake: Collected Poems and Selected Prose. Ed. Carole Gerson and Veronica Strong-Boag. Toronto: University of Toronto Press, 2002.

Full Chronology of Legends of Vancouver

Note: In this list, an "edition" denotes all copies printed from one setting-up of type; an "impression" denotes all copies printed from that same typesetting in a given print run. Once the typeset has been changed, or any significant changes have been made, this constitutes a new edition. In the case of "subeditions," the typesetting remains the same as the initial edition, but the book is distributed by a different publisher.

Johnson, E. Pauline. "Legends of Vancouver." *Mother's Magazine.* Elgin, IL: 1909–1912.

———. "Legends of Vancouver." *The Daily Province.* Vancouver: 1909–1911.

———. *Legends of Vancouver.* First Edition. Vancouver: Privately Printed, 1911.

———. *Legends of Vancouver.* Third Edition (Illustrated). Vancouver: The Thomson Stationary Company, 1912.

———. *Legends of Vancouver.* Fourth Edition (Illustrated). Vancouver: Geo. S. Forsyth and Company, 1912.

———. *Legends of Vancouver.* Sixth Edition (Illustrated). Vancouver: The Thomson Stationary Company, 1913.

———. *Legends of Vancouver.* Sixth Edition (Illustrated). Subedition. Toronto: McClelland and Goodchild, [1913].

———. *Legends of Vancouver.* Seventh Edition (Illustrated). Subedition. Vancouver: Geo. S. Forsyth and Company, 1913.

———. *Legends of Vancouver.* Eighth Edition (Illustrated). Vancouver: Saturday Sunset Presses, 1913.

———. *Legends of Vancouver.* New Edition Illustrated. Toronto: McClelland, Goodchild and Stewart, [1914].

———. *Legends of Vancouver.* New Edition (Illustrated). Subedition. Vancouver/Victoria: David Spencer, [1916].

———. *Legends of Vancouver.* New Edition (Illustrated) (Second Impression). Toronto: McClelland and Stewart, 1920.

———. *Legends of Vancouver.* New Edition Illustrated (Third Impression). Toronto: McClelland and Stewart, 1922.

———. *Legends of Vancouver.* New Edition Illustrated (Fourth Impression). Toronto: McClelland and Stewart, 1924.

———. *Legends of Vancouver.* New Edition Illustrated (Fifth Impression; Third Printing). Toronto: McClelland and Stewart, 1926.

———. *Legends of Vancouver.* New Edition Illustrated (Sixth Impression; Fourth Printing). Toronto: McClelland and Stewart, 1928.

———. *Legends of Vancouver.* New Edition Illustrated (Seventh Impression; Fifth Printing). Toronto: McClelland and Stewart, 1931.

———. *Legends of Vancouver.* New Edition Illustrated (Eighth Impression; Sixth Printing). Toronto: McClelland and Stewart, 1936.

———. *Legends of Vancouver.* New Edition Illustrated (Ninth Impression; Seventh Printing). Toronto: McClelland and Stewart, 1941.

———. *Legends of Vancouver.* New Edition Illustrated (Tenth Impression; Eighth Printing). Toronto: McClelland and Stewart, 1944.

———. *Legends of Vancouver.* New Edition Illustrated (Eleventh Impression; Ninth Printing). Toronto: McClelland and Stewart, 1949.

———. *Legends of Vancouver.* New Edition. Toronto: McClelland and Stewart, 1961.

———. *Legends of Vancouver.* New Edition (Second Impression). Toronto: McClelland and Stewart, [?].

———. *Legends of Vancouver*. New Edition (Third Impression). Toronto: McClelland and Stewart, 1973.

———. *Legends of Vancouver*. New Edition (Fourth Impression). Toronto: McClelland and Stewart, 1986.

———. *Legends of Vancouver*. Kingston, ON: Quarry Press, 1991.

———. *Legends of Vancouver*. Second Impression. Kingston, ON: Quarry Press, 1994.

———. *Legends of Vancouver*. Third Impression. Kingston, ON: Quarry Press, 1995.

———. *Legends of Vancouver*. Vancouver: Douglas and McIntyre, 1997.

———. *Legends of Vancouver*. Second Impression. Vancouver: Douglas and McIntyre, 1998.

———. *Legends of Vancouver.* Québec: Presses de Bras-d'Apic, 2012.

———. *Legends of Vancouver.* Vancouver: Midtown Press, 2013.

Archives Consulted

British Columbia Archives and Records Services. Victoria, BC.

E. Pauline Johnson collection. Special Collections and Rare Books, Simon Fraser University. Burnaby, BC.

E. Pauline Johnson fonds. City of Vancouver Archives. Vancouver, BC.

E. Pauline Johnson fonds. The William Ready Division of Archives and Research Collections, McMaster University Library. Hamilton, ON.

Haweis Family fonds. University of British Columbia Library Rare Books and Special Collections. Vancouver, BC.

McClelland and Stewart Ltd. fonds. The William Ready Division of Archives and Research Collections, McMaster University Library. Hamilton, ON.

North Vancouver Museum and Archives. North Vancouver, BC.

Secondary Sources

Akrigg, G.P.V., and Helen B. Akrigg. *British Columbia Place Names*. Vancouver, BC: UBC Press, 1997.

Alfred, Taiaiake. *Peace, Power, Righteousness: An Indigenous Manifesto*. Don Mills: Oxford University Press, 1999.

Selected Bibliography

Ashwell, Reg. *Coast Salish, Their Art, Culture and Legends*. Surrey: Hancock House, 1978.

Baker, Simon. *Khot-La-Cha: The Autobiography of Chief Simon Baker*. Compiled and edited by Verna J. Kirkness. Vancouver: Douglas and McIntyre, 1994.

Barman, Jean. *Stanley Park's Secret: The Forgotten Families of Whoi Whoi, Kanaka Ranch and Brockton Point*. Madeira Park: Harbour Publishing, 2005.

Carlson, Keith Thor. *The Power of Place, the Problem of Time: Aboriginal Identity and Historical Consciousness in the Cauldron of Colonialism*. Toronto: University of Toronto Press, 2014.

———. "Rethinking Dialogue and History: The King's Promise and the 1906 Aboriginal Delegation to London." *Native Studies Review* 16, no. 2 (2005): 1–38.

Canadian Federation of Libraries. "Position Statement: Indigenous Knowledge in Canada's Copyright Act." *CFLA-FCAB - Copyright*, May 2018. cfla-fcab.ca/wp-content/uploads/2018/05/CFLA-FCAB_Indigenous_knowledge_statement.pdf.

Commemorative Biographical Record of the County of Kent, Ontario: Containing Biographical Sketches of Prominent and Representative Citizens, and of Many of the Early Settled Families. J.H. Beers and Company, 1904.

Clifford, James. "The Others: Beyond the Salvage Paradigm." In *The Third Text Reader on Art, Culture, and Theory*, edited by Rasheed Araeen et al., 160–65. London/New York: Continuum, 2002.

Curtis, Edward S, photographer. *Canoeing on Clayquot Sound*. Photograph. Retrieved from the Library of Congress, www.loc.gov/item/2006676263/.

Deloria, Philip J. *Playing Indian*. New Haven: Yale University Press, 1998.

Fisher, Robin. "SU-Á-PU-LUCK." *Dictionary of Canadian Biography*, vol. 13, University of Toronto/Université Laval, 2003–, http://www.biographi.ca/en/bio/su_a_pu_luck_13E.html (accessed 10 November 2021).

Foster, Mrs. W. Garland. *The Mohawk Princess: Being Some Account of the Life of Tekahion-Wake (E. Pauline Johnson)*. Vancouver: Lions' Gate Publishing Company, 1931.

Francis, Daniel. *The Imaginary Indian: The Image of the Indian in Canadian Culture*. Vancouver: Arsenal Pulp Press, 2011.

George, Thomas. *Raven and the First People: Legends of the Northwest Coast*. Edmonton: Eschia Books, 2009.

Gerson, Carole. "Periodicals First: The Beginnings of Susanna Moodie's *Roughing It in the Bush* and Pauline Johnson's *Legends of Vancouver*." In *Home Ground and Foreign Territory: Essays on Early Canadian Literature*, edited by Janice Fiamengo, 45–66. Ottawa: University of Ottawa Press, 2014.

Gerson, Carole, and Alix Shield. "Picturing E. Pauline Johnson/Tekahionwake: Illustration and the Construction of Indigenous Authorship." *The Cultural Performance of Authorship in Canada,* special issue of *Authorship* 10, no. 1 (2021). https://doi.org/10.21825/aj.v10i1.20629.

Gill, John Kaye. *Gill's dictionary of the Chinook Jargon: with Examples of Use in Conversation and Notes Upon Tribes and Tongues*. Portland: J.K. Gill & Co., 1902. http://dx.doi.org/10.14288/1.0222360.

Goulet, Louis, et al. *Kent Historical Society: Papers and Addresses*. Vol. 5, Kent Historical Society, 1921.

Gray, Charlotte. *Flint & Feather: The Life and Times of E. Pauline Johnson, Tekahionwake*. Toronto: HarperCollins, 2002.

Hale, Horatio, editor. *The Iroquois Book of Rites*. Philadelphia: D.G. Brinton, 1883.

Johnson, E. Pauline. *E. Pauline Johnson, Tekahionwake: Collected Poems and Selected Prose*. Edited by Carole Gerson and Veronica Strong-Boag. Toronto: University of Toronto Press, 2002.

———. *Tekahionwake: E. Pauline Johnson's Writings on Native North America*. Edited by Margery Fee and Dory Nason. Peterborough: Broadview Press, 2016.

Johnson, E. Pauline, and Marcus Van Steen. *Pauline Johnson: Her Life and Work; Her Biography Written by/ Her Prose & Poems Selected by Marcus Van Steen*. Toronto: Musson, 1965.

Johnstone, Sheila M.F. *Buckskin and Broadcloth: A Celebration of E. Pauline Johnson Tekahionwake, 1861–1913*. Toronto: Dundurn Press, 2008.

Keller, Betty. *Pauline: A Biography of Pauline Johnson*. Vancouver: Douglas and McIntyre, 1981.

King, James. *Jack, a Life with Writers: The Story of Jack McClelland*. Toronto: Alfred A. Knopf Canada, 1999.

Lutz, Hartmut. "Canadian Native Literature and the Sixties: A Historical and Bibliographical Survey." *Canadian Literature* 152/53 (1997): 167–92.

McRaye, Walter. *Pauline Johnson and Her Friends*. Toronto: Ryerson Press, 1947.

Miranda, Louis. "Interview by Ruben Ware, Tape 0001," Item AAAB8169. BC Archives, 16 February 1979.

Monture, Rick. "'Beneath the British Flag': Iroquois and Canadian Nationalism in the work of E. Pauline Johnson and Duncan Campbell Scott." *Essays on Canadian Writing* 75 (2002): 118–41.

———. *We Share Our Matters: Two Centuries of Writing and Resistance at Six Nations of the Grand River*. Winnipeg: University of Manitoba Press, 2014.

Morton, James W. *Capilano: The Story of a River*. Toronto: McClelland and Stewart, 1970.

The Native Voice: Official Organ of the Native Brotherhood of British Columbia. Special Commemorative Issue. 1961.

Quirk, Linda. "Labour of Love: *Legends of Vancouver* and the Unique Publishing Enterprise that Wrote E. Pauline Johnson into Canadian Literary History." *Papers of the Bibliographical Society of Canada/Cahiers de la Société Bibliographique du Canada* 47, no. 2 (2009): 201–51.

———. "Skyward Floating Feather: A Publishing History of E. Pauline Johnson's *Flint and Feather*." *Papers of the Bibliographical Society of Canada/Cahiers de la Société Bibliographique du Canada* 44, no. 1 (2006): 69–106.

Ruffo, Armand Garnet, and Heather Macfarlane. "Preface: Opening a Window." In *Introduction to Indigenous Literary Criticism*, edited by Ruffo and Macfarlane, xi–xvii. Peterborough: Broadview Press, 2016.

Ruoff, A. LaVonne Brown, and E. Pauline Johnson. Introduction to *The Moccasin Maker*, 1–37. Edited by Brown. Norman: University of Oklahoma Press, 1998.

Rymhs, Deena. "But the Shadow of Her Story: Narrative Unsettlement, Self-Inscription, and Translation in Pauline Johnson's *Legends of Vancouver*." *Studies in American Indian Literatures: The Journal of the Association for the Study of American Indian Literatures* 13, no. 4 (2001): 51–78.

Shklanka, Diana. "Two Collections of Native Stories." Review of *Legends of Vancouver*, by E. Pauline Johnson (Quarry Press, 1991). *Canadian Children's Literature (CCL)* 75 (1994): 61–62.

Sinclair, Niigaanwewidam James. "Taking Identity: Knowing Who We Are Despite How Others See Us." *Winnipeg Free Press* (Winnipeg, MB), 29 December 2012.

Steele, Richard M. *The Stanley Park Explorer*. Vancouver: Whitecap Books, 1985.

Strong-Boag, Veronica, and Carole Gerson. *Paddling Her Own Canoe: The Times and Texts of E. Pauline Johnson (Tekahionwake)*. Toronto: University of Toronto Press, 2000.

Thomas, Edward Harper. *Chinook: A History and Dictionary of the Northwest Coast Trade Jargon*. Oregon: Metropolitan Press, 1935.

Thornton, Mildred Valley. *Potlatch People: Indian Lives & Legends of British Columbia*. Surrey: Hancock House, 2003.

Threndyle, Steven. *The Greater Vancouver Book: An Urban Encyclopedia.* Vancouver: Linkman Press, 1997, 155.

Viehmann, Martha L. "Speaking Chinook: Adaptation, Indigeneity, and Pauline Johnson's British Columbia Stories." *Western American Literature* 47, no. 3 (2012): 259–85.

Willmott, Glenn. "Modernism and Aboriginal Modernity: The Appropriation of Products of West Coast Native Heritage as National Goods." *Essays on Canadian Writing* 83 (2004): 75–139.

www.ingramcontent.com/pod-product-compliance
Lightning Source LLC
Chambersburg PA
CBHW020926310726
48980CB00005B/399

9781772840209